NORWAY–SWEDEN

UNION, DISUNION, AND SCANDINAVIAN
INTEGRATION

A PUBLICATION OF
THE CENTER FOR RESEARCH
ON WORLD POLITICAL INSTITUTIONS
PRINCETON UNIVERSITY

Publications of the Center are
Listed on Page 299

Norway-Sweden

UNION, DISUNION,

AND SCANDINAVIAN INTEGRATION

By Raymond E. Lindgren

PRINCETON, NEW JERSEY

PRINCETON UNIVERSITY PRESS

1959

The Library of Congress has
cataloged this book as follows:

Lindgren, Raymond E. 1913— Norway–Sweden:
union, disunion, and Scandinavian integration.
Princeton, Princeton University Press, 1959. 289
p. 23 cm. (A publication of the Center for Research on World Political Institutions, Princeton
University) Includes bibliography. 1. Norway—
Pol. & govt. 2. Sweden—Pol. & govt. 3. Scandinavia—Politics. i. Title. JN7041.L5 (342.48) 58–
7127 ‡ Library of Congress

Printed in the United States of America
by Princeton University Press, Princeton, New Jersey

TO

PROFESSOR WALDEMAR WESTERGAARD

FRIEND, MENTOR, AND COLLEAGUE

◇◇

PREFACE

◇◇

THIS case study of the Norwegian-Swedish union, and subsequent Scandinavian integration, seeks to make clear some forces in international conflict and peaceful change. As part of a larger research project, it inevitably has taken on interpretations which might conflict with traditional views. I hope, however, that such variations—based as they are upon recent historical analyses by Norwegian and Swedish scholars—may result in a broader understanding of the past. Reduction of symbols, stereotypes, and false interpretations to their true stature is difficult, if not impossible, and the fate of this work will probably differ in no way from that of older and wiser historians.

To readers expecting all three phases of Scandinavian integration to be treated with equal emphasis, the study may seem uneven, its title perhaps misleading. However, a word of explanation may clarify the tripartite organization and treatment. The first section (Chapters II-IV) compares the general background of the two countries from the formation of the union in 1814 to the appointment of the fourth, and last, union committee in 1902. The materials for this section, as well as for the third, come from secondary accounts presumably familiar to most users of this volume. The period from 1814 to 1905, in particular, has been so well covered by historians of Norway and Sweden that it seemed unnecessary to do more than interpret their accounts in the light of our inquiry. The middle part (Chapters VI-XIII), comprising the bulk of the study, is concerned with the troublous times from 1902 to 1908. This phase of union relationships is explored at greater length in order to demonstrate some of the forces involved in international disputes. The materials for this period, from primary sources, were made available to the author as a research scholar on a Fulbright grant to Norway. They are here incorporated into a monograph for the first time. In the third section, the period of Scandinavian integration (Chapters xIV-xvI), I have tried merely to indicate broad trends in the development of peaceful cooperation among the Scandinavian countries rather than to elaborate details.

The obligations of an historian are a heavy burden on his conscience because mere citation in these lines seems inadequate. Thanks are due the Department of State, the Norwegian foreign office, the Fulbright Office in Oslo, and others for the research grant to Norway. The American-Scandinavian Foundation's Gustaf V Fellowship allowed me to devote the summer of 1951 to studies in Sweden, and the Social Science Research Council's travel grant gave me a chance to work at the Archive étranger in Paris and the British Foreign Office Library and the Public Record Office in London. For publication of this study as part of the history-of-political-integration project sponsored by the Center for Research on World Political Problems, I am grateful for the grant made by the A. W. Mellon Charitable and Educational Trust. The financial obligations are not entirely all, however, that the historian must recognize.

Innumerable persons in Norway, Sweden, and England have assisted in countless ways in this study. A special debt is owed Dr. Reidar Omang of the Norwegian foreign office; Dr. Uno Villers, librarian of the Swedish Royal Library, formerly chief archivist of the Swedish foreign office; and his successor in the latter post, Mr. Åke Kromnow. The aid given me by the librarian and staff of the British Foreign Office Library was most necessary, and thanks are due Mr. E. J. Passant, Mr. S. H. Gellatly, and Mr. C. H. Fone. Professor Torvald Höjer most graciously secured permission for me to use the Bernadotte Arkiv in Stockholm; and Dr. Jonas Samzelius was of great assistance at the library of Uppsala University after Professor C. A. Hessler had given permission for documentary collections in his possession to be used. Archivist Ingvar Andersson of the Royal Swedish Archives is especially remembered for his assistance in using manuscripts under his jurisdiction. To Professor Folke Lindberg I am indebted for even more than the use of the materials which he gathered for his own study of Swedish foreign policy; and to

Professor Arne Wåhlstrand I owe a special debt for his advice and for the use of certain materials under his care in Göteborg.

I am especially grateful to Professor Waldemar Westergaard, friend and guide, and Professor Andrew F. Rolle for their reading of the manuscript before its submission. The aid of Professor Richard Van Wagenen, formerly Director of the Center for Research on World Political Institutions at Princeton University, and colleagues of the "team" at the Center, has been sincerely appreciated. The skillful editorial assistance of Mrs. Polly Hanford, of Princeton University Press, has removed many errors, and the writer's gratitude is wholeheartedly given for this most pleasant cooperation.

But debts and obligations are always the lot of any historian. In the interests of brevity, I have neglected to mention a great number of persons, and I hope that they will pardon my failure to give them credit they deserve. I cannot, however, neglect the historian's eternal debt—that to his wife. And so I repeat with sincere meaning the familiar words, "More than any other, my wife's counsel and assistance have been invaluable."

Los Angeles, California   RAYMOND E. LINDGREN
August 1958

CONTENTS

CONTENTS

NORWAY–SWEDEN

UNION, DISUNION, AND SCANDINAVIAN
INTEGRATION

CHAPTER I

INTRODUCTION

THE Scandinavian countries occupy today a special place in the society of nations. For nearly a hundred and fifty years Sweden has not been involved in a war, and the other four countries have been drawn unwillingly into wars only because of the politics of larger countries. These five Nordic states—Denmark, Finland, Iceland, Norway, and Sweden—have lived in amity with each other for a century and a half and have sought during the twentieth century to create a community which will maintain peace among themselves and with other nations. They have constructed institutions to implement this northern peace and have shown a common front so often that other nations usually regard the north of Europe as comprising an integrated area. In spite of language differences, ethnological variations, and competitive economic systems, these five states have settled their disputes by peaceful means.

Two of these countries, Norway and Sweden,[1] occupy a special place among the Nordic states. They were joined in a union from 1814 to 1905; twice during that period they nearly went to war with each other, both times within the last two decades of the union. After their political separation in 1905, however, these two small countries, buffeted by power politics and fearful of involvement in further war, created a "security-community" for accord and cooperation. It failed to sustain the burden of protection when war came in 1940, but that was an external attack. Internally, the security-community has constantly maintained its vitality, and has in fact become a model for the pacific settlement of controversies and for certain other forms of cooperation. Competent authorities agree that chances for war between these two independent states, even in the long future, do not exist.

[1] An alphabetical arrangement has been used throughout where technically feasible so that Norway appears first, even in the "Norwegian-Swedish union."

It is for these reasons that the union, disunion, and integration of Norway and Sweden take on major significance in any series of studies concerned with political community or with alternatives to war as a method of settling international disputes. In terms used by the Center for Research on World Political Institutions, the two countries form a pluralistic security-community.[2] This statement can best be explained by a definition of terms used throughout the study.

We are dealing here with political communities. These we regard as social groups with a process of political communication, some machinery for enforcement, and some popular habits of compliance. A political community is not necessarily able to prevent war within the area it covers: the United States was unable to do so at the time of the Civil War. Some political communities do, however, eliminate war and the expectation of war within their boundaries. It is these which call for intensive study.

We have concentrated, therefore, upon the formation of "security-communities" in certain historical cases of which this is one. The use of such a term starts a chain of definitions, and we must break in here to introduce the other main links needed for a fuller understanding.

A *security-community* is a group of people which has become "integrated."

By *integration* we mean the attainment, within a territory, of a "sense of community" and of institutions and practices strong enough and widespread enough to assure, for a "long"

---

[2] These terms are used in the other studies of the Center for Research on World Political Institutions. The explanation which follows is taken directly from *Political Community and the North Atlantic Area: International Organization in the Light of Historical Experience*, by Karl Deutsch, Sidney A. Burrell, Robert A. Kann, Maurice Lee, Jr., Martin Lichtermann, Raymond E. Lindgren, Francis L. Loewenheim, and Richard W. Van Wagenen (Princeton, N.J., 1957), 5-6. Further explanation of the problem we are dealing with and the methods used can be found in this work, 3-8 and 10-21. Note also Nils Herlitz, "Nordens problem," *Nordisk tidskrift*, New Series, xxx (1954), 1-13, for analysis of Nordic collaboration where he uses integration, however, in the sense of amalgamation and emphasizes pluralism as an approach to integration.

time, dependable expectations of "peaceful change" among its population.

By *sense of community* we mean a belief on the part of individuals in a group that they have come to agreement on at least this one point: that common social problems must and can be resolved by processes of "peaceful change."

By *peaceful change* we mean the resolution of social problems, normally by institutionalized procedures, without resort to large-scale physical force.

A security-community, therefore, is one in which there is real assurance that the members of that community will not fight each other physically, but will settle their disputes in some other way. If the entire world were integrated as a security-community, wars would be automatically eliminated. But there is apt to be confusion about the term "integration."

In our usage, the term "integration" does not mean necessarily only the merging of peoples or governmental units into a single unit. Rather, we divide security-communities into two types: "amalgamated" and "pluralistic."

By *amalgamation* we mean the formal merger of two or more previously independent units into a single larger unit, with some type of common government after amalgamation. This common government may be unitary or federal. The United States today is an example of the amalgamated type. It became a single governmental unit by the formal merger of several formerly independent units. It has one supreme decision-making center.

The *pluralistic* security-community, on the other hand, retains the legal independence of separate governments. The combined territory of the United States and Canada is an example of the pluralistic type. Its two separate governmental units form a security-community without being merged. It has two supreme decision-making centers. Where amalgamation occurs without integration, of course a security-community does not exist.

Since our study deals with the problem of ensuring peace, we shall say that any political community, be it amalgamated or pluralistic, was eventually *successful* if it became a security-community—that is, if it achieved integration—and that it was *unsuccessful* if it ended eventually in secession or civil war.

The framework may be summarized in its essentials by the following diagram:

	NON-AMALGAMATION	AMALGAMATION
INTEGRATION	Pluralistic Security-Community EXAMPLE (Norway-Sweden today)	Amalgamated Security-Community EXAMPLE (U.S.A. today)
	...............INTEGRATION	THRESHOLD..................
NON-INTEGRATION	Not Amalgamated Not Security-Community EXAMPLE (U.S.A.-U.S.S.R. today)	Amalgamated but not Security-Community EXAMPLE (Habsburg Empire 1914)

(AMALGAMATION THRESHOLD separates the left and right columns.)

The reader will notice the absence of the term "union" in this chain of definitions, despite its use in the title of the book. To use our chosen technical terms would have reduced the likelihood that the title alone would convey any idea of the contents of the book. There was a Norwegian-Swedish union, after all, recognized by all nations of the world, under which two peoples lived for a time in common association. The term "union" is, therefore, used in this study in a twofold sense: it refers both to the historic association of these two peoples and to their political amalgamation. But if the reader translates "union" as "amalgamation," keeping in mind the definitions outlined above, he will be on safe ground.

In these terms, the central purpose of this study is to explore the reasons why the political amalgamation of Norway and Sweden between 1814 and 1905 did not result in their integration. In other words, why did they become a security-community after they were separated politically but not while they were politically amalgamated?[3] A second purpose is to provide new information on a unique case of dissolving a union without bloodshed. The point of view I have adopted is one held by many Norwegians and Swedes during the union's controversies: that the union itself formed a barrier, and that its dissolution opened the way for an integration impossible under pre-1905 conditions.

In 1814, then, the union began its ninety-one-year life.

[3] The case has been very useful in revealing unsuspected strengths demonstrated by pluralism. See especially the section on "Special Features of Pluralistic Security-Communities," in *Political Community and the North Atlantic Area*, 65-69, and also the index to that work for further references to the Norway-Sweden case in the broader study.

CHAPTER II

◇◇

FORMATION OF THE UNION

◇◇

THE union of Norway and Sweden had its origins in Sweden's loss of Finland to Russia in 1809 and in the great coalition against Napoleon in 1812-1813.[1] As a replacement for Finland, the Swedes wishfully substituted Norway, although she had been associated with Denmark from the Union of Kalmar in 1397. During the last quarter of the eighteenth century, Gustaf III and others devised various schemes aimed at such a conquest, but until 1809-1810 such ambitious dreams seemed hardly possible of achievement. Under the stimulus of war and its privations, the three Scandinavian countries drew closer to one another, and it appeared for a time as if the Union of Kalmar might be revived. But the death of the heir apparent to the Swedish throne, a Danish prince elected by the Swedish Riksdag, ended such hopes as had existed for a brief moment.

The new crown prince of Sweden was elected by the Riksdag in 1810; his is a success story worthy of fiction. Jean Baptiste Bernadotte, a French soldier, rose from the ranks to command armies under Napoleon and to receive a marshal's baton. As Karl Johan, adopted son of Karl XIII and crown prince of Sweden, he embarked upon an aggressive foreign policy to retrieve Sweden's past glory and to guarantee his hold on the royal crown. He resolved also to seek compensation for the loss of Finland, and revived imperialistic ideas for the conquest of Norway. In 1812-1813 Karl Johan arranged military alliances with Russia and England in which he agreed to share in the risks attendant upon

---

[1] For studies of Swedish policy and Norwegian history in 1813-1814, see Torvald Höjer, *Carl XIV Johan* (2 vols., Stockholm, 1939-1943); Sverre Steen, *Den norske folks liv og historie gjennem tidene* (10 vols., Oslo, 1929-1935), vii; Wilhelm Keilhau, *ibid.*, viii; Arne Bergsgård, *Året 1814* (2 vols., Oslo, 1943-1945); Sam. Clason, *Karl XIII och Karl XIV* in *Sveriges historia till våra dagar* (15 vols., Stockholm, 1916-1936), xi; Sverre Steen, *1814* in *Det frie Norge* (Oslo, 1951); Jörgen Weibull, *Carl Johan och Norge 1810-1814* (Lund, 1957).

Napoleon's defeat, and in certain anticipated gains. In these agreements Sweden was promised Norway to offset her loss of Finland. Denmark, which controlled Norway, in effect cooperated in the process by unwisely maintaining her alliance with Napoleon. Accordingly Karl Johan led Swedish troops in the coalition against France in 1813 and fought through Germany into Denmark in pursuit of those objectives which would, he thought, endear him to the Swedish people.

At Kiel the Danish government and king reluctantly capitulated. A treaty of January 14, 1814, transferred Norway to the Swedish king in return for illusory promises of monetary compensation and possession of Western Pomerania. For Sweden the Treaty of Kiel was supposed to mean the acquisition of Norway without reservations. Swedes at the time envisioned a union which would have one parliament, the Swedish; one king, under the succession act of 1810; one government, the Swedish council and king.

Yet, events in Norway during the first six months of 1814 altered entirely the character of the union. Even before signature of the Treaty of Kiel, Danish Prince Christian Frederik, who had arrived in Norway in 1813, prepared for trouble.[2] Three alternative courses of action seemed possible: to maintain the Danish-Norwegian union unchanged without war; to defend Norway against Swedish attack and preserve the existing political organization; to resist a Swedish invasion and, if necessary, to create an independent Norway. Norwegian leaders naturally preferred the third course and only if it were clearly impossible would they choose another. Danish weakness, combined with the growing strength of Sweden and increasing pressures from England, Russia, and Prussia, left Norway no course of action having any real expectation of success.

But Norway escaped for a time from Swedish enforcement of the Treaty of Kiel because of Karl Johan's involvement in Euro-

---

[2] On the Treaty of Kiel and Danish policy up to February 15, see Axel Linvald, "Omkring Kielerfreden," *Historisk tidsskrift* (Danish), Series XI, IV (1954), 165-231. For Christian Frederik see the same author's *Kong Christian VIII*, Volume II: *Norges statholder 1813-1814* (Copenhagen, 1952).

pean politics. Only in June 1814 could he turn to the task of making Swedish claims effective in Norway. In the intervening six months, Christian Frederik created a new state, a new monarchy, a new constitution, and a new government. According to Sverre Steen, the most recent Norwegian historian writing upon the subject,[3] the movement for an independent Norway was conceived, organized, and accomplished by Christian Frederik and, weak as his position might be, the new regime hung entirely on his fate. Before the Kiel agreement he journeyed from Oslo[4] to Trondheim, both to consult with army leaders and to arouse the Norwegian people to an awareness of the Swedish threat. His speeches stirred the awakening nationalism of the Norwegians and increased his own popularity—both almost beyond his greatest expectations. Stimulated by his own oratory and swept along by the plaudits of his people, Christian Frederik planned and schemed for a new monarchy which would be supported both at home and abroad by virtue of its legality, the loyalty of the Norwegian people, and foreign opposition to Karl Johan. Advised by his council (*statsraad*) to complete his task speedily, he issued a call in February for a constitutional assembly to meet at Eidsvoll near Oslo.

Here, in cramped quarters and under great tension, Norwegian leaders came to grips with the dangers facing their country. The convention represented only the upper classes, for franchise limitations denied the vote to either workers or small farmers. By special arrangement personnel of the fleet and army elected thirty-two delegates—a sensible decision, since they would defend the new constitution and nation. Twenty-seven civil servants joined them in the assembly, and thus these fifty-seven officials held a majority at Eidsvoll. Business interests were represented by sixteen members, and *bønder* (farmers) by thirty-seven. However, the latter played but a negligible part, for during the entire assembly only one *bonde* spoke.

[3] *1814*, 278.

[4] The modern name of the Norwegian capital will be used throughout, rather than Christiania, the older form, which was discarded after World War I.

These delegates, who met in the opening religious service on April 10, divided into two unequal groups. A minority of twenty-five to thirty desired a union with Sweden and shared similar, though not identical, views. In most instances they favored such a union because an independent Norway could hardly resist Swedish military power or avoid foreign intervention. Foremost among the so-called unionist party was Johan Caspar Herman Wedel Jarlsberg[5] who had conferred with the commander of Swedish troops on the frontier about peaceful negotiations for a Norwegian acceptance of Kiel. Because of his noteworthy experience in politics, his prestige as the only baron in Norway, and his personal wealth and family prominence, his influence was imposing. Wedel's reasons for favoring a union with Sweden were shared by many of his own party: union would mean peace with England and free trade with her, a Norwegian-Swedish defense community, and intimate cooperation between the two countries. Wedel heartily favored acceptance of a constitution, for it would guarantee Norwegian liberties and make possible, through equality of status with Sweden in the union, the intimate relationship which he desired.

Other unionists varied in their motives. Nicolai Wergeland was a pastor whose dislike of Denmark blinded him partially to the dangers of Swedish dominance in the union. He thought there was slight chance of Norway's becoming a completely independent state and, therefore, he was willing to choose union with Sweden. Wergeland believed that such a combination would be based on mutual respect and cooperation if Norway first established her own sovereignty by adopting a constitution and electing a king. Jacob Aall favored ties with Sweden on grounds similar to those of Wergeland. His reasoning, starting with the premise that union was inevitable, was based on the consideration that Norway's small resources ought to be husbanded to bolster the new government's resistance against Swedish coercion.[6] In de-

[5] Yngvar Nielsen, *Lensgreve Johan Caspar Herman Wedel Jarlsberg* (3 vols., Oslo, 1901-1902).

[6] Cf. Jacob Aall's *Erindringer som bidrag til Norges historie fra 1800-1815* (Oslo, 1858).

liberations in the assembly these men were important, for they spoke often, and both Wergeland and Wedel sat on the constitutional drafting committee.

In contrast the independence party expected more than could be realized. They reasoned that Norwegians might hope for power politics to separate England and Russia, with the former intervening in favor of Norway. In London, Carsten Anker, member of a Norwegian commercial and landholding family, sought to augment this division among the powers. His report of the failure of his mission, however, Christian Frederik concealed from the representatives at Eidsvoll. Others counted on Karl Johan's election as king of France, in the event of Napoleon's defeat, to remove him from the scene and, in his place, the election of Christian Frederik as heir to the Swedish throne. Realization of this dream would revive the Kalmar Union and thus create a Scandinavian kingdom. Some, having heard of Metternich's opposition to Karl Johan and Alexander I of Russia, hoped that Austria might support an independent Norway as a curb on Sweden. But the independence party, in voting for a king and a constitution, rested their case on Norway's sovereign right to be free. They held that Norway had been independent during the Kalmar Union with Denmark, which was technically correct, and that now the moment had come for full independence. Without arms and foreign aid, they resolved to resist Swedish efforts to carry out the provisions of the Treaty of Kiel.

Norwegian acceptance of the constitution on May 17, 1814, and the election of Christian Frederik as king of Norway, compelled Sweden to exert political pressure. Under its stress Christian Frederik began to waver and to seek an escape from the dilemma of war. As he was writing ringing phrases about his willingness to die with his people in defense of their liberties, he was simultaneously engaged in negotiations with the commissioners, representing England, Russia, Austria, and Prussia, on the best terms for an eventual Norwegian-Swedish union. After June 9 he no longer sought his own aggrandisement or protection of his new crown, but strove to guarantee Norwegian independence and sovereignty in a union with Sweden.

The commissioners and Karl Johan endeavored likewise to find a formula which would give Sweden the union she desired and, at the same time, not offend Norwegian sensibilities. At the time of the Treaty of Kiel, Karl Johan had made clear his willingness to accept any reasonable conditions for the creation of a union by peaceful means. Even if international tensions demanded immediate action, a union, based on peace and equality, could be created. Despite the extensive concessions of both Karl Johan and Christian Frederik, the curious result of the negotiations of May and June proved to be war. For this, Karl Johan must bear full responsibility, although his yielding to the pressure of Swedish leaders is understandable in light of the fact that they were, after all, his supporters within his adopted country. War was imperative for Karl Johan's purposes. By a display of military force he could increase his prestige and diminish Christian Frederik's in Norway by proving him an ineffectual and incompetent military commander. War would also convince the Swedes of the reality of their past fame and bolster their national pride. The Danes might also be denied a claim to the remainder of the one million *riksdaler* promised at Kiel by a Swedish charge of Danish complicity in Norwegian armed resistance to the formation of the union.

The two weeks' war proved, surprisingly, not a bloodless victory of Swedish hopes. Norwegian defenses stiffened after the first fighting and the entire invasion at one point nearly came to a halt in the face of courageous opposition. But the Swedes, with better equipment and combat experience in Germany, could not be permanently stopped. In addition, representatives of England, Russia, and Prussia strove to convince the Norwegians of the hopelessness of expecting foreign aid. Britain even threatened to blockade Norwegian ports if resistance continued. As a consequence, the Norwegian *statsraad* accepted the Swedish proffer of negotiations for the formation of a union.

The Convention of Moss, which resulted from these negotiations, was arranged between Karl Johan and the Norwegian *statsraad*, entirely excluding Christian Frederik. The document's omission of references to the Treaty of Kiel, its failure to nominate Karl XIII as Norwegian king, and its nonrecognition of Christian Frederik showed the Swedish wish to avoid troublesome issues rather than to solve them. By its terms, the Swedish king was instructed to negotiate through commissioners with the Storting and to accept and maintain the Eidsvoll Constitution, except for changes necessary for the union's formation. All these alterations must be approved by the Storting. No person or group would be punished for their utterances or their part in the war against Sweden. A separate convention effected an armistice for an interim period lasting until fourteen days after the opening session of the Storting and lifted the blockade of the Norwegian coast. Neither Swedish garrisons nor Norwegian forces could approach closer than three miles (twenty-one English miles) to the capital. Only regular Norwegian troops could remain under arms; volunteers must return immediately to their homes. This Convention of Moss was finally signed, with all its provisos, on August 14, 1814.

Its terms, which the Swedes were even then prepared to extend, showed Sweden's eagerness to please. They allowed Christian Frederik to remain in Norway until two days after the opening of the Storting in October. Swedish troops occupied only the Norwegian fort of Fredrikssten, while those forts with Norwegian garrisons were retained by Norway. A time limit on the convocation of the Storting was withdrawn, so it met in October with an entire winter ahead in which to defy Sweden because military operations could begin only in April. Actually many Norwegians, among them military leaders, urged procurement of military provisions and supplies with a view to resumption of war.

Most observers, including the foreign envoys in Oslo, assumed that the Convention of Moss completed the formalities required to establish the union. But final terms were not written until late in the fall when an extraordinary Storting met. From the middle of August until its opening session strident partisan debate filled the air, although no serious incidents marred the armistice period. Swedes supplied a fund of 100,000 *riksdaler* for publications and for payments to agents both to write and to speak in favor of the union. Strangely, the union party, headed again by Wedel, avoided a public display of prounionism as at Eidsvoll. Perhaps its members sensed that an open exposition of their views might result in personal attacks and reverse the begrudging assent which most Norwegians had given. The writings and speeches of this period avoided anti-Swedish sentiments and refrained from any reproaches or praise for events of the summer.

In the Storting, which numbered seventy-nine, only eighteen Eidsvoll men found seats. And, as at that assembly, the independence party easily won control. Members of the civil service held the largest number of seats, but military and naval representation dropped to four. Eighteen *bønder* and nine businessmen found places, but declined in influence and numbers. In strange contrast to the several brilliant personalities at Eidsvoll, only W. F. K. Christie seemed their equal in the Storting. His unmatched abilities as an orator and leader gained him the speakership, and he showed superb qualities in days when fine tact and parliamentary maneuvering were necessary. Wedel, whose speeches, personal magnetism, and prestige had exerted considerable influence at Eidsvoll, refrained almost entirely from assumption of leadership in the Storting. Bergen's delegates came with instructions to resist the union, and not even Christie's most effective persuasion could convince them to disobey their orders. As a modern paraphrase might put it, Bergen had nothing to lose but Norway.

The Storting met under the eyes of dubious Swedish commissioners who believed rumors of a large hostile delegation. But in the end, as Christie kept reminding his colleagues, the decision to associate with Sweden had been made earlier, and the Storting's duty was to arrange the best possible terms. Its opening session immediately debated Christian Frederik's abdication and sent him a resolution of thanks via a sizable delegation. In spite of its drama and tears, the meeting passed off well and the same day, October 10, Christian Frederik departed for Denmark. His brief historic reign and a short moment of Norwegian monarchism ended without incident.

Storting deliberations, only briefly interrupted by this event, turned to the union's formation. Under Christie's presidentship, the delegates worked at changes in the constitution necessitated by the Swedish proposals. On October 20 the Storting, after first carefully skirting the problem, finally came to direct discussion of the union's acceptance and the election and recognition of Karl XIII as king of Norway. Even then it complied simply by a letter handed to the Swedish commissioners. As was to be expected, the Storting approved it with only five dissenting votes, so that the deputation could honestly tell the Swedish commissioners of nearly unanimous approval of the union's formation. The Swedish commissioners showed their enthusiasm over the Storting action by tears and by embracing and kissing the embarrassed Norwegians. Approved by Karl Johan and the commissioners, the letter served as an acceptance of the union.

Two main issues remained after the letter's approval which showed some aspects of the nature of the union. The first problem was the extent of the king's authority over the army and navy. After prolonged debate, the Storting placed stringent restrictions on the king's use of Norwegian military forces, but later these limitations were lifted to make way for a compromise on the second great point at issue.

The Swedes proposed, without understanding its real meaning, that the king be empowered to naturalize foreigners by royal decree. Norwegians quickly saw in the proposal a plan for forcing them to accept Swedes into their civil service. Karl Johan had indeed designed this plan to achieve a merger of the two governmental administrations, but had failed to warn his commissioners. The Storting, having perceived the Swedish crown prince's intent, denied the king any power over naturalization except a veto on any Norwegian grant of citizenship—the very opposite of what Sweden wanted: i.e., naturalization powers in royal hands with a Storting veto. Eventually, however, compromises increased military forces for a defense of the united kingdoms and checked any entry of Swedes into the Norwegian bureaucracy.

The Storting proceeded slowly through the constitution, making alterations compelled by its agreement to the union. Christie's motion during the opening debate limited these modifications to those required by the act of union. On November 4 the Storting approved the revised constitution in its entirety and elected Karl XIII king of Norway. The vote on his election revealed clearly three divergent attitudes in the Storting. Some members voted directly in favor of Karl XIII as king of Norway. Other members, the smaller group, agreed to elect and recognize him as king, in order to date his sovereignty from his election rather than from the Treaty of Kiel. Any recognition of the treaty would approve the Danish right to transfer Norway to Sweden—a right which most Norwegians denied. A third contingent merely agreed to recognize Karl XIII as king of Norway, thus ignoring the Treaty of Kiel and any Swedish claim to rights derived from Denmark, and making no pretence of elective legalisms which would mean a more authoritative position for the new king. They accepted the fact of Swedish invasion and force, and made as few alterations in the constitution as possible.

These final alterations, and November 4, mark the beginning of the union of Norway and Sweden. Formal acceptance of the *Riksakt* (Act of Union) and coronation of the king both came in 1815. The Storting session which accepted the union was marked by the relative silence of the unionist group and by Christie's dominance of almost every important action. Silence of the union party can be easily explained. The union's friends approved of the combination, but only on the basis of recognition of Norway's independence within it. They were not committed to a program of weakening Norway's position to make Sweden strong, and were, after all, just as good patriots as the independence party with whom their only quarrel, they felt, stemmed from the apparent impossibility of resisting union. Wedel, for example, insisted upon strengthening Norwegian constitutional institutions, not only because of his admiration for English parliamentarianism, but also because he believed that in them lay protection of Norway's sovereignty. He saw the union as a necessity "on grounds of propinquity, on grounds of popular 'common culture, common religion, common race, common wisdom, common love of freedom, common old laws, common old institutions, common old speech . . . , common political and commercial interests.' "[7]

Psychologically, however, the Norwegians lacked preparation for the end of their short-lived independence and they bowed reluctantly to Swedish imposition of the union. The union itself, according to the late Norwegian historian Arne Bergsgård, was intended by many Swedes to be a complete merger giving absolute control to Sweden—a situation which Norwegians felt they must prevent at all costs.[8] Some Swedes did claim Norway as a conquered province, as the Swedish nobleman, Axel Gabriel Silverstolpe, stated in the Riksdag debate on the union. From the outset, Norwegians feared Swedish intrusions, especially in military and naturalization issues, and thought that the preservation of their constitution, representative government, and other institutions depended upon vigorous resistance to the creation of union agencies which would tend toward more extensive amalgamation.

The partners in this new union had points of difference and similarity. Norway in 1815 had a population of 885,000 and Sweden numbered some 2,300,000. These people lived within the Scandinavian peninsula which, in Norway, consisted of mountains, fjords, and some river valleys in which the bønder clung to thin soils hardly bearing enough for self-sustenance.[9] Sweden's coastal line, indented by gentle bays on its southern littoral, presented a broad sweep of farming land which grew rich crops without difficulty. Norway's mountains made agricultural cultivation on a large scale either difficult or impossible, and even her forests could not flourish on ice and rocks. Sweden's mountains piled up along the western border and in the north, and these made the area impossible for farming. These natural barriers to agriculture along the frontiers of the two countries left only a band of sparse settlement and prevented growth of mobility between the two peoples in an age when transportation was yet

[7] Steen, *1814*, 246.   [8] *Året 1814*, II, 322.

[9] On the general social, agricultural, and political picture see B. J. Hovde, *The Scandinavian Countries 1720-1865. The Rise of the Middle Classes* (2 vols., Ithaca, N.Y., 1948), 220-302, and for the changes in politics, land, and economy, see pp. 510-572, 617-649.

undeveloped. The central plain, together with the richer southern coast, contained the greater percent of Swedish population and provided the foodstuffs essential for the country's domestic economy. The lakes of the region furnished food and transport. Using this chain, the Göta Canal was built to link Stockholm with the west coast and the port of Göteborg. Norway, on the other hand, possessed few lakes of commercial importance and no navigable rivers. The climate of Norway, milder than that of any other part of northern Europe, was more fortunate, but rainfall and milder winters could not increase productivity of either soil or forest. Sweden's natural resources exceeded those of Norway, for she owned the iron, copper, and other minerals which Norway lacked. In both, however, the forests and mountain waterfalls constituted an important reserve. Both used the sea for transport and food, but eventually Norway forged ahead in her merchant marine and fishing industries. Her fortunate location in relation to offshore cod and herring banks meant a resource denied to Sweden.

In 1814 the economy[10] of the two countries consisted of fishing, agriculture, shipping, and forestry. The fishers, farmers part of the year, were increasing their share in Norwegian economy. Even in the seventeenth century, Norwegian dried and salted fish were familiar sights on Amsterdam's docks and in the Catholic countries to the south. Agriculture composed nearly ninety percent of the nation's economy, and the government and nation leaned heavily upon the agricultural classes.

During the Napoleonic wars both countries went through cycles of prosperity and depression according to restrictive policies of the warring powers and of their own governments. Generally the period from 1800 to 1808 was an era when farmer, merchant, and shipper alike enjoyed relative prosperity. From 1808 to 1812, however, with restrictions at home and abroad, the last two classes suffered greatly. If England had not winked at the smuggling trade through Sweden to the continent, Swedish merchants would have experienced difficult times. Domestic restrictions, remnants of the disappearing mercantilist system, were complete-

10 For Sweden see Eli Heckscher, *An Economic History of Sweden*, trans. Göran Ohlin (Cambridge, Mass., 1954), 130-208.

ly ignored in Norway during the free period of 1800-1808, except where the guilds insisted upon their retention. The two countries differed in that Norway was isolated from the center of authority in Copenhagen, lacked a strong central control within the country, and possessed an English market for her goods. Sweden, hampered by foreign control of sea lanes in the Kattegat and the Sound, and by watchful Danish eyes, could not as yet afford to take advantage of trade with England. Only in 1812 was trade resumed and Swedish merchants briefly permitted prosperity before the post-Napoleonic depressions.

In agricultural landholding the two countries differed considerably. In Sweden, large farms of 100 acres or more prevailed, and large labor groups were available to till them. The average size of farms in Norway was quite small: the majority in 1907 were of less than 15 acres; only 35 farms were over 250 acres. The larger landholders of Sweden were often nobles whose estates were entailed. Among the Norwegian nobility, however, only Severin Løvenskiold held extensive properties. Norway had never experienced serfdom, and her *bønder* remained free of economic and legal controls. In southern Sweden, long under Danish control, a system arose in which the peasants assumed obligations to the landlords unless they held their own property. Out of this system developed a type of landless agrarian class. The greater role of Sweden's aristocracy, landed estates, and larger agrarian holdings, as compared to those of Norway, naturally meant less economic democracy. The controlling Norwegian bureaucracy, which owned little land, manifested less hostility toward extension of political rights to lower income groups as agitation for franchise reforms developed in the last part of the century.

The many comparisons which existed in the economy had no parallels in the governments of the two countries, for they differed both in ideology and practice. Norway had been ruled from Denmark since the end of Queen Margaret's reign (1412). The Danish representatives in Norway had been either the local governor (*amtmand*) or, nationally, the *statholder*. The latter often failed to reside in Norway, and the office served frequently as a sinecure to pay for political debts of Danish kings. Decrees emanated from Copenhagen and their restrictions on a mercantilist pattern satisfied the interests of Danish merchants and ignored wishes of the Norwegian towns. The civil service of political and religious officials came mainly from Danish rather than Norwegian backgrounds, and *bønder* naturally eyed them with suspicion and resentment. In the period of neglect caused by the Napoleonic wars, administration from Copenhagen lapsed and a native bureaucracy arose from the Norwegian professional and middle-class groups who intermarried with the old Danish civil service families.

In Sweden the personnel of government could trace its traditions, on both local and national levels, back to the sixteenth century. Its center of authority and function was the king, his court and councilors, and the Riksdag. Methods of government matured in the eighteenth century and by 1814 Swedish officials could reasonably say that they knew how to govern, whereas the Norwegians lacked experience. The constitution of 1809 began parliamentary government in Sweden, but it was on a reactionary, aristocratic basis. The Riksdag's organization into four estates, or houses, of *bönder*, burgher, clergy, and nobility led to constant deadlocks, for each estate jealously guarded its autonomy. The frequent compromises arising from this arrangement favored most often the house of nobles because of their greater prestige and training in government. The four houses of the Riksdag not only conflicted in their interests, but the monarchy possessed considerable powers over their members. Authority over the army, navy, finances, laws and courts, foreign affairs, and many other matters rested with the crown.

The Eidsvoll Constitution, in establishing the Storting, added parliamentary government to the Norwegian system in effect during the Danish regime. Drawing its inspiration mainly from French, American, and Spanish sources, Norway's new constitution put her politically so far in advance of other European states that often she was regarded as a "Jacobin" among conservative governments. The Storting itself was an anomaly among European parliamentary forms because of its unicameral organization and because of the degree of control given it over political, economic, and social matters. Even though the political franchise was limited and the commercial interests dominated sessions of the Storting, nevertheless the fundamental law of Norway was most liberal.

Contrasts between the Eidsvoll Constitution and Sweden's constitution of 1809 were varied and deep. On the one side was Norway, with her limitation of royal power through constitutional checks and her sovereignty vested in Storting and people. And on the other was Sweden, whose constitutional and political organization reflected the traditions of a monarchy which had not been entirely discarded in 1809 and a nobility which remained the bulwark of the crown.

In the decade preceding union, social development hung at dead center in both Norway and Sweden, largely because of class rigidity, the agrarian character of their economy, and the economic depression both suffered in the wake of the Napoleonic wars. Of polite society Norway had little, unless the small middle-class "courts" of Bergen, Oslo, or Stavanger could be counted. Inspired by the French Revolution, leading citizens of these towns organized dramatic societies, some journals and newspapers, and discussion and debating clubs. For the most part, however, pleasures were rustic and refined culture nearly absent. In Sweden, on the contrary, there was a court with long traditions, an Opera made famous by Gustaf III, and a royal palace in which the nobility and royal family enlivened the long winter of the capital. It was there that the Norwegian delegation appeared to inform Karl XIII of his election as king of Norway; foreign observers and the Swedish queen noted the startling comparison of plainly-dressed Norwegians with Swedish courtiers and officials in their court regalia. In particular the Danish minister commented favorably on the impressions conveyed by Christie's speech and by the native costumes of the bønder in the delegation.[11]

Contrasts between the social classes of either country showed gaps which in the end proved obstacles to real understanding. The landed and wealthy nobility of historic heritage headed the

11 Steen, *1814*, 273-274.

Swedish social list. They were numerous, cultured, and politically powerful. In sharp contrast was Norway, which had only two nobles, and even they were eliminated from any class privileges by the Eidsvoll Constitution which abolished their status as an hereditary class. Norway's bureaucracy paralleled the entrenched position of Sweden's nobility. It was composed of professionally trained people: lawyers, teachers, clergymen, and politicians who, though educated and cultured, were disinclined to venture abroad for training or to seek new concepts. The scope of bureaucratic class traditions and philosophy was, consequently, fixed within the narrow Norwegian orbit.

The middle class of both countries, while small in numbers, possessed considerable wealth. Both this class and the bureaucracy could hardly be separated in Norway because of family, intermarriage, and cultural ties. Wedel, for example, was nobleman, middle class, and bureaucrat all in one, while others fell only within the latter classification. The middle class played a dominant role in Norwegian economic and social life and "liberties" of the laissez-faire period meant usually the extension of middle-class influence and control over the countryside.

The *bønder* of Norway and Sweden shared many similar characteristics. Both were superstitious, religious-minded, narrow in most concepts, hard-drinking (especially in those days of home distilling of *brennvin*), frugal, and impervious to change. In Norway a free peasantry could date its traditions in local legal rights from earliest times, while the southern Swedish *bönder* had lost some of their freedoms. Roughly farmer classes in both countries separated into three groups: the large *bønder* of considerable wealth and material possessions; the small *bønder* who always verged on bankruptcy because of hazards in making a living; and the small crofter owning an acre or two of land and eking out a living through fishing and forestry during the winter months. Differences between these three groups in Norway and Sweden were matters of degree, for the truly large *bønder* hardly existed in Norway while in Sweden they were important both economically and politically. Most Norwegian *bønder* fell naturally into the second category of small farmers, but without the precarious

economy of their Swedish parallels. The crofter of Norway possessed greater potentialities and greater security against want than
Swedes of the same class. In both countries a fourth category of
the landless was growing in size. They were essential in rural
economy for they worked as a roving labor force in the forest during the winter and in harvests in the summer.

In both Norway and Sweden, the *bønder* missed the cultural
and political mainstream. For farmers, reading was a luxury they
could ill afford, and was confined to the Bible and Luther's
Catechism; they did not read newspapers until the 1860's. Although they possessed inherent traits of independence and democracy, they had as yet developed no class consciousness[12] and
as a consequence had no political power. Willing to bow before
superior education, social position, and tradition, the *bønder*
were content through the first part of the nineteenth century to
be governed by intellectuals.

Education as well as society in Norway seemed contentedly
isolated from the continent. The upper classes received their education in Denmark because their own university began operation
only in 1813, while Swedes trained either at Lund or Uppsala
or in Germany. Attendance at any university was most unusual,
however. The education of the average Norwegian or Swede consisted of the confirmation class or the "dame" schools where nearly all children were taught to read and write. In 1814 the rate
of illiteracy was low in both countries, as each pastor was required
to ensure that the children in his parish could read, interpret,
and write the Holy Scripture. In this way, the clergy assured
themselves of creditable performances by pupils at their confirmation exercises.

The official church of both states was Lutheran, and the clergy,
as members of the civil service, derived their salaries from the
state. As a force in political and social life within each country,
the clergy ranked with the upper classes. Their activities in the
parishes naturally gave them an insight into the life of the
farmers and agrarian workers, but, on the whole, the clergy of

---

[12] Halvdan Koht, *Norsk bondereisning. Fyrebuing til bondepolitikken* (Oslo,
1926).

both Norway and Sweden buried themselves in routine and contented themselves with perfunctory performances of their official duties. The two churches were completely separate, and they resisted efforts to forge one Scandinavian religious body.[13]

The language of the Norwegian upper class, and the written speech of the country, was Dano-Norwegian or *riksmaal*, as it came to be known, and marked differences existed between the official language and regional dialects. The speech of a citizen of Bergen or Trondheim, while intelligible to the resident of Oslo, differed from the latter's dialect in the same fashion as did the Swedish spoken by the resident of Skåne from that of a citizen of Dalarne. All Swedes accepted the official language (*bokmål*), but in common speech its use would be an affectation. The dialects of western Sweden and eastern Norway often combined elements of both languages, and a citizen of Jämtland could more easily understand a Norwegian across the border than his fellow countryman from Stockholm.

Language remained a distinctive cultural characteristic, for ethnically the two peoples composed a single unit. Studies of physical characteristics show no marked differences and, except for language, even a native of one country could not identify with certainty his fellow countryman in the midst of Scandinavian "foreigners." Homogeneity of population was marked, for political barriers to the entry of Jews, and the absence of Slav migration, prevented their intermixture. Numbers of Germans, Dutch, English, and Scots fitted naturally, after short residences, into the local population. The Finns and Lapps constituted the main non-Scandinavian elements in the two countries and their small numbers gave them no social or political significance. Intermarriage of Norwegians and Swedes was uncommon, not for ethnic reasons, but because of communication difficulties. On the border in contiguous areas marriages across national boundaries occurred in some numbers because Swedish migratory workers thought Norwegian wives more industrious than Swedish. Yet these isolated instances did not alter the general separatism of the two union partners.

[13] Cf. Hovde, *op.cit.*, 303-347.

The union of these two kingdoms by the *Riksakt* (officially signed in 1815) produced no changes in Swedish governmental institutions or in Norwegian institutions of the Danish period. Norway was left autonomous, and her Eidsvoll Constitution was retained with the alterations voted by the Storting to bring the union into being. Her language, customs, religion, and culture underwent no change. Structurally, the symbol of union in Norway was the king, who resided there part of the year, or who designated a *statholder* (until 1856) to act for him. The king's powers were broad: he could, and did, open parliament; he signed all legislation and had the power of veto over it, according to the constitution, though subsequent heated disputes revolved around the issue of an absolute or suspensive veto. He appointed cabinet officers, usually with the advice of Storting leaders.

The king also possessed full powers over the conduct of war and foreign affairs. He commanded the Norwegian army and navy, though its officers had to be Norwegians. His command of the defense forces was restricted to operations within the territory and waters of Norway; the Storting could grant authority for the use of Norwegian forces outside the country, but it was never necessary. In foreign affairs the king was free of any Norwegian control except that of the purse, since the Storting voted in each budget an annual sum for the foreign office. His freedom meant that the minister of foreign affairs in the Swedish cabinet (who was responsible solely to the king) was entrusted with the conduct of the union's foreign relations.

Actually, the king occupied the position of a dualistic sovereign. When in Norway, he must be Norwegian; when in Sweden, wholly Swedish. He used the Norwegian language and belonged to the Lutheran faith. He took an oath to maintain the Norwegian constitution. All officers of the armed forces, government, and courts likewise took an oath of loyalty to uphold the monarchy and its representative sovereign. Norwegian officers accompanied the king and male members of the royal family on their tours, and ladies in waiting attended the queen during her residence. At least one Norwegian adjutant returned with the king to Sweden. The Storting voted annually a civil list for the royal

family which could be refused, as was done on at least two occasions.

But no distinct line marked his royal functions as monarch
of the united kingdoms, as Norwegian king, or as the sovereign
of Sweden. Neither parliament could check the power of the
king in the other state, and neither country's ministers could
advise him on his duties and functions in the other nation. Norwegian cabinet officers, however, resided in Stockholm, when the
king was in residence there, to consult and advise him on all
legislation pertaining to their country. Although most Norwegian
writers fail to mention it, the king was likewise accompanied by
Swedish cabinet officers on his visits to Norway for the same purpose. At first Swedish ministers had expected that the king would
exercise his powers in Norway through them, as had been done
in negotiations with the Storting in 1814, but this technique
never developed.

In other respects Norway was free and independent. An independent civil service, cabinet, and parliament prevented the
creation of a joint governmental system. No Swede gained any
authority within or over Norway and he could not enter the
Norwegian civil service. Local administration and the courts remained completely free of even royal control, although the king
might pardon criminals and civil offenders with the consent of
the cabinet. Appointments to local administrative posts were
made and approved by the cabinet and Storting with the king's
signature *pro forma*. In general the king confined himself to
major questions touching the union itself and avoided interference in strictly Norwegian affairs. He was a constitutional monarch in name and fact, which was quite different from his position in Sweden.

Norwegian laws remained intact and subject to no outside
interpretation or court. There was not even a union court or
legislative body superior to the Storting or Riksdag. The Act of
Union established procedures for the election of a king, should
there be no heirs, and for its own dissolution, but these powers
were intended to be exercised jointly and a meeting of leaders
of the two countries would have to decide on a course of action.

The Norwegian currency was separate from that of Sweden and
entirely different; not until signature of the Scandinavian mint
convention in 1875 did the two kingdoms have a common currency. Each national bank was subject only to its own parliament
and its governors, and financial policies for each country originated in Oslo and Stockholm.

The union, therefore, was an amalgamation in which the main
link between the two separate kingdoms was their common king.
As Norwegian jurists argued, the association of the two countries
was a personal and not a real union, and they recognized only
the authority of a limited monarchy.[14] The ties forging this union
were not only fragile, at times they seemed hardly to exist.

But weak as these bonds might be, they were important, and
needed to gather strength if the union were to endure peace-
fully. Disputes over politics, separatism, and jurisdiction often
appear picayune and theoretical, but they assumed an ever-in-
creasing role in the relations of the two countries. In addition the
methods for establishment of the union and the ambitious and
thwarted views of Swedish political leaders led to friction, misunderstanding, and the growth of symbols effecting a warped
attitude of both peoples toward the union and its problems. Almost from the beginning the union distilled the poisons responsible for its eventual demise.

[14] Cf. articles in *Historisk tidsskrift* (Norwegian), xxxvi (1953), 449-512, by
Hans Meijer (Swede) and Reidar Omang (Norwegian). See also the latter's
summary in his *Norsk utenrikstjeneste grunnleggende år* (Oslo, 1955), 17-28.

◇◇

CHAPTER III

CULTURAL AND ECONOMIC PROBLEMS
OF UNION

◇◇

THE separatism of the two countries, symbolized politically in
the *Riksakt* and in the status of the monarchy, became increasingly apparent during the last half of the nineteenth century,
especially in cultural and economic aspects of their union relationship. Tendencies toward both integration and disintegration could be discerned, with more emphasis on the latter. Hardly any cultural institutions with vitality and strength enough to
act as carriers for integration came into being or flourished. Some
integrative economic institutions, on the other hand, emerged at
various times, even during the decade of defeat after the failure
of amalgamation. Exploration of these cultural, social, and economic phenomena indicates possibilities for growth of both integration and amalgamation, but not at a rate constant enough
to enable leaders and governments to make systematic use of
these currents.

Representing as they did two nationalistic and separate traditions, milieus, and cultural patterns, the people of Norway and
Sweden stressed individuality in language, although in reality
linguistic barriers might have been easily overcome.[1] In the 1840's
a new language, constructed from country dialects, aided in both
the development of nationalism and the movement for independence from Dano-Norwegian and Danish influences. This
nynorsk of Ivar Aasen represented a revolt, not against Sweden
but against Denmark. Although the struggle between adherents
of the new language and the old *riksmaal* stressed anti-Danish
sentiments, this linguistic nationalism perversely increased friction between Norway and Sweden. The Norwegian language con-

---

[1] Elias Wessén, "The Scandinavian Community of Language," *Le Nord*, IV
(1941), 221, 225-226.

flict, or *maalstriden,* as exemplified in the bitter argument between two Norwegian novelists—Bjørnstierne Bjørnson and Arne
Garborg—found these opponents of the union savagely trading
verbal blows whose end product was Norwegian-Swedish friction.
Garborg's dictum, "Language is the nation," showed the personal feeling that he and his followers had not only toward adherents of *riksmaal,* but also toward the union.[2]

Naturally language contained attributes of cultural superiority
within both Norway and the union. The Swedish of Bellman,
Geijer, and Strindberg and the Norwegian of Garborg, Bjørnson, Ibsen, and Ivar Aasen must be "protected" and "kept pure."
Language evidenced most clearly the uniqueness and separate-
ness of each nation. In small ways it became a part of the inner
conflicts of the union: kings were liked or disliked for the fluency
of their Norwegian; documents must be in either Norwegian or
Swedish, depending upon their use; letters must be translated before their official acceptance, although friends corresponded each
in his native tongue. The connection between language and
union conflict depended upon linguistic consciousness, a feeling
projected with comparative ease into political strife.

Both peoples belonged to the Lutheran faith, and no important
changes developed during the first half of the union's existence.
The two national churches infrequently collaborated, except at
the level of bishops, for the Norwegian clergy out of national
considerations refrained from any association with the Swedish
clergy. Religious currents ran similar courses: both developed
fundamentalist circles; both suffered with "liberals" such as
Bjørnson and Strindberg; both endured evangelists, Baptists,
temperance societies, Grundtvigians, and other evidences of fervor or fanaticism. None of these movements crossed national
lines, even if Bjørnson's philosophy was strikingly close to that
of Vitalis Norström or Victor Rydberg, because publications of
the church in one country were not read in the other and no
interreligious groups existed until late in the nineteenth century. Danish religious leaders did influence Norwegian and
Swedish thought, but few Swedish philosophers affected either

2 Keilhau, *Den norske folks* . . . , x, 198-202.

Norway or Denmark. Søren Kierkegaard and N. F. S. Grundtvig were well-known Danish names in Norwegian churches, while the Swedish Rydberg and Norström were inconsequential there. In an indirect way, fundamentalism and conservatism among the clergy in both countries indicated common sources of ideas in Germany, but no apparent approach on an interunion basis could be discerned. The social historian seeks evidence of clerical unity in opposing "radicalism," atheism, Darwinism, and the free churches, only to find each clergy distrusting the other and fighting alone. Since both were national churches, funds for their support came from national legislatures, and national councils of bishops served as sources of authority to which prospective clerical candidates looked. Neither corps of pastors needed to direct their attention beyond their own political horizon. While other professional groups often deplored antiunionism, a bare handful of the clergy resisted the movement toward separation. The case of Christopher Bruun, who defended Scandinavianism and unionism, was unique enough to be discussed in the Norwegian cabinet in 1905. The two countries were identical in religious form and thought, but a movement to combine their churches would have caused a veritable revolt.

Late nineteenth century changes in the social structure of the two countries showed some important differences. The *bønder* class, which for the whole of the century made up the majority of both populations, began to struggle for political power. In Sweden, where farmers wielded a great influence on development of parliamentary powers, they fought middle class, aristocrats, and workers at various times. In Norway, their class and economic unity in *Venstre* (Left) furnished *bønder* with a political program, and the creation of the *bonde* lodges gave them a cultural center around which they could develop pride in their accomplishments. Swedish farmers maintained their nondemocratic control over the country *statare*, crofters, and day laborers —all of whom, because of the Swedish system of large landholdings, were economically and socially dependent upon the good will of the *bönder*. Social and economic discontent arose within these lower rural classes, who comprised 30% of the farm population between 1840 and 1900, but any efforts to improve their conditions or to give them recourse to the ballot were resisted by the farmers with large holdings. Norway continued her tradition and even increased her practice of small proprietor farms. Consequently, the subordinate landless groups, because of their improved economic and political conditions, were disappearing after 1870, except in the forest industries where they became the nucleus of a new labor force after industrialization. The increase in personal ownership of farms and a parallel decline of the landless group influenced the rise to power of *Venstre* and increased the political weight carried by cultural and other farm organizations. At the same time as this trend developed in the decades after 1870, along with Norway's industrial and economic growth, a unified Norwegian middle class evolved.

This middle class, with its liberal program, slowly emerged during the late nineteenth century. In Norway depressed economic conditions, prevalent in the 1820's, forced changes in composition of the middle class, as migrants from Germany, Holstein, and Copenhagen gradually outnumbered, and thus replaced, the older, more aristocratic-minded gentry.[3] Joined with them were the bureaucratic and professional men: politicians, officeholders, pastors, teachers, and lawyers. During the mid-century years, this middle class dominated a slowly-awakening Norway, only to lose power when the lawyers and teachers shifted their political allegiance to the new *Venstre* party. In the last two decades of the century, an entirely new industrial-commercial middle class arose from the merchant marine owners, the forest product millowners, and fish processors. It was a new aristocracy of wealth.

The Swedish aristocracy, which had controlled political, social, and economic life until mid-century, retreated to fight a social-political battle. They eventually lost their dominance, however, with the growth of the Liberal Party and the rise of the workers in the Social Democratic and labor movements. Until the Riksdag reforms of 1865-1866, the House of Nobles held almost absolute power through their alliance with the clergy, their political ex-

---

[3] Theodore Jorgenson, *Norway's Relation to Scandinavian Unionism 1815-1871* (Northfield, Minn., 1935), appendix, 427-432.

perience, and their endowment with wealth and prestige. Their
social-political concepts rested on the assumption that they ruled
by right and knowledge and that only they knew the ultimate
good for society.

Social communication of these various groups across national
boundaries was not only uncommon but would have transgressed
class traditions. Swedish aristocrats found no nobles in Norway
with whom to associate, and the Norwegian bureaucrats sought
cultural and social affinity with their fellows in Sweden in vain.
In spite of their need for supranational support to maintain their
position, the two bureaucracies found no ground for collaboration: they held no common views; in fact, they hardly spoke the
same political language. Norwegians viewed with suspicion the
nationalism of Sweden's upper classes and believed that they
grasped selfishly for political supremacy over both kingdoms.
Some friendships were formed, but not at the expense of Norwegian nationalism or pride. The Swedes reluctantly admitted
Norwegians into their social circles; a notable exception was
Georg Sibbern, Norwegian member of the joint council in Stockholm, who made friends with Baron Louis de Geer and his liberal colleagues. No Swedish officials or government leaders resided for any length of time in Norway, except for the *statholder*
who failed to take part in social affairs and who was heartily disliked because of his office.[4]

Norwegian *bønder*, neither reading about nor interested in
their Swedish parallels, attempted feebly to seek cooperation after 1860. Working class and farm laborers failed to make any
mark on Norwegian-Swedish relations until the last decade of
the union's life. Only in the 1890's, under the leadership of Hjalmar Branting, Carl Jeppesen, and Christian H. Knudsen did the
labor unions and Social Democrats forge new ties, but too late
to affect the union's quarrels. Even then, their willingness to
cooperate with each other made some impression on the eventual

---

[4] Von Essen, the first Swedish *statholder* in Norway, asked Karl Johan for
a transfer or relief from his duties because he considered it "a sentence of
death if his fate were to live and die in Norway." *Sveriges historia* . . . , XI,
376-377.

outcome of the movement toward dissolution of the union. As a social class the bourgeoisie were the first to find a bridge in economic and cultural collaboration and to found groups, associations, committees, businesses, and other organizations with a union character.

Communication of individuals or groups saw little friendship, little intensity, and no depth. If correspondence was necessary—and it rarely was—it revealed no understanding or association with the respondent's viewpoints. Letters between Norwegians and Swedes often contained a formal note, expressing the reserve felt for one another. Even such a dedicated unionist as Francis Hagerup, when he was prime minister, wrote with reservations to Ivar Afzelius, his close Swedish friend. Adolf Hedin and S. A. Hedlund, prominent Swedish liberals—the latter a famous editor of *Göteborgs Handels-och Sjöfartstidning*—criticized Swedish views on Norway without restraint, but their letters to Norwegian friends were scarcely friendly. The paucity of nonofficial correspondence between Norwegians and Swedes, and of the ordinary intercourse to build better relationships, indicated the lack of real communication.

The main media of communication proceeded from political associations based on compulsion, since this was a union, and were of such a nature as to impress Norwegians with their subordinate position. The main groups forced to associate with each other were those most opposed—Norwegian bureaucrats and Swedish political leaders. Little fruit could be expected of such prejudiced sources, where the Swede thought the Norwegian to be inferior, legalistic-minded, stubborn, dishonest; and the Norwegian believed the Swede to be militaristic, aristocratic-minded, insufferably egotistical, narrow, and stiff-necked. Individual familiarity usually changed general concepts only to this degree—that one Swede (or one Norwegian) was not like the others.

In their forced dependence upon each other, the peoples of the two countries remained either antagonistic or neutral. For prestige, Swedish Conservatives demanded Sweden's dominance in order to match her greater size and historic greatness. Norwegians accused Swedes of still living in the period of their

European glory in the sixteenth and seventeenth centuries; a favorite cartoon in Norwegian newspapers pictured a pigmy Swede in Karl XII's famous jackboots, wearing his enormous sword. Swedish ministers, who accompanied the king to Norway on his visits, were regarded as foreigners, which they were. The story is often told in Swedish memoirs of how carefully and painstakingly Norwegians avoided association with these ministers for fear of being charged with currying favor or, worse yet, of being pro-Swedish. The Norwegian ministers in Stockholm visited with Swedish middle class-liberal friends, and were deemed by even those as socially inferior. Constantly on the defensive, they made a reputation for themselves as boorish, distant, and unpleasant.

Even more than personal and individual communication, the rise of newspapers and their quickening of the intellectual life of both countries fostered disintegration by their full participation in the union's controversies. Their editors held in their hands powerful weapons for and against the union. Unfortunately, from the union's viewpoint, the intellectual origins of Norwegian editors were either *Venstre* political circles or the university, where antiunion sentiment was strongest. These editors sympathized with *Venstre* viewpoints, although they might direct an opposing paper. The Norwegian foundation of *Vort Land*,[5] *Verdens Gang*, and *Dagbladet* in the years 1867-1869, and their subsequent attacks on the union, were closely linked to the failure of revisionism in 1871. The willingness of newspapers and editors to adopt strong stands arose from the close linkage of individual papers to political parties. The *Venstre* press naturally adopted party attitudes toward the union, charging it with placing hindrances in the path of franchise reforms, parliamentary government, and greater democracy. Even the Conservative papers could not avoid involvement in the incessant "press wars" with their emphasis on hostility and bitterness and the worst elements in Norwegian-Swedish relations.

[5] Note especially how the Conservative *Vort Land* followed an anti-Scandinavian, anti-Swedish, and antiunion program, despite its rural, conservative origins. Helge Dahl, " 'Vort Land—Dølens Femte Aargang,' " *Historisk tidsskrift* (Norwegian), xxxvi (1953), 579-601.

In Sweden, similarly, the press multiplied in number during the middle years of the century. Published mainly in Stockholm, the major papers stood for party programs and voiced partisan Swedish views on the union. *Nya Dagligt Allehanda, Vårt Land, Svenska Dagbladet,* and *Aftonbladet,* for the union's last decade, filled their columns with verbal brickbats and defensive forays against Norwegian refusals to face facts. The Swedish press either denounced the Norwegians, or worse yet, disdainfully treated them with contempt. The first exciting experience of a real public press was fruitful in argument and debate but most destructive of unionist sentiments.

In some respects the press could not occupy a middle ground. A few newspapers attempted, however, to cast light rather than heat upon the controversy. *Morgenbladet,* the leading Norwegian Conservative paper, maintained a steadfast unionist position, but made quite clear Norway's equality with Sweden and her sovereign character. Its chief rival, *Aftenposten,* also assumed a double role. In Sweden the great liberal *Göteborgs Handels-och Sjöfart-stidning,* under the editorship of S. A. Hedlund, tried to develop a closer union relationship in order to increase the strength of the dual kingdoms and to maintain peace on the Scandinavian peninsula. With the rise of the Social Democratic press after the 1880's, a new political contingent entered the arena and found itself embroiled in the union's quarrels. During the 1890's the Norwegian *Social-Demokraten* became as ardent a supporter of nationalism as the *Venstre* papers, while its Swedish counterpart held firmly to international socialist principles. Toward the end of the union the Swedish *Social-Demokraten* advocated the dissolution of the union and favored a new relationship based on equality and peace. The Swedish labor press, however, received no cooperation from the Norwegian Social Democratic party. Needless to say, local labor papers followed the lead of the major party newspaper, and thus what was said in Stockholm or Oslo was echoed throughout the country for the benefit of the working class.

The newspapers occupied an important role in the development of intellectual and cultural life and opened the outside world to the gaze of Norwegian and Swede. At the same time they stimulated interest in domestic affairs which, combined with economic, social, and cultural advances toward mid-century, turned the attention of both peoples inward. For Norwegians, especially, this self-analysis led to emphasis on nationalism and national sovereignty which, it was claimed, were thwarted by the union's existence. Papers exchanged news and magnified friction, so as the century progressed reports from each country came out with increased embellishments and invective. Antagonisms already close to the sensitive core of the union were deepened.

Just as the press and social communication furnished poor avenues for union collaboration, so the economic interests failed to provide easy paths to fuller integration. Norwegian economy felt some effects of the union's formation, but not to the extent expected by her middle class. Peace with Sweden and the lifting of the blockade were supposed to regain England's markets for Norwegian fish and forest products, and did so for a brief time. The general depression following the Napoleonic wars, however, closed both English and Swedish markets to Norwegian merchants. Economic contacts also proved to be socially unprofitable, i.e., a Norwegian sailor on board a Swedish ship would not fraternize with Swedish sailors. Economic aid and technicians were borrowed from England or Germany, not from each other;[6] Stephenson engineers from England, for example, built the first Norwegian railroads. Swedish capital, which after 1888 was legally on an equal footing in Norway, represented to Norwegians an investment whereby their industry would become a mere adjunct of Sweden's greater industrial plant. In both countries, however, capital remained almost exclusively at home. While Norway borrowed from abroad, Sweden exported capital in small quantity and when she imported, drew mostly upon German sources.[7] A notable exception was the building (1897-1903) of a railroad, the *Ofotenbanen*, to carry iron ore from northern Sweden to Narvik;

[6] Torsten Gårdlund, *Industrialismens samhälle* (Stockholm, 1942), discusses foreign influences in the development of Swedish industries in the late 19th century and finds Norwegian factors or techniques only in the sawmill and textile industries.

[7] Cf. chart in Gårdlund, *op.cit.*, 195.

in this enterprise capital and consultants from both countries actually cooperated.

Trade and commerce of the two countries retained their autonomy, except for joint tariff laws effective from 1825 to 1897. These applied only to a few specific items and their acceptance in 1825 was natural, since Sweden, as the larger partner with trade connections, protected the commerce of both countries. In 1857 the Storting refused to consider extension of the agreement to previously exempted articles on the ground that it would constitute a serious threat to Norwegian sovereignty, especially when accompanied by schemes for amalgamation. On the other hand, when Norwegians wished alterations they were able to secure them as the comprehensive changes in 1874 showed. At that time, for example, Norwegian textiles, which sold widely in Sweden, remained on the free list despite Swedish complaints.

After 1874 economic and industrial changes in both countries produced agitation for tariff revision. In Norway the trend was toward free trade after political battles in which Anton Schweigaard, Ebbe Hertzberg, and T. H. Aschehoug represented both free trade and unionist principles. The antiunionist *Venstre* mainly favored protectionism. In Sweden the tariff struggle of the 1880's, crossing both party and national lines, resulted in a narrow victory for protectionists, while in Norway just as close a margin was won by the free traders.[8]

Warning signals on the meaning of free trade-protectionist strife for the union appeared in 1886. The Riksdag approved revision of the joint tariff laws and protectionists won a notable victory. In 1895 the Riksdag asked the cabinet to abandon the joint trade laws and, because of a bitter union crisis that year, the proposal was approved. The ensuing discussion and negotiations on the laws in 1895-1897 reveal the specific interests at work. Norwegian textile manufacturers sought to protect their profitable markets, while agricultural groups wished the laws repealed because of competition from foreign grain imported into Sweden and sold either as flour or bread in the Norwegian market. In

8 Cf. *Sveriges historia* . . . , xiii, 121ff., and Keilhau, *Den norske folks* . . . , x, 347-349.

March 1897, Norwegian businessmen, chiefly those of Bergen, negotiated with Swedish colleagues and arranged a tariff law which the Swedish government and king refused to bring before the Riksdag. As a result, the joint tariff laws automatically lapsed on July 12, 1897, and as one Norwegian remarked: "When the tariff union binding the united kingdoms in economic relations was eventually removed, the foundation itself for the political union was thrown away."[9]

Just as the history of the joint tariff laws revealed weaknesses of union economic ties so the foreign trade of both Norway and Sweden displayed the absence of strong intra-union bonds. After England and Germany the next important nation in either country's import-export economy was either the union partner or Denmark. Swedish shipping in Norwegian ports between 1880 and 1910 ranked either third after England and Germany, or fourth after Denmark; similarly Norwegian shipping in Swedish ports was fourth after Germany, England, and Denmark, but declining in proportion to Swedish shipping. But the gross amounts of Norwegian tonnage in Swedish ports consistently outdistanced that of Swedish shipping in Norwegian ports. A common opinion, perpetuated through most textbooks, is that German markets and industries were imperative for Sweden's economy, as English markets and industries were to the economy of Norway. However, Sweden's import-export balance with England and Germany, respectively, shows England leading until 1904, when iron ore shipments to Germany via the *Ofotenbanen* and Narvik reversed their position. Norway's volume of trade with England was greater than that with Germany by only a comparatively small margin; after 1890 this slight gap began to decrease. During these years Norwegian politicians denounced Sweden's German orientation and emphasized Norway's English ties in order to defend their argument that the union's consular service favored Swedish trade with Germany to the exclusion of Norway's British connections.

Neither country found the other essential to its economy to

---

[9] Sigurd Grieg, "Omkring mellomrikslovens opphevelse, 1885-1897," *Nordisk tidskrift*, xxiv (1948), 404.

any considerable degree. On the other hand, competition seems
to have been no source of economic conflict since none materialized during the highly competitive period of the 1880's and
1890's.[10] The growth of a Norwegian merchant marine, which in
1900 was fourth in the world, thrust Norway farther away from
Sweden. Her ships brought products from English industries to
Sweden and reaped what Sweden either could not or did not wish
to develop. Since steam and iron freighters could not be built
in Norway, both English and Swedish shipbuilding yards profited
from Norwegian purchases of vessels. Throughout the first part
of the nineteenth century, England was the major source of such
purchases, since she was the cheapest market. In the last two
decades of the century, however, a small increase in numbers of
Norwegian keels laid in Sweden appeared to offset the general
trend away from dependence on each other.

The industrial separation of the two countries was most strikingly evidenced in their banking facilities. National banks (*Riksbank* and *Norgesbank*) controlled the financial life of each nation
even when private banking arose in the 1840's. Capital funds
came from foreign banks in Hamburg, London, and Paris;
Sweden used German sources and Norway used the French and
British, although there are exceptions such as the *Stockholms
enskilda* dependence upon the *Crédit lyonnais*. The complete
separation of both private and public banking systems meant an
absence of joint economic growth. At the same time the two
countries could agree on the signature of a mint convention in
the 1870's. As a Scandinavian agreement it became valid in 1875,
but only after considerable argument. When first attempted the
Norwegian Storting rejected it and an explanation lies, perhaps,
in Johan Sverdrup's words: "I vote against it because it is a
foreign growth without root in our domestic situation."[11] Although his opposition killed the proposal at first, Sverdrup eventually bowed before election reverses and the need for a change of
the awkward coinage system. In 1875 the Storting passed the
Scandinavian mint convention by a comfortable margin of 82 to
28. The new joint Danish-Norwegian-Swedish currency was now

[10] Cf. Keilhau, *Den norske folks* . . . , IX, 368-408.
[11] Halvdan Koht, *Johan Sverdrup* (3 vols., Oslo, 1918-1925), II, 117.

the *krone* of 100 *øre* with a gold standard. Exchange went through the national banks and few complaints arose from business and banking institutions until World War I's inflation.[12]

In the most important economic sphere of agriculture, changes in Sweden were more marked than in Norway. Cyclical movements did not reveal quite the same trends in both countries, although both suffered much from Russian, Canadian, and American grain imports in the 1870's and 1880's. Norwegian agriculture showed a more marked downturn in the 1870's, while Swedish farming continued to expand for at least another decade. Neither Norway nor Sweden competed in world markets for grain, for neither grew exportable surpluses in any appreciable amount. Both, in fact, imported quantities of foodstuffs.

Farming methods and economy lacked significant differences, although Swedish farmers, notably those of the south, steadily improved equipment and land. Farm equipment improved technically, and Sweden, with larger farms and more industrialization, advanced more rapidly. Dairy products constituted the essential mainstay of both farm economies, and steadily new agricultural schools increased popular interest in soil improvement and pure-bred cattle. The formation of farmers' cooperatives and their rapid expansion in the 1880's and 1890's created the economic unity necessary for an export industry and increased the strength and stability of farm groups in both countries. The acquisition of agricultural supplies through purchaser cooperatives, of capital from cooperative banks, and the sale of farm products through domestic and overseas organizations eventually resulted in providing greater farm capital strength and productivity. By 1900, except for backward areas, dairying had become the main economic foundation of farms and technically the most advanced.

Changes in the agricultural economy came at about the same

12 Attempts to continue the currency convention during World War I failed because of inflation in Denmark and Norway, and Sweden dumped the system by her restrictive legislation. In 1924 the convention was completely abrogated. For fuller details on the mint convention see Keilhau, *Den norske folks . . .* , x, 313-318; for the war period see Eli Heckscher, Konrad Bergendahl, *et al., Sweden, Norway, Denmark, and Iceland in the World War* (New Haven, Conn., 1930), 129-131, 191-197, 265.

time as the beginning of industrialization in Norway and Sweden. With superior material resources Sweden's expansion began earlier and showed greater rapidity and greater breadth. In the main, industrial growth in the two countries originated from the same basis, but differed in the separate industries which marked their rise to some prominence. Beginning in the 1870's with the lumber industries, both countries expanded into pulp and forest products with some rapidity in the two decades prior to 1900. Norway also expanded her merchant marine much faster than Sweden and developed fishing and chemical industries into export trades of some prominence. Sweden, on the other hand, turned to electrical, machine, and steel industries which made her a leading exporter of these products for the world market. Her iron ore, shipped via Narvik, came to assume an important place in German industry. The remarkable aspect of this industrial development was the rapidity with which Sweden outdistanced Norway and the degree to which she utilized natural resources.

Vitally important in the industrial development was the creation of a land transport system. Norway began with the building of the first railroad from Oslo to Eidsvoll in 1854. Sweden, inspired by Baltazar von Platen and the Göta Canal, also built numerous canals in the 1830's and 1840's, a feat which Norway could not duplicate. She also expanded her railroad system rapidly after 1850. Inter-Scandinavian transport and communication began with the Oslo-Karlstad telegraph in the 1850's and the opening of the Oslo-Stockholm railroad in 1867. From the first, both governments assumed responsibility for construction and ownership of main roads while private companies built spur lines. Towards the end of the century, and notably in the building of the Ofoten railroad, alterations in this policy allowed the government to pay building and financing costs and to retain control. At the same time, the Swedish government began to purchase private railroads—an action to which it was forced partly by their weak financial condition—until only a small fraction remained in private hands. In Norway public financing of railroads started her transport system, for engineering difficulties, lack of capital, and urgent need compelled government ownership. Lines were first built northward into the Gudbrandsdal, then south from Oslo on either side of the fjord. Extension of northern rails to Trondheim, although a matter of real importance, was delayed by Storting reluctance to finance the exceptional costs, by local "politicking," and by arguments over rail gauge. The west coast remained isolated, except by sea, until completion of *Bergensbanen* in 1907, a remarkable financing and an amazingly intricate engineering problem. In Sweden such difficulties were minimal, the needs greater, and improvements more rapid than in Norway.

Even when railroad lines connecting the two countries were fully opened, heavier traffic continued to be routed by sea. Shipment of heavy machinery from Oslo to Bergen by rail, for example, would have been considered foolish since marine freight costs were only a fraction of those overland. Similarly, shipments from Göteborg to Stockholm, or the opposite, went through the Göta Canal or by sea. Only the interior in either country depended upon the railroads, but they were essential for the maximum utilization of each country's resources. Both nations faced the sea and used waterways for communication and food, and each developed a merchant marine of considerable proportions for transport.

Intra-union ties remained few and fragile and dependence upon them for prevention or modifications of the union's controversies would have been unrealistic. Yet the cultural and economic ties of union show that the association of the two countries was not necessarily doomed to failure at its inception. Ethnic, linguistic, and religious similarities of the two countries might have assisted and certainly would not have harmed cooperation in a greater amalgamation scheme. Growth of large-scale industrial enterprises in the last quarter of the century in each country heightened possibilities for economic rivalry, but none seems to have developed and their continued need for imports, especially in agriculture, showed the two nations to be largely noncompetitive. The notable absence of any pronounced economic, cultural, or social intra-union associations offers a clue to the union's shallow roots among a sizable proportion of the citizens of either country. As a Swedish politician predicted in 1815, the union neither developed those political ties which were indispensable, nor achieved the broad economic, cultural, and social supports which were so imperative for integration.[13]

[13] Hans Järta as quoted in Jorgenson, *Norway's Relation* . . . , 23-24.

◇◇◇

CHAPTER IV

THE TESTING AND FAILURE OF INTEGRATION

◇◇◇

THE new social and cultural forces within the union during the late nineteenth century never became as important in the union's preservation as did the political factors. It was at the level of ministers, governments, and parliaments that the failure of integrative processes occurred. The grounds for growth of integration might have been better prepared if the social, economic, and cultural institutions had developed; but, since they did not, attempts at greater amalgamation during the mid-century could not but fail. As the union's first troubles and economic difficulties passed, leadership and governments of both countries sought to find means to enlarge the existing amalgamation. By union committees, by reform proposals, by compromises and negotiations, the monarchy sought to bring about a greater amalgamation, but these efforts floundered on divergent sets of values and inconsistent political systems. The failure of integration in the 1870's was not inevitable, although it can now be easily forecast in light of the attitudes of leaders, governments, and large groups of the people. Within these various groups constant minor controversies arose, indicating the absence of bases for integration.

These issues of conflict could hardly be avoided in the course of negotiations relating to the Treaty of Kiel, and the first incidents stemmed from Norway's former union with Denmark. Swedish commissioners at Kiel had agreed to secure from the Norwegians payment of part of the Dano-Norwegian public debt. The Norwegians objected on the grounds that they had not been represented in the Danish administration and felt great distaste for the payment of obligations about which they had not been consulted. Furthermore, they objected to the disproportionate size of the amount and to Swedish haste in negotiations. The

Storting refused to pass the requisite legislation, and thus blocked a settlement. In negotiations with Denmark, where Norwegians assumed an important and active role, Sweden defended the right of the Norwegian parliament to approve or reject payment of the contribution, but also realized the necessity of fulfilling treaty obligations even if it meant payment by Sweden herself of the portion of the debt assigned to Norway. Eventually the Danish debt case was amicably solved, but not before the foreign powers threatened to take diplomatic measures, not against Norway, but against Sweden who had failed to fulfill her obligations.

Sweden's eagerness for a solution of the vexatious problem was handicapped by a serious restriction of the powers of the foreign office. By accidental circumstance, foreign office administration passed from Christian Frederik to the Swedish king and the Swedish minister of foreign affairs without the accompanying authority to compel the Norwegian Storting to support an action taken by either the king or the foreign minister. Although actually a joint official in the sense that he acted as a union foreign minister, the Swede occupying the ministry of foreign affairs could never be a Norwegian official or recognized in Norway. His authority derived solely from his identification with the king whose powers did extend over Norway. This most confusing administrative procedure arose from the nature of the union, and foreign powers found it difficult to understand.

This confusion became even more apparent in the second serious incident—the Bodø affair—which may be sketched briefly. English smugglers escaped from Norwegian authorities at Bodø and, as a result of British pressure on Sweden and private falsification of documents and testimony, were freed completely by the union foreign office.[1] A representative of the smugglers even had the effrontery to demand an indemnity, which the Norwegian government and Storting refused to pay. England presented Sweden with a near-ultimatum demanding immediate indemnification and, after prolonged negotiations, the money was finally paid in 1821.

[1] For documents on the Bodø affair, see *British Diplomatic Correspondence Relating to the Bodø Affair*, ed. G. M. Gathorne-Hardy (Oslo, 1926).

Both cases created a legend of Swedish disregard of Norwegian interests and left a marked stigma on the "Swedish foreign office." Actually the handling of the two cases might well have left the impression that Norwegian policies and views dominated the foreign office, for Norway nominated negotiators for both discussions and her demands were met. Likewise, in negotiation of a treaty in 1827 with Russia and in the passage of a joint union law on partial free trade between the two kingdoms in 1825, Norwegian interests and not Swedish were mainly involved.[2]

Other issues arose in the 1820's, of little significance then but of some importance as symbols of "Swedish tyranny" in the union. An attempt of students and the Oslo public to celebrate May 17 (Constitution Day) in 1829 met with harsh treatment from troops dispatched by the authorities to quell the disturbance. This "Market Fight" (*Torgslaget*) of 1829 became an historic event not unlike the Boston Tea Party. Popular lithographs depicted the market square in Oslo with countless corpses lying bleeding or lifeless on its stones and with cavalrymen, obviously the "Swedish" garrison although no Swedish soldier was allowed in Norway, riding over their prostrate bodies. In a similar vein, Norwegian attempts to procure a national flag, without the union emblem in one corner, aroused patriotic sentiment more quickly and easily than had more than a generation of inflammatory books and pamphlets. When Norwegians in 1838 received the right to fly a "clean flag" on merchant ships "at their own risk," jubilation in Oslo and public admiration of Norwegian leaders of the movement showed the nationalistic weight of this symbol.

Belief in Swedish neglect of Norwegian foreign interests, properly spiced by the "Market Fight" and Constitution Day celebration, became a delicate political matter. With this background, Anton Jonas Hielm's Storting resolution of 1830 for a separate

[2] See Magnus Mardal, *Norge, Sverige og den engelska trelasttoll 1817-1850* (Oslo, 1957), for an exhaustive examination of a special problem—that of timber imports into England—and the question of which country exercised the greater influence. Mardal's conclusion is that English domestic factors resulted in restrictions on Norwegian lumber exports, even while earnest efforts were made by the union's foreign office to overcome this handicap. Cf. his English summary for condensation of this viewpoint.

foreign service assumed a serious aspect.[3] In justification of Norwegian apprehensions about foreign relations, it might be noted that Swedes displayed little concern for their desires and interests; if Norwegian cabinet officers objected, some slight modifications might be made, not as a right but as a special privilege. Eventually Swedes agreed to take problems affecting both countries to the joint council and granted some authority to Norway over consular officials.[4] Forced to retreat from their previous stand by the mounting pressure of Norwegian public opinion, the Swedes began to appoint Norwegian diplomatic officials, yet refused to consider these arrangements as rightfully within Norwegian expectations. An alternative would have been the establishment of a Norwegian foreign office, or, as in a later stage of union conflict, the creation of a separate consular system. Grist for official debates and fierce public vituperation was furnished for the last two decades of the union.

With rising *bonde* representation in the Storting, economic progress, and prosperity, some friction disappeared. Karl Johan, weary of the controversy, appointed a joint Norwegian-Swedish union committee in 1839 to discuss conduct of foreign affairs, appointment of diplomatic and consular officials, and other problems. The committee was still debating on its report in 1844 when Karl Johan died. The new king, Oscar I, requested legislation on two questions: a union coat of arms and a flag. Passage of these items allowed a program of union revision to die.

At the same time a trend of another nature was fraught with possibilities for integration. A movement for development of closer cooperation and fraternal feeling, begun in the 1830's by prominent Danish and Swedish leaders, culminated in meetings of students of Uppsala, Lund, and Copenhagen. In 1844 a great gathering at Copenhagen of students, professors, and other interested persons initiated popular Scandinavianism. Intertwined with ideas of northern union, of a defense community, of dynastic confederation, and of other will-o'-the-wisps, Scandinavianism reflected both benefit and harm upon union relationships. It was

[3] See Jorgenson, *Norway's Relation* . . . , 51-53, for Hielm's resolution.
[4] *Sveriges historia* . . . , XII, 138-139.

the impetus for the creation of a branch of the Karl Johan Society in Oslo in 1848 and the celebration there, six years later, of Union Day (November 4) for the first time, although the monarchy had pressed Norwegian leaders for its inauguration as early as 1821. Some Norwegians accepted stronger pro-Swedish and prounionist programs because of their Scandinavianism; T. H. Aschehoug's defense of the union, both in committee and in the Storting in 1871, arose largely from his sympathy for it. His Scandinavianism found itself in good company with that of Anton Schweigaard, Georg Sverdrup, Henrik Ibsen, and even Bjørnstierne Bjørnson, who were among its enthusiastic adherents. Mixed with a somewhat mystical idea of Scandinavian brotherhood was a firm belief in liberal principles as represented in the events of 1848-1849 in Denmark. Support for liberalism was interpreted naturally by Norwegians as advocacy of a freer and looser union, but by Swedes as greater union solidarity and creation of joint institutions.

The failure of Norway-Sweden to aid the Danish cause in the war with Prussia in 1863-1864 killed political Scandinavianism. Cultural groups continued their programs through *Nordiska nationalförening, Skandinaviska sällskap, Nordisk samfund,* and the publication of propaganda works, including *Nordisk tidskrift,* but the old impulse was gone.[5] From this period dated the strong Danophilism and exile of Ibsen, whose *Peer Gynt* and *Brand* evidenced his bitterness toward his homeland. Bjørnson, just as angered, turned to composing plays and songs embodying an intense Norwegian nationalism. To Norwegian radical and liberal leaders, Scandinavianism constituted not a single, but a twin, danger. Johan Sverdrup, *Venstre* leader in Norway, said the " 'enemies of our independence and nationality live not in Germany and Russia but in Sweden and Denmark,' " and he organized a Norwegian society to protect Norwegian language and literature.[6]

This hostility stemmed from a movement, begun in the 1850's

[5] Hans Lennert Lundh, *Från skandinavism till neutralitet* (Trollhättan, 1950), 23-28, 64-70, 71-77, 79-83.

[6] Koht, *Sverdrup,* I, 372.

by Karl XV, for an expansion of amalgamation. His plan proposed the enlargement of the existent union governmental administrative agencies to include a union parliament, a joint defense establishment, and other reforms. The united parliament
was Karl XV's, and possibly Christian Birch-Reichenwald's,[7]
suggestion. It envisioned a bicameral legislature with an upper
house of thirty members (fifteen from each state) and a lower
chamber of fifty-one elected on a basis of population (thirty-six
from Sweden and fifteen from Norway). This parliament, whose
members were to be chosen by Riksdag and Storting, would be
vested with authority over defense, foreign affairs, and other
problems common to both kingdoms. The plan was never made
public because of Swedish ire over the Storting's passage of a new
law abolishing the *statholder* office. Although the law had received the tacit approval of Karl XV, the Riksdag was incensed
at this offense against its authority. It censured both Norwegians
and the king for proposing changes in the *Riksakt*, and thus
stifled real possibilities for further amalgamation. In the fall of
1859, Carl Henrik Anckarsvärd, Swedish ultra-Conservative leader, proposed in the House of Nobles the revision of the Act of
Union—a maneuver bluntly intended to keep Karl XV from
sanctioning the *statholder* law. Anckarsvärd pointed to Norway's
position in the union, which violated a principle in the first draft
of the Treaty of Kiel providing for incorporation of Norway into
Sweden. The *Riksakt*, he insisted, ought now to be revised to
place Norway in her proper subordinate status. No Norwegian
public figure dared voice pro-Swedish or prounion sentiments
when a leading Swedish statesman publicly spoke in this fashion.
In place of opportunities for integration, sore questions arose
between the two countries.

Karl XV's attempts at increased amalgamation and political
Scandinavianism continued to fail. His Swedish ministers rejected an alliance with Denmark in 1864 because they wanted no

---

[7] A copy was in Karl XV's, and another in Birch-Reichenwald's, handwrit-
ing, thus indicating the seriousness of the proposal. See *Sveriges historia* . . . ,
xii, 139-140, and Jorgenson, *Norway's Relation* . . . , 45-47, for other special
revision efforts, such as the committee for army and defense of 1856, the joint
kingdom proposal committee of 1855, etc.

fight on the southern Danish frontier, and his military reforms were never initiated, since Norway refused to adopt Swedish army organization. If military reforms had been accepted, the defense forces of both kingdoms would have been amalgamated into a military unit of respectable proportions and, as specified, could have been used outside the respective countries. But Norwegians resisted stubbornly Karl's strong unionist program.

The multiplicity of projects, Karl's urging, and a sincere wish to accomplish something for the union forced the two governments in 1865 to appoint a union committee, which worked for two years. Its report recommended the combination of military and naval defenses, the creation of a joint council (*statsraad*), to which matters of common concern could be brought, and the appointment of joint consular and diplomatic officials responsible to a foreign office removed from control of either Riksdag or Storting. In brief these reforms were based on fifty years of experience and designed to create a new, durable union which might avoid subsequent strife. The Riksdag constitutional committee approved the report and the Swedes knew that their parliament would accept. Yet, as everyone acknowledged, the Storting decision would be the most important, for, if Norwegians refused their consent, nothing but physical force could move them. In 1871 the Storting debated on the report and on the entire problem of amalgamation; and Aschehoug and other members of the union committee presented a good case for it. The death of one committee member, Ole Gabriel Ueland, converted a possibility for victory into a defeat. If he had lived, his voice would have been decisive with the *bønder*, who turned instead to Johan Sverdrup for guidance and accepted his program of refusing changes in the *Riksakt*, except those dissolving the union. The Storting answer was unmistakable when it voted 92 to 17 against consideration of the revision committee's report. Although the decision was accepted quietly by the Swedish Riksdag, Louis de Geer expressed very well the feelings of his colleagues of that body when he said:[8] "From that moment I gave up hope that the union by some constitutional method might become something

[8] Louis de Geer, *Minnen* (2 vols., Stockholm, 1906), II, 93-94.

entirely different from what it was; if alterations should be accepted, I declare that those soon would end in dissolution [of the union]." Integration had failed.

Several changes in both Norway and Sweden influenced the Storting in 1871. In Sweden aristocratic-bureaucratic-monarchical control of government received a serious setback when local government and national reform acts were passed. The old Riksdag organization into four estates was finally abolished in 1865-1866 and a bicameral parliament, with new laws on elections and electors, substituted. By the reform, members of the Second Chamber were elected through a restricted franchise, and First Chamber representatives by municipal and district electoral boards. As a result the new delegates, reflecting more nearly opinions of the whole country, launched a slow struggle for governmental control. Strengthened liberal forces in the Riksdag, the "Old Liberals" as Rustow[9] calls them, favored a limited franchise, military and defense reforms, and strict economy in government. At the same time they hardly matched the more advanced Norwegian *Venstre* for they were not ready to adopt the "radical" liberal program of parliamentary responsibility, universal manhood suffrage, factory legislation, and the like. The "Old Liberals" did advocate a broad and elastic view of the union which, perversely, made the question more and more a struggle between the two parliamentary bodies. In the attainment of a limited parliamentary responsibility and in the implicit alterations of the *Riksakt*, they touched involuntarily one sore point of the relationship of the two countries: the matter of legislative control over foreign affairs.

In Norway similar political changes had preceded Swedish reforms by two to three decades, and the concept of popular control of government had existed from 1815. Municipal reforms, alterations in local administration, extension of the franchise for farmers and urban workers, and economic reforms of the 1840's and 1850's caused Norwegians to reflect upon their

[9] On the confusing difference between "Old" and "New" Liberals see Dankwart A. Rustow, *The Politics of Compromise: A Study of Parties and Cabinet Government in Sweden* (Princeton, N.J., 1955), 20ff.

greater democracy and relatively greater political advance. In the decade of revolution in the 1840's, the Norwegians saw their progress with some pride and looked doubtfully at the slow pace of reforms in Sweden. But those liberals in Norway were nationalistic and anti-Swedish and encouraged a more stubborn stand on union politics. Under the leadership of Ole Gabriel Ueland, Søren Jaabaek, and, most important of all, Johan Sverdrup, in the late 1850's the liberals acquired a program and a purpose. An agreement between Sverdrup and Jaabaek in 1869 formed the liberal Norwegian *Venstre* party, while in Sweden political groups still floundered in disorganization. The Norwegian *Venstre* in the next thirty-six years decided the vital question of the union's existence.

These rising liberal parties and the atmosphere of change and uncertainty caused debates between Norwegians and Swedes to become increasingly complicated. Both sides refused to recognize mutual equality in amalgamation. To the Norwegians equality of the two kingdoms meant independence from any Swedish controls. After 1850 this view drove king and Storting into conflict over real principles: the *statholder* question, parliamentary government, and the royal veto. The ideological contrast reflected popular loyalty: in Sweden attachment was to king and country; in Norway, to country alone. The union won some popular support in Sweden, but became more and more either an abstraction or a nuisance, potentially useful, but never containing enough vitality for positive action. The absence of union symbols with real meaning or of material value for national self-interest weakened the groundwork for a real union. Norwegians sought to limit integrative activity rather than to expand it, while Swedes wished subordination of Norwegian institutions in an amalgamation. Without growth of a Norwegian tradition of loyalty toward the ruling royal family, even monarchy became another symbol of Swedish superiority, always present and ever reminding Norwegians of their subordinate status. The king represented a symbol to Norwegians, not of loyalty, but of the union; in J. E. Sars' words: "The Bernadottes were good men, but after all Swedish men." In judging whether union or nation exerted the greater pull, the decision would be overwhelmingly in favor of the latter. Nationalism's hold in Norway converted bonds of union into chains of subjugation to Sweden.

In these decades of hope and pessimism, integration and anti-integration parties became more confirmed in their principles. Swedish aristocrats and large landholders supported the union for reasons stemming from their own nationalism, prejudice, and desire for Swedish dominance and prestige. Without the union Sweden would appear to foreign eyes as a very small country endangered by great power expansion. The neutral role of the middle classes arose from their interest in political reforms and economic growth, which the union either did not benefit or actually hampered. The Swedish farmer, vainly seeking leaders until mid-century, upheld the union, partly from his sense of nationalism, partly from economic interest—i.e., his desire for expanded markets—but his attraction to it was far slighter than that of the upper classes.[10] Lower classes lacked any voice and, therefore, could not exert any influence on union relationships.

After the 1850's, fear of the growing political strength of the farmers gradually forced the upper classes to change their attitude. They approved of the union, and urged its maintenance without modification because it assisted them to retain special political positions in which the bureaucracy could use the government as a shield against the *bønder*. The *bønder* themselves, under Sverdrup's leadership, had become strongly nationalistic and, therefore, opposed either integration or amalgamation. Their leadership came from an intelligentsia of university graduates of professional rank; gown and farm in the *Venstre* party of 1869 formed an alliance which dominated Norwegian politics. Norwegian middle classes at first viewed the union with apathy, but after they were merged with teachers, lawyers, and other professional groups, they favored either dissolution or Norwegian equality within the union.

The three classes in Norway could hardly cooperate in any

[10] For farmer politics and conservatism in Sweden, see Edvard Thermaenius, *Lantmannapartiet* (Stockholm, 1928).

fashion with their opposite number in Sweden. Norwegian upper classes dissented in principle from Swedes of the same social class because their interpretations of the union diverged so widely. Similarly, Swedish Conservatives and Liberals differed in their political views from Norwegian middle-class ideology, although they shared some common ground. *Bønder* of Norway and Sweden held greatly different opinions on the union, and lacked means for social or political communication or understanding.[11] The working classes, of little import until the century's end, agreed in principle, but varied in means to achieve accord. In the 1890's Norwegian laborers wanted separation from Sweden by peaceful means if possible, but even by military means if necessary. Swedish workers desired cooperation but, in case of an acute crisis, dissolution by peaceful procedures. An estimate of the relative influence of the various groups would place as most powerful the Swedish aristocratic-bureaucratic-farmer alliance in favor of union, but with some variance in opinions as to its maintenance. The Norwegian class with most power after 1884 was the *bonde*-intellectual group with strong nationalistic traditions and views hostile to the union.

Swedish leaders in their views on amalgamation and integration represented largely this class division. The Swedish upper-class attitude was reflected in the views of men like Carl Henrik Anckarsvärd, in ill repute for his revision motion in 1859 which demanded both recognition by Norway of Swedish dominance and constitutional amendments to implement Norway's subordinate status. He privately favored military pressure, if any sizable minority in Norway favored revision, and the Riksdag approved his motion. Later his viewpoints received partial support from the historian Oscar Alin.[12] On the other hand, Baron Louis de Geer mirrored the moderate views of mid-century. Peace and

---

[11] A curious exception was the Selmer crisis in 1884, when *Lantmannapartiet* (Swedish Farmers' Party) and Norwegian *Venstre* cooperated; cf. Liss Olof Larsson's letter to the king asking agreement with the principle of the suspensive veto, and the dinner for the Norwegian "agitator," Viggo Ullmann, in Stockholm. *Sveriges historia . . .* , XIII, 110-111.

[12] Cf. Alin's work on the union published in 1889; in reality his proposals were not extreme, but they assumed a considerable degree of amalgamation. *Sveriges historia . . .* , XIII, 145-148.

amity within the union, he said, required both countries to give up some elements of their "rights." Equality should be recognized, and Norway should have her own consuls, for nothing mechanical or technical prevented it. De Geer's suggestions, indicating a broad policy, envisioned a greater amalgamation, with mutual abandonment of older interpretations. His plan, however, ran counter to the majority views of both Norwegians and Swedes and, therefore, stood no chance of success.[13]

A radical wing of the Liberals, represented by Adolf Hedin, pleaded for peace, and in Riksdag debates Hedin supported the unpopular Norwegian side by his speeches advocating a recognition of Norwegian equality. He favored the union's peaceful dissolution to end political discord and to make way for future integration, and he wrote vigorously in pamphlets, letters, and newspapers[14] in his efforts to achieve his program. The most important leader among Swedish lower classes was Hjalmar Branting[15] who advocated separation of the two kingdoms, because he believed that such an act would have its rewards in greater peace and stability and in the alleviation of political tensions both internally and externally.

Conservative Norwegian leaders at mid-century, such men as Frederik Stang, Schweigaard, Sibbern, J. H. Vogt, T. H. Aschehoug, and Birch-Reichenwald, were all willing to support revisionism, if it did not mean subjugation of Norway to Sweden. They were willing to abandon some abstract principles for the sake of integration. Their rationale was best expressed in Bernhard Dunker's *Om Revision af Foreningsakten mellem Sverige og Norge* in 1868 or in T. H. Aschehoug's series of articles in *Morgenbladet* of the same year. Without retreating from the task of guarding Norwegian constitutional liberties, conservatives emphasized strongly the need for political unity and its advantages

---

[13] De Geer, *Minnen*, II, 274-276.

[14] Cf. his *De ministeriella målen och unionen* (Stockholm, 1892); letters to Bishop Gottfrid Billing in the latter's *Anteckningar från riksdagar och kyrkomöten, 1893-1906* (Stockholm, 1928), 92-95. See also Hedin's *Tal och skrifter*, ed. Valfrid Spångberg (2 vols., Stockholm, 1904-1915).

[15] Zeth Höglund, *Hjalmar Branting och hans livsgärning* (2 vols., Stockholm, 1928-1929).

in European affairs. A genuine union would be a defense alliance and a power factor, as well as an efficient governmental and economic organism.

Their opponents claimed Conservative views to be selfish and narrow, for amalgamation would protect their bureaucratic powers. Amalgamation, said Johan Sverdrup, threatened Norwegian democracy; yet Sverdrup's coleader of the *bønder*, Søren Jaabaek, flatly stated the union controversy to be "higher politics" with no value for the farmers. Sverdrup,[16] liberalism's leader for over forty years, opposed unionism as Norway's greatest danger. If he orated on threats to Norwegian liberties from Swedish proposals, a majority of Norwegians joined him against king and Riksdag. He directed Liberals in 1869, in 1871, and in the parliamentary question in 1882; he became Norwegian prime minister in 1884 when Oscar II admitted defeat.

From 1850 to 1890 Sverdrup was aided, pushed, and coerced by the inflammatory speeches and writings of Norway's great literary leader, Bjørnstierne Bjørnson. Bjørnson's career ran the political gamut from radical to conservative to liberal. He praised republicanism in the 1880's, and monarchy in 1905. A bitter antagonist of the union during the nineteenth century, he advocated its retention in 1903 as the best protection for Scandinavia against Europe's power politics. Condemned in the 1870's by the Lutheran church for his radicalism, he was its supporter at the end of his life. Bjørnson's vital pen produced an arsenal of nationalistic newspaper articles, pamphlets, letters, plays, novels, songs, and poems against the union in the decades between 1850 and 1890. He composed the lyrics to Rikard Nordraak's music for the national anthem, *Ja, vi elsker dette landet*, and he wrote the republican play, *Kongen*, in 1877. In the forefront of political and social conflicts, he led, and most of Norway followed, even in 1903's retreat. Never a Storting member, never in a cabinet, yet electing representatives and making cabinet ministers, Bjørnson was the voice of national and patriotic conscience most devastating to integration.

Leadership of class and party in both countries showed a singu-

16 See Koht's three volume biography of Sverdrup.

lar absence of transnational communication. In the conduct of union affairs Sverdrup shared power with Swedish representatives to whom his words seemed meaningless. When Norwegian Conservatives Francis Hagerup and Emil Stang led Norwegian negotiations, they spoke an ultraliberal language compared with the principles of Swedish Prime Minister E. G. Boström. Swedish "New Liberals," not in power until 1905, understood and backed Hagerup's program, but opposed much of the dogmatism and obstinacy of *Venstre*, the party representing their closest parallel in Norway. The victory of parliamentarianism in Norway in 1884, with its double meaning as to democracy and the union, forced the dominant Swedish Conservatives and Norwegian *Venstre* into supporting irreconcilable and contradictory programs and views.

Political dependence of one country upon the other remained marginal. Although Norwegian philosophy and political theory came largely from France, Denmark, and Germany, the strong pull of English parliamentarianism and of economic ties with the British Empire formed an integral part of Norwegian trade and social systems. Norwegians sought safety in recourse to English sources of capital, in English and imperial markets, and in support by British Liberals.[17] On the other hand, the main source of Swedish political philosophy was Germany, and Swedes felt that their safety, and Scandinavia's, depended upon strong political ties against a hypothetical Russian menace.

After the Norwegian refusal to approve an amalgamation scheme for the union's defense forces, Norwegian-Swedish interests and policies in foreign affairs diverged. Norway remained unstirred by Swedish fears of Russian aggression and resisted every effort to build a strong Scandinavian alliance. Sweden's fear of "sinister Russian ambitions" in Finnmark, where Russo-Finnish spies purportedly accomplished their work, left Norwegians unmoved. The long, undefended Russo-Norwegian border contrasted strangely with Swedish heavy fortifications built in the 1890's along the Swedish-Finnish boundary. Norway's re-

---

[17] Cf. comments by Paul Knaplund, *British Views on Norwegian-Swedish Problems, 1880-1895* (Oslo, 1952), introduction, x-xii.

luctance to assist by approving a greater military contingent arose from her desire to protect the integrity and independence of domestic institutions even at the risk of offense to Sweden or of attack by Russia.

In desperation, though with some willingness because of family connections, the Swedes turned to Germany after 1871 as a substitute for the missing union defense community. As Germany's military might showed her new power and influence in Europe, Sweden naturally leaned upon her for protection against Russia's expansion and rumored aggressive designs. Without firm pledges of aid from Norway, even under the minimum conditions of the *Riksakt*, Sweden moved consciously toward a rabid Russophobia which Norway did not follow.

As foreign policy illustrated to some degree, the decade from 1871, the year of decision on amalgamation and revision of the *Riksakt*, to 1881 was filled with serious portents for the union. In this decade *Venstre* made its bid for power in Norway, only to find the king, through the royal veto, blocking adoption of a true parliamentary system. The issue seemingly concerned only the king and Storting, but in such a situation Swedish Conservatives and Riksdag felt that alterations contemplated in Norway were revisions of the *Riksakt* and the Norwegian constitution without their consent. Differences in theories regarding the union were responsible for Norwegian-Swedish conflicts at this point. The Swedes always considered the *Riksakt* to be unamendable and held that it conferred upon the Riksdag a voice in Norwegian parliamentary and constitutional changes. Norwegians, naturally, denied any authority on the part of either the Swedish government or people over the Norwegian constitution—a position entirely justified on juridical grounds. They thus assumed that a crisis over the royal veto was of no concern to Sweden, and, indeed, that Swedes possessed no rights even to discuss it in the Riksdag.

In 1872 the Norwegian Storting passed a law, amidst general applause, providing for admission of cabinet officers to parliament. A similar law in the 1850's had been vetoed by the king, whose decision the Storting then accepted. Circumstances surrounding the 1872 law, however, differed considerably, for Johan Sverdrup and Søren Jaabaek had formed *Venstre*, and an effective *Venstre* press extolled the virtues of parliamentary government. Bjørnson rose to his greatest efforts in behalf of the party, and Sverdrup himself persuaded the farmers to give up their earlier antagonism toward admission of officials to the Storting. The attainment of Storting control over the cabinet was assured by the farmers' approval of the new law, for with their consent the main obstacle was removed.

The act passed without difficulty by a resounding majority of 80 to 29. When presented to the king in Stockholm for his sanction, the Norwegian ministers in the *statsraad* urged him to veto it, which he did. In Oslo, therefore, the Storting approved a resolution forcing the cabinet's resignation, the first step in the long process of achieving parliamentary responsibility. But the old controversy of whether the act itself transgressed the *Riksakt* arose anew. Norwegians insisted that it could not be debated by the joint council and in 1873, after prolonged argument, the king upheld them. Therefore, Norwegians won a victory over the Swedes, and *Venstre* blooded its colors in a purely union question. Passed a second time by the Storting, the law again was vetoed by Oscar II. Norwegian elections in 1879 became, therefore, a trial of strength between Conservatives who favored the union and king, and *Venstre*, in which the cabinet issue predominated. Voters gave *Venstre* a popular mandate and, consequently, the Storting passed the law a third time only to have Oscar II refuse his signature again and insist upon an absolute veto which would permanently kill the measure.

Man's inventive mind finds devious ways to accomplish desired ends. The one for Norwegians at this moment, oddly enough, was suggested by Aschehoug, a Conservative and a strong unionist, who proposed the impeachment of cabinet officers appointed without a majority in the Storting. In the fall of 1882 Oscar II named Christian Selmer as prime minister with a bureaucratic cabinet having neither popular nor Storting support. Elections in October 1882, revolved around this issue and resulted in a clear victory for *Venstre*. In 1883 the Storting impeached

Selmer and his colleagues in the cabinet, and in 1884 they were convicted. In reality the Storting tried Oscar II and Sweden, not Selmer, who was only an agent. Both Norway and the Storting by their solidarity in action against Selmer illustrated clearly their refusal to be content with a subordinate status in the union. Confronted with a determined majority against him, Oscar II submitted; from that time, cabinet officers entered into Storting debates, they could be summoned by that body, and their appointment had to be approved by a parliamentary majority. A secondary issue, involving the king directly, was his right to a suspensive or an absolute veto on legislative acts; the royal privilege of an absolute veto was quietly dropped.

In 1885, a year after Selmer's conviction, Sweden also began her slow advance toward parliamentarianism. Adolf Hedin, strong friend of the union and, for his time, ultraliberal, proposed in the Riksdag a law placing foreign relations partly under parliamentary control. Previously, the Swedish foreign minister owed responsibility solely to the king whose status as monarch, governing both kingdoms, was entirely acceptable to the Norwegians. The Swedish reform perturbed the Norwegian government which asked for an arrangement whereby the foreign office might be placed above national jurisdiction, possibly responsible to a joint council, or, as a third choice more pleasing to themselves, a completely separate and independent consular system for Norway.

When the Swedish Riksdag voted for partial parliamentary control of foreign affairs the union's controversies turned to a single and bitter core of debate. Henceforth *Venstre* concentrated upon the attainment of an independent consular, or at best a diplomatic, system. Solution of this contradiction between Norwegians and Swedes depended upon the creation of an administrative system capable of elevating problems to a level where separate national factors were subordinated to integration.

CHAPTER V

◇◇

A DECADE OF CONFLICT

◇◇

THE first steps toward parliamentarianism in Sweden in 1885, when the Riksdag gained greater control over foreign affairs, introduced a new phase into the union's conflicts. The ensuing strife rose to a crescendo in 1895, then subsided until 1905 when negotiations failed. Issues at stake were concerned with the question of where constitutional control of diplomatic and consular officials should be lodged, and with Norwegian refusal either to permit diminution of the Storting's parliamentary powers in domestic matters or to acknowledge Riksdag authority in nonunion issues. Whether the Norwegians made their case or not, the controversy came close to the heart of union relationships when the Swedish Riksdag altered the spirit of the *Riksakt* without the consent of Norwegian officials or Storting. While Swedes insisted on superiority of the *Riksakt* to the Norwegian constitution, and, therefore, dogmatically demanded that not a comma of it be changed without Riksdag approval, they consistently failed to acknowledge similar Storting privileges in cases of revisions of the Swedish constitution. Swedish extension of partial parliamentary control over foreign affairs in 1885 clearly infringed upon the system laid down in 1814. On strictly legal grounds the Norwegian complaint about Swedish interference with union institutions contained much substance. In retrospect, however, legal arguments sought another desired end: complete liberation of Norwegian institutions from Swedish interference.

In defense of their insistence on a separate consular system, the Norwegians marshalled an impressive array of arguments. They contended that they were all but ignored in appointments to diplomatic and consular posts and that their shipping interests and trade were mishandled by Swedish consuls, who showed favoritism to Swedes where competing goods were marketed. In brief, Norwegians felt that they suffered economically from Swedish attempts to relegate them to an inferior status. In reality, however, these arguments served only to prove a case of suppression of Norwegian political liberties. In their own eyes, they were capable of and possessed the right to foreign representation as one independent country in a union postulated on the merger of two sovereign states.

To meet this argument the Swedish government and Oscar II expressed their willingness to revise the *Riksakt* in 1885 by permitting a special status for the foreign minister. A general statement, tentatively accepted by Norwegian members of the joint council, formed the basis for Sverdrup's discussions of alterations in the *Riksakt* that same year at Stockholm with Swedish representatives and the king. The Norwegians, Ole Richter and Sverdrup, and the Swedish ministers, in the presence of the monarch, accepted a final draft which substantially conformed to Norwegian views but left unspecified the nationality of the union foreign minister.[1] Acceptance of the protocol bound neither party, but historically it was a step toward agreement. Unfortunately, Sverdrup either failed to read the protocol carefully, or, having read it, permitted the following words to pass unnoticed: ". . . that ministerial matters shall be executed for the king by the minister for foreign affairs in the presence of two other members of the Swedish together with three members of the Norwegian council."

A vehement and wordy debate in Norway echoed in Sweden and centered around "two other members." Only one interpretation was possible for these words: the foreign minister must be Swedish and, therefore, subject to supervision by the Riksdag. Since foreign affairs fell clearly within the category of union matters, Norwegian leaders demanded a statement which would read, "three Swedes and three Norwegian members of the joint council," leaving the nationality of the foreign minister undefined and permitting him to be either Norwegian or Swede. The Storting,

---

[1] In this historical argument the author has taken Richter's, Oscar II's, and the Swedish view; cf. Keilhau, *Den norske folks . . .* , x, 205-209; and *Sveriges historia . . .* , xiii, 145.

when asked to pass an act converting the agreement into law,
naturally refused, and the Swedish press and public, not to mention government and king, interpreted its action as a violation of
a contractual obligation. Blame for the incident, which might
have been avoided by a scrupulously careful reading of the agreement before it was made public, must be shared by Sverdrup,
Richter, and the Swedish members of the council. Oscar II should
likewise have ascertained more precisely the nature of the protocol, for its possible injury to the union and to the Norwegian
and Swedish people could scarcely have been overlooked.

In reply Sverdrup now proposed a project resembling an
earlier Swedish proposal: a joint foreign minister, either Norwegian or Swede, controlled through a delegation drawn from
the Storting and Riksdag. But Sverdrup's fortunes had waned
in the meantime because of a purely Norwegian issue, and elections in 1886 saw *Venstre* split into two factions, one of which
claimed to be the "pure" *Venstre*. Although the contingent backing Sverdrup received a majority at the polls, his Storting support could hardly face a fight on any union issue. Yet Sverdrup
went ahead to a fruitless defense of his program in a most
magnificent speech in 1886. Sentiments of the "pure" *Venstre*
were expressed in a studied aside of Jørgen Løvland: "Norway
out of your grasp, Johan Sverdrup." Through crisis after crisis
Sverdrup moved swiftly to his political defeat in 1889, and his
death in 1892 ended an era.

The new cabinet that replaced Sverdrup was composed of Conservatives under the politically astute Emil Stang. After clearing
the way for negotiations on the status of the foreign ministry,
variants in an agreement received careful, close scrutiny to eliminate possible duplication of blunders. In 1891 a two-member
committee reported, on the basis of an earlier draft of Sverdrup's,
that an administrative neutrality might be achieved by leaving
the nationality of the foreign minister undefined and by making
him responsible to an enlarged union council of three Norwegians and three Swedes. Approved by the joint council, the
report went to the Storting where Wollert Konow of Hede-
marken, Carl Berner, and other "pure" *Venstre* members tore it

to shreds. Berner's resolution, in reality a vote of no confidence in the government, dogmatically laid down the principle that the Norwegian people would never agree to hindrances in their acquisition of full rights, or, in other words, a separate Norwegian diplomatic service and autonomy in conduct of foreign affairs. The Conservatives had to resign, and Johannes Steen and a *Venstre* ministry were appointed. The crisis of 1891-1892 was on.

Hidden behind these sparse details lay venomous debates, vitriolic press warfare, Bjørnson's emotional utterances, and an unwise remark of Swedish Prime Minister Gustaf Åkerhielm. In a private meeting at which revision of the *Riksakt* came under discussion, he made the statement that the Swedes should speak Swedish both eastward and westward. He meant military "speech" in terms of navies, soldiers, and cannons, not plain conversation, and his remark was a pointed reminder of both Russian and Norwegian dangers.[2] Adolf Hedin, Swedish liberal and pro-Norwegian member of the Riksdag, purportedly gave the statement to *Dagens Nyheter*; if true, then Hedin with the best of intentions served his own country badly and the Norwegians worse. In June 1891, an angry Storting in retaliation passed a resolution stating its right to legislate on a Norwegian consular system; refused to pay expenses for the union's legation at Vienna; and then, since there appeared to be no opposition from Sweden, voted a law for separate consuls and appropriated the funds necessary for preparatory work. When the Norwegians brought the last part of the law to Oscar II for his approval, he refused, since, as he claimed, this was not the real intent of the Norwegian proposal and he could not bind himself by approving Norway's appropriation and expenditure of the funds.

In Norway the greater share of the population favored continuation with the proposed legislation. Steen's popularity increased appreciably after his speech in the Storting which outlined the program for *Venstre* action.[3] "The difficulties we have

---

[2] Hugo Hamilton's *Hågkomster* (Stockholm, 1928), 235, has two versions: *med norrmännen* (with Norwegians) and *både västerut och österut* (both to the West and East). Cf. *Sveriges historia* . . . , XIII, 148. Note also Hamilton's assertion that Åkerhielm's statement was printed in *Aftonbladet*.

[3] J. E. Sars, *Norges historie* (6 vols., Oslo, 1909-1915), VI, 116.

to fight against . . . lie not in laws but outside them, and these problems must be overcome with the aid of legal means, so far as these operate, and thereafter— (a long pause)—yes, thereafter, I do not doubt that forms will be found and means sought that are necessary to achieve success, but within the law—within the law it must certainly be." This speech, and Steen's careful, judicious pause on the word *thereafter*, expressed all the pent-up emotion of the consular controversy.

Norwegian sternness drew out Swedish willingness to negotiate and in January 1893, E. G. Boström and Carl Lewenhaupt, the Swedish prime minister and minister for foreign affairs, issued an invitation to discuss terms. They conceded Norwegian and Swedish equality in the joint council and promised agreement to the appointment of a common foreign minister who could be either Norwegian or Swede. But Norwegians refused further negotiations, for they were convinced that discussions would end in the same blind alley as before. Jørgen Løvland's resolution of March 17 stated again Norway's clear right to her own consuls and the nonnegotiable nature of this claim.

At that point the Riksdag began its debate on ministerial plans for negotiations with the Norwegians. In the course of the arguments, the cabinet program gained strong support, but the Swedish strategy at this point was to utilize a Second Chamber vote in favor of the ministerial proposals to show Norwegians the unity across the border. The Riksdag committee, appointed to examine the proposition, went so far as to propose a study of the entire diplomatic service, since consuls owed responsibility to a minister of foreign affairs.

Fortunately for the Swedes and the union these peace gestures came at a time when the Norwegian cabinet could not budge. Steen needed either a consular law or approval by Oscar II of the funds for an inquiry commission to go ahead. Instead Steen resigned in April 1893, hoping to force the king's submission. *Venstre* expected Oscar to seek in vain for a ministry among the Conservatives, and the party's tactic, the famed "crisis line," was designed to create a Norwegian domestic furor which would sweep the king from his throne. But the Conservative Emil Stang promised the monarch to form a ministry, and Oscar II, sure of his ground, accepted Steen's resignation and appointed Emil Stang. The crisis of 1892 was over.[4]

In both Norway and Sweden recriminations, ill feeling, and overt threats were everywhere abundant. Animosity between conservatives and *Venstre* became a vital ingredient in Norwegian elections in 1894. Conservatives naturally hoped for positive results to enable the union to remain as it was; the "clean" *Venstre* wished passage of the consular legislation to gain independence for Norway; the moderate *Venstre* desired the same result, but without strife with Sweden or the king. Election debates flayed individuals and parties unmercifully and developed intense friction. Newspapers added to the din of debate with their shrill emphasis on the decisive importance of the elections and consular legislation. Naturally in such press debates stereotypes and symbols of all kinds were used and uncomplimentary epithets were exchanged not only with fellow Norwegians, but with Swedes as well. Pamphlets were published by the score defending on either historical or emotional grounds each country's side of the argument; and Norwegian rifle clubs, organized during the crisis of the preceding decade, became threats to amicable solution of the confusion. Throughout these two years public opinion reached an inflamed point where reason vanished and emotion reigned.

Venstre won its expected parliamentary majority in elections in 1894, and Stang asked to be relieved. Oscar II went to Oslo for negotiations on a new ministry, but returned to Stockholm before their completion. Pessimistic about the outcome of the negotiations and irritated with the Norwegians, he decided to consult with Riksdag leaders and to ask for the creation of a secret committee (*Särskildt utskottet*), a procedure last used during the Crimean War, to examine ways and means for solution of the crisis. After three sessions in March 1895, the committee decided to support the king in whatever course he might recommend; and from its context, this could even mean war. The alarm-

4 Thanks should be expressed here to Bengt Grimlund for the use of his manuscript study of "Emil Stang i hans kamp for unionen, 1889-1895."

ing tension of the moment was intensified further by numerous meetings of the king with members of Swedish military and naval staffs and with leaders both in and out of the Riksdag. The press of both countries carried stories of projected military preparations and other rumors, such as Christian W. E. B. Olssøn's recall from Stockholm to handle defense problems in Norway, purported mobilization orders for the Swedish army, commands for the Swedish fleet to be combat ready, and removal of furniture, art objects, and furnishings from the queen's Norwegian residence at Skinnarbøl. Neither Norwegian nor Swede would budge and, unless military means were used, Sweden could not hope to coerce Norway into signing away her rights of free legislative action.

The Swedes first yielded by passing a resolution in May 1895, which offered an escape. Nearly unanimous support of the Riksdag resolution showed openly the state of mind of Sweden's political leaders: the First Chamber accepted it without balloting and the Second voted 164 to 51 in its favor. The resolution's wording was sufficiently ambiguous to give freedom of interpretation to both Norwegians and Swedes: the *Riksakt* should have a full and early revision to furnish a system of foreign representation for Norway and yet leave Sweden some control over foreign affairs. Credits voted by the Riksdag (seven and a half million *kronor*) were without limitation as to use. Norwegians interpreted them to be for military measures against themselves in case they did not accept the Riksdag proposals.

Emil Stang, the Norwegian prime minister, could convey little information to alleviate Norwegian fears. In his report to the Storting he commented on the alarming seriousness of Swedish preparations for war. A series of meetings with Storting leaders, ministers, and military officers only continued and deepened the pessimistic impression left by Stang's report and led to suggestions for a retreat. *Venstre* leaders, in close touch with the situation, also began to waver. In June a resolution was offered which stated the willingness of the Norwegian government and Storting to negotiate on "an entirely free basis." With some relief and considerable reluctance, the Storting made its strategic withdrawal in the face of superior Swedish resources and military strength.

In the fall of 1895 a new ministry was appointed from moderates and Conservatives, with Francis Hagerup, professor of jurisprudence at the university, at its head. In the Norwegian view, the crisis of 1895 ended ignominiously, but its experiences might be valuable for future crises. The Storting, in an unmistakable answer to the Riksdag defense appropriation, voted credits of eight million *kroner* for the purchase of two armored naval vessels and borrowed an additional twelve million to put fortifications at Trondheim, Bergen, and Christiansand in order. But more important for the future, *Venstre* leaders came to a realization that they must have first a united country, and second, the defenses and military forces to protect Norway against a Swedish attack. On these two premises *Venstre* based its whole policy for the next ten years and excused both its domestic and its defense policies on grounds of hostility toward Sweden and the union.

The Swedish monarchy and some government leaders retained their thoughts of an attack on Norway and substitution of a new *Riksakt* to force subordination of Norway to Swedish control. In June 1895, shortly before passage of the Storting resolution, the pro-Norwegian Lewenhaupt lost his post as foreign minister, and Count Ludvig Douglas, known both in Norway and Sweden as an ardent advocate of Swedish supremacy in the union, replaced him. Despite the joint council acceptance of a proposition for a union revision committee in November, the Swedish government persisted in its attempts to secure foreign assistance for an attack on Norway. In the summer of 1895 Kaiser Wilhelm visited Oscar II and indicated to him his willingness to support Sweden. Questions regarding the attitudes of the Kaiser's ministers or of the Swedish government and Riksdag were not explored. These discussions resulted in Oscar's refusal of German aid. It is problematical whether or not such help would have been actually forthcoming in view of the general European situation and the recognized undependable character of the Kaiser's promises.[5] While lacking full knowledge of the serious intent of

5 Cf. Folke Lindberg, *Kunglig utrikespolitik* (Stockholm, 1950), 145-175.

events in Stockholm, Norwegian leaders sensed their importance and expected the worst.

The alleviation of the tension, made possible by the Norwegian retreat and Oscar II's reluctant turning down of the Kaiser's offer, permitted the appointment of a union committee for a study of the *Riksakt* revisions. The committee, appointed in November and consisting of seven representatives from each country, continued its work from 1896 to 1898. A general air of amiability surrounded the sessions, for each side could quote verbatim the main opposing arguments and saw little point in prolonging debate.

In its report of 1898 the committee contradicted the impression of good will shown during its sessions. It succeeded in confusing issues even further than before. Instead of a single statement, it issued four, which revealed nearly complete disagreement among its individual members. One report proposed a new *Riksakt* with precedence over both Norwegian and Swedish constitutions; a foreign minister of either nationality, responsible to a joint ministerial council elected from both parliaments; and royal authority over defense, subject to parliamentary supervision. The other five Swedish members favored a foreign minister responsible to both Riksdag and Storting through committees appointed by these bodies for this specific purpose. The majority (4) of the Norwegians consented to a *Riksakt* amendment for implementing the second Swedish proposal, but refused to accept any plan on defense issues. The minority Norwegian report dogmatically insisted on Norway's having her own foreign minister and consular service. Both Johannes Steen, now prime minister for the second time, and his *Venstre* colleagues agreed with the minority. Under such circumstances the king's acceptance of the report and his tabling it, even if with petulance, were wisdom itself. The Swedish cabinet added a complementary phrase to the effect that no changes would be made until a settlement of the consular question could be reached by negotiations. Norwegians and Swedes used this position of status quo in opposing senses: the former to connote Swedish obstinacy and highhandness, and the latter to define a virtuous and sensible method of guarantee against rash Norwegian action.

Both the Norwegian and Swedish public seethed with the events of these two portentous crises. The Norwegians managed to achieve one long-cherished goal in 1898 by complying with constitutional provisions and passing a law for the third time on a merchant marine "clean" flag. Oscar II bowed to the rules and Norway flew her "clean" flag, leaving the despised union mark only on the colors flown on state and formal occasions. Naturally, attainment of this prize was hailed in Norway as a great victory. In Sweden Boström, Swedish leaders of the First Chamber, and some of the Second begged Oscar II to veto the law, claiming it was an alteration of the *Riksakt*. If the king had followed the advice of his ministers, another crisis, far worse than that of 1895, would have developed immediately, for the Norwegian government insisted adamantly that the matter was wholly domestic. Boström, angered by the king's refusal to veto, asked for permission to resign. A Swedish cabinet crisis followed in which the king and crown prince persuaded Boström to remain, but Count Douglas, the foreign minister, left the government.[6] Later both Lars Åkerhielm and General Axel Rappe resigned and Boström reconstructed the cabinet. In the process Alfred Lagerheim, former minister to Germany, known to be pro-Norwegian and friendly to a dual foreign office system, was appointed foreign minister. Quiet preparations in both countries pointed to the resumption of negotiations on the consular problem, for its ghost could not be laid.

Although the crisis passed, the Norwegian government continued to increase defense budgets. The *Venstre* military program grew out of the demoralizing defeats in 1895-1896, when its members supported the humiliating resolution to negotiate with Sweden. The first appropriation was approved by the entire

---

[6] Cf. Lindberg, *Kunglig utrikespolitik*, 176-183, and his "Ett svenskt förslag till stormaktsintervention i unionskonflikten våren 1889," *Historisk tidskrift* (Swedish), LX (1953), 258-269, where Austrian and Swedish documents explain efforts of the king in that direction.

Storting in 1896, except for a few Conservatives with faith in the union and some economy-minded *Venstre*. The latter party demonstrated its dislike of Swedes and its insistence on Norwegian sovereignty by a certain ambiguity of program. Early in the 1890's it most ardently favored pacifism and in the last half of the decade, somewhat hypocritically in view of its program of defense expenditures, it urged the king to sign arbitration and conciliation agreements and to limit military budgets. Likewise the Social Democratic party, just beginning its rise to prominence, adopted a resolution in 1895 favoring military expenditures and its prominent leaders defended Norway's cause, even to the extent of war. Hjalmar Branting, Swedish Social Democrat, strongly opposed this belligerent "chauvinism" in Scandinavian party congresses and was roundly condemned by Norwegian socialists. In this feverish decade even strong international socialist programs lost ground to nationalism. At the other extreme, Oscar II approved increases in Norwegian defense budgets because he feared new political crises and was dismayed by them more than by the purposes for which the money would be used. Sweden's position also became more ambiguous and uncertain because of her failure to take aggressive action during the crisis of 1895. After that date the idea began to spread among the Swedes that it would be better to dissolve the union than to maintain it by force.

Norwegians, without qualms as to war, thought of dissolution more frequently than ever before. The altered Steen cabinet after the elections of 1900 introduced two new, dynamic Norwegian leaders. Wollert Konow, who had voted with the twenty-four in 1895 against initiating negotiations with Sweden, advocated firm Norwegian resistance to Swedish demands. The second figure, Georg Stang, as an ardent advocate of military preparedness, proposed the building of a system of fortifications along the Norwegian-Swedish border. His oratory and enthusiasm battered down opposition of pacifists and economy-minded *Venstre*. Johan Castberg, newly-elected member of the radical wing of the party, gave him powerful support in Storting debates. To complaints about harmful effects of the proposed forts on staff plans for a mobile defense strategy, both Stang and Castberg countered by stressing their use for mobile defense. Stang, in his excitement, dwelt unwisely on the utility of the forts as bases for an offensive wartime invasion of Sweden. This ill-advised statement later became effective fodder for Swedish press campaigns and for Swedish delegates at Karlstad in 1905 when they quoted Stang on the offensive utility of the forts. Voting in the Storting on defense appropriations closely followed party lines: *Venstre* in favor; Conservatives, and a small group of moderates, in opposition. The final vote on the appropriation in 1901 showed as fairly as possible the division of Norwegians between prounion and antiunion sentiments.

Norwegian defense plans caused the usual repercussions in Swedish public debate and in the army reforms completed in 1903-1905. Conservative Bishop Gottfrid Billing, in his diary, remarked about the silence of the Riksdag and Christian Lundeberg, another Swedish Conservative, wrote that the reason was Boström's refusal to permit debate. To match Norwegian reforms, the Swedish army command devised a strategy which made greater use of cavalry, mobile artillery, and unity in staff work. The Swedish government, to the enthusiastic plaudits of the First Chamber, purchased or built four new armored vessels. The light torpedo fleet and the length of service of naval cadets were both extended. In conscripts and in fleet size the Swedes held a clear superiority, for they possessed a total army of 400,000, ready for operations in six months, as compared to approximately 100,000 trained Norwegian troops. In naval forces the Swedes outnumbered the Norwegians by two to one both in ships and weight, with even greater superiority in fire power.

At the same time the crises of the 1890's caused the Swedish government to adopt in some respects a policy of appeasement. Norwegian consular officials were entrusted with negotiations of trade agreements with Spain, Italy, Switzerland, Belgium, and other continental countries. Prime Minister Boström in 1900 agreed to equality among Norwegian and Swedish citizens for posts in the foreign service.[7] Swedes remained in control of important legations, but Norwegians headed the Spanish, American, and Belgian delegations. From 1895 to 1902 Norwegian consuls received posts more frequently than Swedes, until they held a majority throughout the world where nationals were used. In Spain, Portugal, and Belgium, staffs of the consular offices were manned by Norwegians. In Norway, to prepare for possible attainment of a separate foreign office, a new department of foreign affairs in the ministry of the interior was created in 1899 with Sigurd Ibsen, son of the novelist-playwright and son-in-law of Bjørnson, as its director. Ibsen figured even more prominently when he proposed a plan for a system of consular representation which met with the approval of Alfred Lagerheim, Swedish foreign minister.

Consular representation symbolized an issue of great political significance for Norwegians, most of whom had come to believe that consular officials aided business expansion in foreign countries. Actually, such arrangements as those of the 1890's for negotiation of trade agreements with foreign countries produced far more economic and commercial benefits than a separate Norwegian consular service might attain, for Sweden's greater bargaining capacity carried more weight with foreign powers. In Norway party alignment on the question of a separate consular system was often confused. Christian Michelsen, one of the two shipowners having a leading role during the union's last decade, did not argue the question on economic grounds but rather on grounds of Norway's need for political independence. A second shipowner, Gunnar Knudsen, also stressed the political aspects of the argument. On the flag issue, associated in Norwegian minds with the consular problem, shipowners manifested a peculiar disposition. After expressing their opinion that nothing prevented the use of a Norwegian commercial flag, they went no further. In other words, they evidenced good Norwegian nationalism, but could see little economic advantage in either a

[7] *Møt frigjørelson*, ed. Sigurd Blehr (2 vols., Oslo, 1946-1948), ii, 298. For a survey of Norwegians in the union's foreign service, see Reidar Omang, *Norsk utenrikstjeneste*, 113-118.

"clean" flag or a separate consular service.[8] Norwegian arguments from 1891 to 1902 contained virtually nothing on the economic advantages of a separate consular system and stressed exclusively the need for manifestation of Norway's political independence from Swedish control.

Signs of both discord and accord could be pointed out in the decade of the crises. In 1897 joint tariff laws lapsed despite certain Norwegian economic interests favoring their renewal and a record of seventy years of commercial and industrial benefits to both peoples. The rise of protectionism in Sweden had something to do with her refusal to continue the acts; but on the other hand, neither Norwegian Storting nor government exerted pressure to maintain them. Norway rated in nowise as a firm advocate of free trade, for the tariff controversy in the Storting ended in only a slim margin in its favor.

In other respects the Norwegian symbols of revolt struck deeper. Two *Venstre* slogans or catchwords of 1892 and 1895 became popular in Norway, while they created alarm in Sweden. Steen's *thereafter* (implying threats or force) and *Norway should take matters into her own hands* both ranked as attention-catching symbols and as evidences of Norwegian pride. The latter represented the strong independence feeling rampant in Norway and also showed the urge to proceed without consultation with Sweden. Growth of a more moderate opinion in both countries toward the union was both aided and hindered by discussion in the press and by arguments raging in both countries over the union's past history. In 1899, the Swedish professor and Conservative Oscar Alin published his study of the union[9] which only led to further debate. Bernhard Getz, a Norwegian jurist,

---

[8] Cf. Keilhau's unsupported evidence in *Den norske folks* . . . , x, 380-381. Much of his logic is dubious. The language question was not a factor; he admits that union officials conducted their business well; and he still insists on stressing the economics of the union controversy. The phenomenal rise of Norwegian maritime interests, such as fishing, shipbuilding, merchant marine, and whaling, during a period of union representation abroad, and when Norwegian-Swedish strife was at its height, seems to be convincing proof that Norway's lack of consular representatives hardly impeded her progress.

[9] In 1925, S. J. Boëthius, writing in Volume xiii of *Sveriges historia* . . . , calls Alin's work "scientific!"

retaliated with an analysis of the union's origins in which he defended nationalist views. The dozen or more brochures and "historical" treatises on the union of the 1890's, and the newspapers which fed on conflict, intensified the polemic and frictional side of the union's quarrels.

The fevers of union controversy in the 1890's left Swedish Conservatives shaken and Liberals ardently pacifist. Almost no Swedish leader, and no member of the royal family after 1900, advocated the maintenance of the union by armed force. A philosophy of "better no union than one maintained by force" spread in the Riksdag and dominated that part of the programs of Liberals and Social Democrats dealing with the union problem. An invasion of Norway would need the assistance, either materially or economically, of a great power. Russian aid was unthinkable; England would most likely support Norway; Germany's Kaiser clearly stated in 1896, after Oscar II had declined his aid, that he would in the future maintain friendly neutrality. Even the most chauvinistic Swedish army officer or political leader saw the diplomatic balance shift to Norway's side.

These changes in Swedish opinions met with no comparable modification on the part of Norwegian parties or their leaders. Rather, *Venstre's* retreats in 1892 and 1895, and Norwegian weaknesses, forced compromises in *Venstre* party programs to achieve unity with Conservatives. The creation of a moderate party meant in reality the growth of solidarity, since it formed the bridge for association of the two traditional parties. Defense appropriations continued to increase in amounts because of the Norwegian determination to succeed. In a new crisis, therefore, Norwegian leaders relied on armament to resist aggression by Sweden and to strengthen their hands in negotiations. But complete political decision on a single program remained to be achieved, and it would come when the Swedes rejected a Norwegian moderate or Conservative proposal for settlement of the union controversy.

The changed atmosphere in Sweden, and the friendliness of Alfred Lagerheim, resulted in Norwegian approval of a plan suggested by Sigurd Ibsen. The Swedish cabinet consented to his proposals in January 1902, and agreed to name a committee to consider them. Both the committee's formation and its basic program received Swedish Conservative support and the full cooperation of Liberals. The committee's plans for a separate consular system, discussed and endorsed by both governments, prepared the way for appointment of a more general and representative body. Private conversations revealed no fundamental disagreement and, as if to increase hopes for success, Boström promised in July 1902, when the committee was appointed, that its recommendations would be put into effect.

In 1902 this fourth union committee initiated its work in an atmosphere of enthusiasm and hope. The emergence of an attitude in Sweden favoring concessions was matched in Norway by a general view that negotiations might and should be attempted once again. Norwegian friendliness depended, however, upon acceptance by Sweden of a basic postulate—that a separate consular system must be created over which neither Swedes nor their parliament possessed authority. In so many words, Norwegians favored integration but not amalgamation; and the Swedes, apparently at long last, agreed with this basic premise.

◇◇

CHAPTER VI

"ONLY NEGOTIATIONS"

◇◇

THE appointment of the fourth union committee in 1902 sprang from sincere and wishful motives. Any new course seemed for the better, and some Norwegians and Swedes wished the committee all possible success and held high hopes for its work. The only outcome certain of approval by *Venstre* would be the creation of a separate consular system and the subsequent establishment of a Norwegian diplomatic service. A satisfactory agreement short of that could, at most, only temporarily preserve the union. At worst, the union committee might end in a stalemate, which would mean a Norwegian resort to its slogan of 1895: "Norway must take matters into her own hands." In that event, the union, and what few institutions remained, would be in shambles.

At the center of the union committee's labors lay the question of whether or not the union could and ought to endure. The majority of *Venstre* wished to separate their country as much as possible from Sweden and, if need be, to dissolve the union in order to gain what they called "independence of Norwegian institutions and full recognition by the world." To a disinterested observer it might seem that the consular question was wholly a minor issue, the importance of which was exaggerated by both sides. But so much significance had been given it by the two crises in the 1890's that the creation of a separate consular system for Norway became a symbol in which the real issues were interwoven. Divergences and similarities in society, culture, and politics became obscured, and neither side could be rational about its position. To Norwegians it was a serious matter of their independence from Swedish controls over domestic institutions, and they deeply resented Swedish opposition which they believed to be rooted in the wish to subordinate Norway to the status of a "conquered province." Swedes, for their part, considered the

Norwegian demand for separate consuls as a violation of the *Riksakt* and an attempt to sever the last remaining bonds of union.

In this conflict of opinion neither leaders nor people mattered a great deal. Rather, the issues involved in decades of dispute, the feeling of inferiority held by most Norwegians, the stereotyped caricatures of both peoples, the antagonism fed by nationalism and pride, the feeling of pressure, and the resentment of old wounds became the forces sweeping individuals along and making them incapable of independent action. While the dissolution of the union might not, perhaps, be inevitable, a majority of Norwegians and Swedes came to accept its end as reasonable and logical. Often the clamor and alarm of this entire controversy appear to be mostly bombast; yet the dispute possessed attributes of a battle for freedom and liberty as clear as those involved in the American Civil War. If the union committee failed to manufacture machinery to accomplish what the Norwegians wanted, then the union would not endure. The committee realized fully its mission, and the Norwegian and Swedish people recognized completely the meaning the elections in Norway in 1903 held for the committee's work and the union. If a party committed to a policy of separation won the elections, and the committee split on its decisions, then the dissolution would come. There would be no turning back once a decision had been made.

Well aware of these prospects, public sentiment and statements continued for some time to stress hopes for the success of the consular committee's endeavors. Boström, Lagerheim, Ibsen, Conservatives in Norway, and even leading Conservatives in Sweden added to the inflation of optimistic hopes by their public utterances. During 1902, and well into 1903, this opinion persisted, and the press of both countries maintained a reserve unknown in earlier negotiations. Chances for positive action seemed most bright.

In spite of desires for early sessions, the committee held its first meeting late in October 1902, with only minor results. Gunnar Knudsen, a Norwegian *Venstre* shipowner, Ole Anton Qvam, a

Venstre lawyer, and Sigurd Ibsen, as members of the joint council in Stockholm, negotiated with the Swedes. The three Norwegians may have lacked wholehearted *Venstre* support, but Conservatives backed them to the limit. They hoped, for their part, to achieve an agreement which would permit the creation of a separate Norwegian consular system outside Swedish control and subject only to the king and a joint foreign minister. The Swedes, on the other hand, intended as never before to accomplish their purpose in arranging for negotiations and hoped to create a new consular system for Norway. Alfred Lagerheim spoke clearly to both Norwegians and Swedes about the technical and administrative problems involved in a solution of the consular question and gave full indication that its independent status and freedom from Swedish control would not be obstacles. His chief aim, and that of Swedes who approved of negotiations, was to preserve the union.

In December, in its second meeting, the committee avoided frictional issues and seemed anxiously desirous of an agreement. But, as Qvam said in a letter to Otto Blehr, Norwegian prime minister and *Venstre* leader, "when we come deeper into questions, the flute can very well play another tune."[1] Yet the amiability in another meeting before the Christmas holidays caused Qvam to write to Blehr that even the difficult problem of the administrative relationship of Norwegian consuls to the foreign minister presented no knotty complications. From private conversations with Lagerheim, Qvam concluded that the Swedes would approve a joint foreign minister.[2]

In January, however, the negotiations were nearly disrupted. Their possible success, which might mean further troubles, caused *Venstre* to propose a resolution insisting on autonomy for the consuls in their relationship to the joint foreign minister.

[1] Blehr, *Møt frigjørelsen*, II, 251. The committee did listen to expressions of pique from Lagerheim arising from newspaper attacks in both countries. He had asked for expressions of opinion from foreign powers as to the reception of consular representatives from both Norway and Sweden. Since the replies favored the Norwegian case, the Swedes blamed Lagerheim, and since the inquiry implied Norwegian inferiority in the union it infuriated *Venstre* leaders and editors.

[2] *Ibid.*, 251-252.

Acting on the *Venstre* recommendation, the Storting on January 23, 1903, demanded that the authority of the foreign minister be legally established only with Norwegian consent. This resolution, in combining consular and foreign administration issues, tied together questions which could lead only to Norwegian-Swedish dissension.[3] Here, perhaps, is the point at which disintegration for the third time became ascendant.

Venstre politics succeeded in getting the resolution passed. Moderate and radical wings of *Venstre* displayed appreciable differences of opinion. Moderates wished the negotiations to succeed and strove energetically to aid attainment of conclusions acceptable to both sides. Radicals insisted on standing firm on the principle of Norway's right to establish separate consuls and an administrative apparatus free of Swedish control. Johan Castberg's conversations with Qvam and Blehr convinced the former that the moderate cabinet contemplated jettisoning this principle by agreeing to make the consuls responsible to the union foreign minister. In this fashion *Venstreforeningen* stated its views, which were binding upon the cabinet if it wished parliamentary support, and, pushed by Berner, Castberg, Konow, and others, the Storting likewise expressed its opinion. Party programs were being fashioned for the fall elections of 1903, and *Venstre* wished it understood that it represented national and patriotic sentiments of all "good" Norwegians. *Venstre* also attempted to negotiate a joint program with the Conservatives, but for them, too, the pending elections were crucial. Francis Hagerup, the Conservative leader, publicly announced his party's policy after a meeting on January 13: no cooperation until clarification of party programs.[4] Collaboration with *Venstre*, however, might

[3] Cf. Heiberg, *Unionens opløsning 1905* (Christiania, 1906), 89-90; for details of the *Venstre* meeting of January 19, 1903, which agreed to Berner's proposals see Castberg, *Dagbøker 1900-1917* (Oslo, 1953), I, 128-130.

[4] In conferences between Hagerup and Venstre leaders the former had insisted on a promise from *Venstre* that if a coalition government were created no policy of crisis would be followed whereby Oscar II would be placed in danger of finding no parliamentary majority in the Storting. *Venstre* policy was just such a course, if negotiations stranded, and therefore, Hagerup's request could not be approved. This was the main reason for Conservative policy until elections in the fall; at all costs a crisis must be prevented for it would place the union in danger.

be discussed later if terms could not be arranged with Sweden. If *Venstre* could force the discontinuance of negotiations, formation of a national coalition of *Venstre*, moderates, and Conservatives would be likely. Members of *Venstre*, especially of the left, more and more sought opportunities to block negotiations in order to proceed to an immediate crisis on the consular question.

The Storting resolution exploded in Sweden, as Bishop Billing expressed it, "like a bomb." Many Swedes wished the Riksdag to return the discourtesy with a stern reprimand. But, instead, it created a committee to study the consular question, which meant in actuality its supervision of the cabinet's handling of negotiations. Swedish Conservative newspapers, especially *Nya Dagligt Allehanda*, blasted Norwegians indiscriminately and called the resolution "the well-known Norwegian action policy." Only the firmness of the cabinet and the disarming candor and friendliness of Lagerheim saved the situation. In spite of a temporary reduction of rancor the royal family was greatly shocked by the Norwegian resolution and by the cold reception given Crown Prince Gustaf in Oslo when he was acting as regent.[5]

As with most troubles within the union, the storm passed by, but left its traces of discord and bitterness. Negotiations continued, but showed little progress in an atmosphere where recriminations became repetitious. At least these arguments on consular responsibility to a foreign minister restricted the volume of verbiage and revealed basic unresolved issues. The main impediment, as Blehr stated in March 1903, was Boström's refusal to separate the responsibility and functions of consuls from an authoritative status for the foreign minister. A consular service removed from control of a foreign minister would be a form of administration unknown among nations of the world, and yet Norwegians objected to consular responsibility to a Swedish administration. A solution of the problem required exceptional measures.

Throughout February of 1903 the negotiators continued their

---

[5] Cf. Folke Lindberg, *Kunglig utrikespolitik*, 184-195, on possibilities of German intervention and the Kaiser's attitude. Gustaf was forced to favor dissolution in preference to military, forceful coercion of Norway.

wearisome exchanges without resolution of this major point. In a meeting of *Venstre* leaders and the cabinet on March 16, Blehr summarized the preceding negotiations and presented comments on a Swedish statement of principles. It laid down four basic points: 1) that separate consuls must be compensated for by Norwegian agreement to certain obligations; 2) that a joint law on the relationship of consuls to the foreign office must be passed with the proviso that this law could not be withdrawn or nullified without the consent of both kingdoms; 3) that a revision of the *Riksakt* would give responsibility through the king to both Storting and Riksdag over foreign affairs; 4) that the position of neither the foreign minister nor the diplomatic administration would be disturbed.[6] Any one of these four proposals could end negotiations. By presenting them Boström yielded to the Swedish Conservatives who wished to force the Norwegians to retreat. The Norwegians in their meeting divided into two camps in which Georg Stang and Wollert Konow, both vigorous and influential cabinet officers, attacked the Swedish demands. Two other *Venstre* sided with them on most points, but still straddled the fence. In this heated debate the radicals made their position clear: that the cabinet shamed Norway by its compromises of Norwegian legal rights and honor.

These March days, before the Swedish ministers returned to Stockholm, were crucial ones both for the negotiations and for the union's future. Not only did the ministers hold daily sessions, but the Storting and press debated freely what was known or surmised of the Swedish conditions. Under attack by Stang and Konow, Sigurd Ibsen's political fortunes began to wane. In retribution, he plotted their dismissal from the cabinet and thus joined his own fortunes, as did both Conservatives and moderates, to those of the negotiations. If they failed, then the radical wing of the *Venstre* party would have proved its case against Sweden.

An agreement, or March communiqué as it came to be known, resulted from the council's labors which approved continuation of negotiations. One of the radicals expressed his disapproval in

6 Cf. Castberg, *Dagbøker*, I, 152-163.

no uncertain terms:[7] "With sorrow and shame I write this. The government majority has now agreed to an arrangement which for the sake of preservation of dear peace breaks with the old Norwegian national policy, which binds our freedom of working for our full independence, which places a Norwegian administration under Swedish control, and which makes Norwegian legislation bound by an absolute Swedish veto." In Sweden the communiqué received an equivocal reception. The Riksdag directly expressed its dissent by requesting that in the future it be kept more fully informed. Privately Bishop Billing, Conservative member of the First Chamber, wrote to his wife that "the Swedish government goes almost as a supplicant. . . ."[8]

Support of or dissent from the communiqué depended upon party orientation. Swedish Conservatives and moderates opposed it because it conceded too much, while Liberals favored the continuation of negotiations because they offered some hope. Norwegian Conservatives approved the communiqué, but would not bind themselves to cooperate with the moderate *Venstre* on a program of implementing it. A majority of *Venstre* and the cabinet grudgingly consented to the basic conditions it laid down, but a vocal and influential minority adamantly opposed it. Stang and Konow were unalterably anticommuniqué and the former's unpremeditated and blunt revelation of his opinion in Storting debate furnished Sigurd Ibsen the lever needed to oust Stang from the cabinet. Konow's resignation followed shortly after.

Newspapers divided along party lines. *Verdens Gang*, moderate *Venstre* in politics, favored resumption of negotiations and complimented the government on its introduction of a "new period" in Norwegian-Swedish relations. The liberal press throughout Norway quickly followed suit. Conservative papers showed more interest in making political profit than in complimenting the ministry. For example, *Aftenposten* bitterly attacked Stang and Konow for their failure to support their colleagues.

In the electoral campaign, and during the oratory which started in April, divergences developed quickly and clearly.

[7] *Ibid.*, I, 163.
[8] *Anteckningar . . .* , 233.

Moderate *Venstre* lost steadily and the radical wing gained a larger and larger following. Conservatives multiplied in strength and increased their hold even more in the fall of 1903. In both Norwegian and Swedish Conservative newspapers the radical wing of *Venstre* came to be labelled the "war party" or the "chauvinists." The Conservatives, of course, called themselves the peace party and in April started the negotiations which led to the working coalition with the moderates called *Samlings-partiet*. In an article in *Aftenposten* on April 12 Bjørnson formally announced his support of this coalition and its program for the continuance of negotiations. It was here that the campaign slogan of "only negotiations" first appeared, only to be repeated again and again during pre-election oratory. The Swedish liberal *Dagens Nyheter* reprinted the whole of Bjørnson's letter, while other Swedish newspapers of both city and country approved highly of what he wrote.

Such widespread comment and approval from this world-famous publicist required an immediate answer and Carl Berner, an old leader in *Venstre*, mounted the platform at Lillehammar on April 26 to charge the Conservatives with playing a double game both in negotiations and in parliament. Berner's defense of his resolution of January and of his party's program was weakened by his questionable statement that *Venstre* sought only to "work for" a Norwegian foreign office and was not belligerently favoring independent action. Conservatives, incensed by Berner's statement that they had agreed to cooperate with *Venstre* in negotiations, charged him with deliberate falsification. Following Berner's speech Bjørnson triumphantly proclaimed in *Aften-posten* that the true program of *Venstre* had been admitted: to break off negotiations and create an independent foreign office.

During the summer and fall the oratory continued its loud clamor unceasingly. The two program speeches of Francis Hag-erup, certain to be prime minister if *Samlingspartiet* won, set the course for the next two years. Selecting Lillestrøm, north of Oslo, for his first speech, he dramatically forced the Norwegian voter to choose between war and peace by accusing *Venstre* of fomenting discord which would result in war. Negotiations with

Sweden, he said, ought to proceed until the consular system was achieved. If Norwegian electors adopted *Venstre* proposals, they must be prepared to sacrifice their blood. As Bjørnson had clearly stated—and Hagerup thus identified the great poet with the new program—the choice was war or peace, and a Norwegian consular system could be bought at too dear a price.[9] A week later Bjørnson joined Hagerup openly by attacking *Venstre* and its "war" campaign platform. Swedes, so Bjørnson believed, would negotiate honestly like gentlemen, and Norwegians must do likewise. "What would be the product of campaign promises of *Venstre?*" Bjørnson asked. "War!" It was Bjørnson's influence throughout Norway and his words which identified *Venstre* in the Norwegian mind with hostile, vain gestures without meaning other than war.

Resentful of Bjørnson's charges and fearful of his influence, Blehr defended the government's loyal defense of Norwegian rights and honor and in turn accused the Conservatives of unpatriotic behavior. Berner also defended his party and, though admitting that negotiations had been initiated by *Venstre*, insisted that the party would not compromise in its demands for national independence. In essence, Berner implied that the Conservatives would submit to Swedish demands. If negotiations failed, *Venstre's* program was to pass a law setting up a Norwegian consular system and to settle with Sweden on that basis. Political oratory increased in volume and vehemence as the elections drew nearer; accusations of disloyalty, lack of patriotism, betrayal, and treason smeared both Conservative and coalition parties. Simultaneously *Venstre* speakers and press scoffed at the fears aroused by Bjørnson when, in a new speech, he warned his countrymen about the danger of war and foreign intervention.

Yet for most Norwegians Bjørnson placed the issue squarely. If negotiations with Sweden failed, then "speak no more on negotiations. We form a party approving the union's dissolution, [for] it has become impossible for us to live in such a union." He estimated that two-thirds of the Norwegian people, under such conditions, would approve passage of a consular law and

9 *Verdens Gang*, May 22, 1902.

accept the subsequent crisis. The Storting, speaking with the voice of the Norwegian people, would decide on action evolved from a variety of alternatives. But first Norway must explore and exploit all the possibilities in negotiations. Until the Swedes illustrated clearly their unreasonableness, Norwegians could not refuse peaceable discussion of any union matters.

The second of Hagerup's campaign speeches was given at Trondheim on August 15. By this time everyone acknowledged him as the next prime minister if the coalition won the elections, and his prospects gave his speech added significance. After reviewing the situation in somewhat academic fashion, he defended his refusal to cooperate with *Venstre* in a stalemate program which could lead only to severance of connections with Sweden. He struck out at "persons of small vision" who dared to lead Norway into a series of crises as in the 1890's. *Venstre* had once clasped the "brother's hand" offered by Sweden and, therefore, "negotiations must continue." He also reiterated Bjørnson's question: Consular system at what price? The speech concluded with two slogans: Conservatives stood for peace, and *Venstre* for war; and Norway must first have "only negotiations." Conservatives further stigmatized *Venstre* as a party of radicals and socialists, and implied that those voting for its candidates must also accept its adventurous social and economic policies.

In the last month of the campaign Conservative leaders also centered their fire on *Venstre* leaders who had been most active in denouncing negotiations. Thus, Konow and Castberg, as the most vocal and most prominent, were especially singled out. At Ringsaker in Konow's own district, Bjørnson accused him and the radicals of bellicose and impractical views, an attack which others followed up by an intense campaign of personal charges. *Verdens Gang* on August 25 associated Blehr and Stang with the other *Venstre* leaders and called them all "saber rattlers." *Venstre*, the paper wrote, sought to destroy the mutual friendship of the peoples of the two nations. Next day it pointed gloomily to the slim prospects of success in negotiations if the present government stayed in office. The heated debate and oratory concluded in a great pre-election appeal which marked the campaign of 1903 as the most bitter in Norwegian political history, with the worst "mudslinging" yet experienced. Only once before, in 1894, had Norwegian elections been waged on so small a field and with such singular attention to a union problem.

With all the charges and countercharges, the stigma of "warmongers" attached to *Venstre*, and the still active hope for successful negotiations with Sweden, the Norwegian voter's choice seemed fairly simple. In October, 49 Conservatives, 9 moderates, and 6 liberals took their seats in the Storting to face the "war party" of 48 *Venstre* and 5 Social Democrats. The latter contingent were its first representatives in parliament. Norwegians decided, therefore, to continue negotiations and to test the thesis of Bjørnson, Hagerup, and Ibsen that the Swedes were willing, even eager, to settle the consular question.

With the vote clearly against it, the Blehr cabinet resigned and Hagerup formed a new coalition ministry of Conservatives and moderates. Its principles, reduced to an "either-or" status, were clearly delineated in a meeting of its prospective members.[10] If the consular negotiations failed to achieve a satisfactory solution, then Hagerup would resign, and a new ministry pledged to the *Venstre* program would be appointed. In such clear and distinct blacks and whites, where alternatives loomed like mountains for all to see, the two choices lay before the Hagerup cabinet. The life of the cabinet hung on the successful solution of the consular question, the outcome of which both the prime minister and Ibsen were confident. So high had political tensions mounted, however, that an emotional response to any proposal had become automatic. Swedish obstinacy or blundering could trigger these automatic responses at any time, and negotiations would fail. *Venstre* then would proceed to find "other means" to solve the union's dilemma, and it was certain in everyone's mind that the dissolution of the union would result.

The hectic political campaign was followed by a general lassitude which even the union committee reflected by holding no meetings until the end of the year. The celebration of Union Day presented an opportunity for Norwegians in Stockholm and for

[10] Sigurd Ibsen, "Da unionen løsnede," *Samtiden*, XVII (1906), 217-220.

Swedes in Oslo to display their faith in the union. On this day a Swedish music concert in Oslo's *Nationalteatret* drew a large, appreciative audience and the capital's newspapers, regardless of their political leanings, warmly praised this performance of the works of Swedish composers. A meeting on a Scandinavian tariff union in the Oslo political economy society showed general approval of this important movement toward integration and its prospects of revival of the defunct Norwegian-Swedish customs law. Norwegians present divided on the topic. Bredo Morgenstierne, professor of political economy at Oslo University, vigorously supported the plan, and Norway's Agricultural Director Jonas Smitt argued that a customs union, with free imports of Swedish and Danish agricultural products, would be a disaster for Norwegian farmers. Some editorials criticized the project adversely, and *Verdens Gang*, which supported moderation in the past elections, led in disapproval of those who would destroy national independence.

Another event displayed in a minor way the depth of feeling and union discord. When Bjørnson received the 1903 Nobel Prize in literature, the union ghost walked with him to mock the honor conferred by the Swedish Academy. Norwegian anti-Swedish circles and some newspapers, either openly or privately, said scornfully that the Judas touch and the "thirty pieces" were for services rendered in the 1903 elections.[11] The Swedish Academy might well have ignored Bjørnson for that year, but, in truth, its decision had been made in June and, therefore, as Lagerheim explained to Ibsen, its action preceded the Norwegian election campaign. The Norwegian literary genius thoroughly enjoyed the festivities in Stockholm. Self-conscious at first in the king's presence, Bjørnson's momentary stiffness was swept away in the warmth of King Oscar's welcome. His speech to the Academy touched only briefly on the Norwegian elections and high hopes for settlement of the consular issue.

11 Cf. Stang's letter in *Aftenposten*, January 11, 1904, attacking Bjørnson for his equivocal position on negotiations with Sweden and his defense of his own policies in 1903.

It appeared in December as if these high hopes might be materialized. Three official Swedish protocols concerning the consular question were handed the Norwegians. These protocols, taken in their entirety, insisted upon discussion of the administrative relationship of the foreign office to the proposed consular system, combined with reservation of an unchanged position for the minister in conduct of foreign relations. The Norwegian cabinet agreed to these and requested that future negotiations center on these problems. Simultaneously, in the belief that a separate consular system was forthcoming, the Storting began drafting a law on the basis of stipulations in earlier negotiations. In January 1904, the Storting referred the proposed law to a committee for thorough study, and it reported favorably. It was understood that an identical law would be approved by the Riksdag.

In May the Storting legislation was handed to Boström. His previous objections, and the several obstacles he had placed on the road to successful solution of the conflict, had made the Swedish prime minister seem a veritable Beelzebub to most Norwegians, who awaited with apprehension his latest response to their attempts. The new law seemed to meet his demands for, although it carefully preserved the independence of the proposed consuls from administrative supervision by the foreign minister, it left to that union official considerable discretion in regulation of the diplomatic functions of consuls. Actually the law went as far as limits of Norwegian self-interest would allow toward satisfying Swedish demands. Having completed their share of conference work the Norwegians waited for the Swedes to act.

In Swedish debates in the spring Riksdag sessions, malcontents in the First Chamber voiced their disgust with concessions to the Norwegians. Some Conservatives felt that Sweden's honor was endangered, for the compromise, from their viewpoint, virtually granted the Norwegians their own foreign office. However, as Sigurd Ibsen wrote to Bjørnson, the Swedes circulated a draft of their own legislation, so there seemed to be some remote possibility for action. Ibsen guessed erroneously that September would see the entire matter clarified to the point where the outlines of the final result could be seen.[12]

The annual Union Day on November 4 was celebrated as usual with expressions of good feeling. *Verdens Gang* stated that apparently no grounds existed for believing in future dangers. It was not expected, continued the paper, that the Swedes and the king "shall love us with any burning love. But it is to be hoped that they will treat us with understanding and tact." The way to cooperation was open and an agreement would be easy, if the right spirit prevailed. Yet, four days later, the same paper, regretfully remarking on Lagerheim's resignation, noted that the entire picture had changed.

From 1903 and the March communiqué, Lagerheim had been most unpalatable to Conservative Swedish leaders in the Riksdag. In addition Boström resented his influence with the royal family and the prime minister's friends urged him to dump this "notoriously" pro-Norwegian foreign minister. A majority of the cabinet sided with Lagerheim in the debate on the union, which did not improve Boström's temper or his equivocal position with either cabinet or monarchy. In October Boström threatened to resign and the crown prince offered his mediation to prevent a split because of its effects on Norwegian-Swedish relations. An open quarrel broke out during the afternoon of October 21 when both Boström and Lagerheim swore that they would not remain in the same cabinet. On October 25 Lagerheim, the victim of an intrigue within his own department, offered his resignation to the crown prince, who evaded an answer. Boström seized the opportunity to force his will upon the monarchy by going to the royal palace to persuade the king, queen, and crown prince to accede to his wishes. They decided to accept Lagerheim's resignation and to appoint Count August Fersen-Gyldenstolpe, who could be controlled by Boström. The "pilot was dropped."[13]

With Lagerheim's dismissal, made public some days later by his

[12] September 4, 1904, Bjørnson Mss., University Library, Oslo.

[13] For details of the Boström-Lagerheim controversy see Arne Wåhlstrand, *Regeringskiftena 1900 och 1902* (Uppsala, 1947), 81, 128, 129, and his "Statsminister Boström och Lagerheimska krisen," in *Festskrift till professor skytteanus Axel Brusewitz* (Uppsala, 1941), 154-179.

resignation, Boström became solely responsible for conduct of Swedish negotiations with Norway. More than that, his personal enmity toward and jealousy of Lagerheim forced future Swedish policy into a strait-jacket from which the only escape was Boström's own dismissal. As a matter of policy Boström had to adopt a course opposed to that of Lagerheim and logically it must offend the Norwegians, unless the Swedish prime minister wished to displease Swedish Conservatives. Boström, faced by a revolt of his own cabinet and with grumbling from his own party, turned most naturally toward a course intended "to preserve Swedish honor and prestige." In a word, Boström, for the part he played in ridding himself of Lagerheim, must be blamed for the cessation of negotiations and the events of 1905. As Ibsen informed Hagerup, the affair presaged a break between Norway and Sweden;[14] almost unconsciously the Norwegian minister noted the time when disintegration won its way.

With Lagerheim gone, Boström took over negotiations in Oslo on the consular question. He brought no Swedish draft of a law as was expected, but only the basis for one which the Norwegian ministry must approve in advance. It incorporated conditions unacceptable to the Norwegians, for the Swedes now insisted upon a direct authority for the foreign minister and diplomatic administration over the consuls. For several years, even in the 1890's, Norwegians had repeated explicitly their objections to a foreign minister's control of the Norwegian civil service or administration, and now the Swedes bluntly asked it. Shaken, yet hopeful, Hagerup went to Stockholm in December where the six-man state council uselessly belabored points of disagreement. Boström's draft of a law, and his statements during the conferences in Stockholm, showed further conversations to be futile and the basis on which negotiations had been initiated in 1902 completely destroyed. In sessions in Oslo and Stockholm Boström made explicit the terms on which Swedish consent to

14 Ibsen in letters of November 3 and 20, "Da unionen løsnede," *Samtiden*, XVII (1906), 200-204. Castberg wrote to Konow, May 1, 1904, Konow Mss., University Library, Oslo, that Michelsen had threatened to leave Hagerup's cabinet because Lagerheim certainly would be dismissed during the summer. Cf. Jakob Schøning, *Dagbøker* (Oslo, 1950), 209-211.

creation of a separate Norwegian consular system would be granted. His six points (the Norwegians called them "the six dependency clauses") insisted upon control by the foreign minister over the consuls, with no clarification of whether he might be Norwegian or not. The sixth point—"that the joint consular system under certain conditions should continue to exist in special foreign countries"—was an entire negation of Norwegian insistence upon complete independence. The Swedes, pressed by the Conservative party, went to the limits of demands; the next step would be to tell the Norwegians that they were denied their separate consular system.

Boström was aware of the probable results of his actions and admitted openly to Hagerup that he lacked the support of either his colleagues or Crown Prince Gustaf who said that the monarchy could not prevent a separation of the two countries, if both wished it.[15] King Oscar II objected to his son's statement, but even he soon realized how accurately Gustaf read the future. When Hagerup returned to Oslo for the Christmas holidays, he expressed his extreme pessimism about chances for even a resumption of negotiations. In a letter to a friend he disclosed his unwillingness to compromise further and his interpretation of the split within the Swedish cabinet. Boström, so Hagerup wrote, would resign if the Norwegian government could arrange a satisfactory accord with the remaining members of the Swedish cabinet. But, without him, as Norwegians and Swedes knew, any agreement would stand a slim chance in the Riksdag. According to Hagerup, a compromise, admitting some Swedish control over the consuls, would be anathema to the Norwegian "chauvinists."[16]

Subsequent endeavors to retrieve from discarded drafts, plans, and projects some pieces upon which to build new foundations called for the labors of a Hercules. Hagerup admitted as much and openly spoke of a "new basis" when he returned to his

15 Cf. Gustaf to Bjørnson, November 16, 1904, especially where the crown prince states: "The union is not a major affair for the dynasty but ought to be that for both peoples; it is a matter of life for their fortune and future." Bjørnson Mss., University Library, Oslo.

16 Hagerup to Vinje, December 26, 1904, Vinje Mss., Royal Archives (Riksarkivet), Oslo.

office after the Christmas holidays. The first meetings of the Storting in January 1905, passed without action, although its members talked much of dissolution, of choices as to procedures, of war fears, and of subjects closely associated with their wish to act. But over all in Norway, and even to an extent in Sweden, a gloomy pall settled. Many waited impatiently for this indecisive moment to pass and for someone to step forward to offer his services for Norway's cause. In Sweden leaders in cabinet, Riksdag, and palace were aware that the time had come for decision. But because of years of acrimonious debate they could not offer those generous gestures necessary to preserve the union.

CHAPTER VII

◇◇

A TIME OF DECISION

◇◇

THE gloom and pessimism caused by Boström's startling alteration of basic principles lasted for over a month. The slow pace
in dispersing this gloom benefited *Venstre*, whose members heartily wished the resignation of the Hagerup cabinet. But beyond
that, *Venstre* desired the agreement of the Conservatives to a
separation of the two countries, and, to gain the desired goal, it
waited for events to move moderates and Conservatives towards
it. Boström's proposals put the Swedes into the unhappy position
of ending the negotiations, and few Norwegians argued the point.
The moment had arrived for operation of those automatic responses leading to severance of ties with Sweden—a process which
Venstre shrewdly recognized could not be hurried. The first step
was the hardest of all—to let events take their natural course
without interference. If *Venstre* stirred the brew too vigorously,
both moderates and Conservatives might concede some points
in order to continue negotiations with the Swedes.

For the Hagerup cabinet, January was a disturbing month.
Lengthy discussions on courses of action continued unremittingly
without resolving differences of opinion.[1] Their alternatives covered familiar ground from debates of the past ten years. Since
negotiations were not to be resumed, then the union must be
dissolved. The cabinet had been formed in 1903 on the condition
that it would resign when negotiations stranded. But, inspired

[1] In letters from Oscar II to Hagerup, the king lamented the effects of
Boström's actions and asked Hagerup to persuade the Norwegian cabinet, by
all possible means, to continue negotiations and to prevent a crisis. In addition, the king wrote that Boström was willing to retire from office, if he
were an obstacle to peace between the two countries, and that Crown Prince
Gustaf had no share in framing the six points. Hagerup's answer quite
formally expressed his displeasure with negotiations and his regrets over the
obvious effects of Boström's proposals. Hagerup Mss., Royal Archives (*Riksarkivet*), Oslo; and *Dagbok ført i 1905 av statsminister Francis Hagerup*, ed.
H. Falck Myckland (Oslo, 1951), 20-23.

by a false sense of leadership, Hagerup sought to avoid a resignation in order to pursue one of the several alternatives for action.

These multiple choices presented some confusion but little room for bickering. First choice was the "long law line," whereby a bill passed by the Storting three times would become a law over the king's veto. The obvious deterrent to this method was its snail-like pace. Some of its adherents argued the merits of its slowness because military defenses could be improved. On the other hand, the expense of the "long law line," and its fomenting of bitterness between the two countries, forced recognition of its impractical nature. Second choice, with two separate avenues to the same objective, was passage of either a resolution or a law on the consular system and precipitation of an immediate cabinet crisis when the king refused his sanction. Such a crisis, which meant dissolution of the union, would be strategically planned by Storting, government, and party leaders for the most opportune moment. A third choice was for the Storting to declare the union dissolved and to propose negotiations with Sweden for an achievement of a reasonable settlement. The last choice deserved some consideration, for Swedish Liberals generally accepted it, and it conformed to requirements written into the *Riksakt*. However, any proposal for negotiations by now implied to the Norwegians a distasteful "begging" for independence and carried a stigma in its tacit recognition that Sweden must be asked to dissolve the union. In all probability, Swedish delays might also frustrate Norwegian desires.

Years of argument in party caucuses, in Storting debates, and in newspaper wars, during which various details of these three main courses of action had evolved, left Norwegian political parties little room for debate. The Conservatives, most prounion of the four parties, prepared a strategic retreat: to defend the union as long as humanly possible, to continue deliberations with Sweden, and to propose negotiations on the dissolution. The "long law line" could be approved as an amendment or substitute for this course. *Venstre*, the old party of attack during the 1890's, favored a "crisis line," by passing either a consular law or a resolution, but preferred the former since it was more likely to be clear to all Norwegians and would not be muddied by confusing alternatives. Only the moderates, when it came time to cast their lot with one or another of the several courses, postponed an unequivocal commitment. Social Democrats, with five Storting seats from the election of 1903, favored an immediate dissolution, either by negotiations with Sweden or by the *Venstre* "crisis line." Norwegians might disagree as to alternatives, but they possessed a thorough familiarity with the risks involved and their possibilities for success.

The tactical advantage of having a Conservative-moderate coalition in power when negotiations ended was now clearly revealed, and *Venstre* silence for over a month became quite explicable in these terms. A cabinet crisis could end only on *Venstre* terms, to which Conservatives then must accede. A new coalition could not be formed except on a program of dissolution, or by establishment of a separate consular service. *Venstre* could afford to wait, or even to join a coalition with Conservatives.

Despite promises of resignation and a need for haste if his cabinet stayed in office, Hagerup now proved annoyingly pedantic, even though skilled leadership was needed. The prime minister's incapacity was proved in conferences with A. J. Vinje, leader of the moderates, and with the editor of *Verdens Gang*. Hagerup freed Vinje and the moderates from any obligations and to the editor he spoke of the union's dissolution only after elections in 1906. With several Conservatives Hagerup likewise alienated possible support by refusing to approve cooperation with *Venstre*. Consequently the confidence of his own colleagues began to diminish. By upholding a mild and placating answer to Boström's six points, Hagerup offended directly one cabinet member and caused the others to doubt whether his leadership might prove equal to their great task. Jakob Schøning, one of the three members of the union council, opposed the Norwegian answer to the Swedes, having already adopted the *Venstre* policy of an immediate crisis. Minor changes in the note allowed Schøning to continue in the cabinet, but he had threatened to resign and had cast doubts upon Hagerup's leadership.

Outside ministerial chambers the usual mutual recriminations were exchanged by newspapers of both countries. Stockholm's *Dagens Nyheter* (January 12, 22) condemned Norwegian and Swedish policies alike for not having in any way relieved union tensions. Eventually, it contended, if such policies continued, the union would be broken; therefore, negotiations should be renewed on a broad basis to create a new union. Norwegian papers replied by attacking Boström's conduct and Swedish stubbornness. Sweden held sinister designs on Norway, so Norwegian writers stated, and *Verdens Gang* (January 31) charged that Sweden would not come to Norway's aid if rumors of Russian aggressive plans materialized. *Vårt Land* (January 20) thought talk of war to be a " 'puff in the wind' " and responsibility for the failure of negotiations to rest squarely on the shoulders of the unreasonable and obstinate Norwegians. The Swedes could not relinquish control over consular officials, the paper continued, and therefore Norwegian insistence upon separation of consular and diplomatic functions was pure nonsense. Even the Liberal *Göteborgs Handels-och Sjöfartstidning*, one of the three most influential Swedish papers, blamed Norwegians for the failure to reach an agreement.

Some trace of reason in the overheated atmosphere appeared in *Svenska Dagbladet's* request for cessation of the newspaper agitation. It was a sentiment applauded by the Norwegian liberal press which also asked for public calm during the tense government negotiations. *Svenska Dagbladet* also initiated a provocative series of articles by Professor Harald Hjärne of Uppsala.[2] The premise on which the articles were based was the rapid movement toward dissolution. The union's feeble state, although many wished its preservation, and the fierce debates between governments and peoples neutralized any effectual conciliation. It was better to end fruitless argument and to dissolve the union, substituting some form of defense union in which each country would be sovereign and equal. Hjärne outlined in subsequent articles minimal conditions for dissolution: a Storting election of a Bernadotte as king in Norway, the razing of the frontier

[2] February 1, 10, 14; March 9.

forts, creation of a neutral zone along the border, an agreement on a free and reciprocal transport between the two states, and a treaty protecting the Lapps. The articles reflected the opinions of many Swedes, and Hjärne himself represented Swedish nationalism in the Riksdag. He contributed constructively to the union debate in two ways: by specific suggestions for a dissolution of the union and by revealing some Conservative principles. His articles and opinions influenced Norwegians, especially the Conservatives, during February and March when the Storting deliberated on courses of action and a cabinet crisis was in process. In essence, Hjärne calmly suggested disamalgamation in order to pave the way for integration.

The press warfare revealed the moment's seriousness more clearly than ever before. At this crucial juncture every reader was made to realize that the next step was in the direction of either retreat or separation. Since the press of both countries was controlled by political parties, it exposed most frankly discussions in cabinets, in Storting and Riksdag, and in party meetings. Papers exaggerated small incidents into great debates; illustrative of this tendency was the furore over remarks made by the union minister in Berlin reflecting adversely on Norwegian honor. The indiscretion exploded into a public issue. Hagerup and Ibsen both immediately filed protests with the Swedish foreign minister. This affair, largely a concoction of the press, aroused public opinion and graphically cast light on the "Swedish" foreign office and its "Swedish" personnel. For dubious Norwegians, of whom a small fraction was still wavering, it focused attention on so-called "obvious facts."

At the end of January the Swedish government issued its answer to the Norwegian statement of January 12. With deliberation it insisted on maintenance of the December "six points," and asked for continuance of negotiations. The Norwegian cabinet wasted little time in framing its instructions to the Norwegian councilors in Stockholm; these orders told them to say nothing, and closed the door on further negotiations. On February 1, Ibsen also wrote privately to Boström that any further discussions were impossible in light of the Swedish government's uncompromising attitude.

The Swedish action hastened all parties toward a decision on a future policy. The week preceding the joint council session on February 7, where Norwegian members officially and publicly had to end negotiations, saw all parties setting their programs on their course. Hagerup presented his choice in a cabinet meeting on February 2. He wished the creation of a Storting committee to cooperate with the cabinet and, if possible, with representatives of the Swedish government and Riksdag "to prepare for the question of the union's peaceful dissolution or transformation."[3] In this proposal Hagerup chose the most moderate Conservative course of action. It received no support when Christian Michelsen presented it to a *Venstre* caucus the same day. Ignoring Hagerup, *Venstre* and Conservatives agreed on selection of a committee by the Storting. Casting aside his recommendation as too confined in scope, they agreed to allow the committee complete freedom in its deliberations. The only real contention centered on the number of its members—whether there should be fifteen or nineteen—and gave a minor victory to *Venstre* by adopting the larger number of nineteen.

The rudderless drifting and indecision of Hagerup could be continued only through endless persuasion by the prime minister. Before his own party on February 4 he advised a policy of "wait and see," perhaps because of Michelsen's admonition to use caution. He was prevented from presenting his own personal views, which at least had some merit, by Michelsen's urging the cabinet to insist on general and nonpersonal utterances by the prime minister. Michelsen might not have been Machiavellian enough to lay a powder train to destroy the cabinet, but suspicious signs of preparations surrounded this action.

Opinions in the country became more and more crystallized. A mass meeting of the Student Society (*Studentersamfund*) on February 4, attended by officials and prominent private persons, approved a radical policy of immediate action. A *Venstre* caucus of the same date, in choosing three extremists for the Storting

[3] Hagerup, *Dagbok*, 51.

Special Committee, revealed the party's determination, for these men bore special grudges against both the union and Sweden.[4] On the other side of the peninsula the Swedish press, especially *Vårt Land* and *Stockholms Dagblad*, seemed bent on forcing Norwegians into action by its dogged insistence upon accepting the Swedish note of January 30. Sven Hedin, famed explorer and expert on Russian affairs, expostulated gloomily on the results which termination of the union would have on Scandinavian defense. In *Stockholms Dagblad* an editor wrote on February 7 that ". . . what we ought to do is to wait cold-bloodedly and prepare to discuss different future programs when such discussions can be quiet and reasonable. Let us assume a defensive position at least until we can prepare ourselves in advance about the force and plans for dissolution of the union." If "cold-blooded," "defensive position," and "force" are wrenched from context and added to the "thereafter" of *Svenska Dagbladet*, as the Norwegians did, then an ominous sound of rattling sabers and noisy muskets seems audible above the hum of human voices.

On February 7, 1905, the joint council met in Stockholm to hear the Norwegians. Personal correspondence between Boström and Ibsen, telegraphed messages and telephone calls between the Swedish prime minister and Hagerup, and royal attempts to explain the monarchy's position preceded this most important conference. The Norwegian pronouncement expressed tersely their determined stand: "The Norwegian Council has found no grounds to differ from what previously has been presented, orally and in writing, on the subject." Officially the king, the Swedish and Norwegian governments, and both peoples were now informed of the break in which the Norwegians took the initiative. The Swedish press seized upon that advantage to proclaim its wholesale condemnation of the union partner. But, tactically, Norwegian assumption of the initiative meant that the Swedish Riksdag and government sat idle for four months while Nor-

---

[4] The members chosen were: Johan Castberg, Sophus Arctander, Aaslev O. Bryggesaa, Wollert Konow, Carl Berner, H. K. H. Foosnaes, J. T. Hoff, and A. J. Langeland. Those generally regarded as "radical" were Castberg, Konow, and Bryggesaa.

wegians busied themselves with ending the union. The very nature of the problem forced Swedish negativism. Only a radical political reversal on the part of Boström or a change of ministry offered any hopes for preservation of the union, but neither the ministry nor the Riksdag dared venture such an about-face with the Conservative majority of the First Chamber threatening retaliation against those who dared speak for Norway.

Norwegians initiated the offensive against the union when Hagerup announced in the Storting on February 8 the cessation of negotiations with Sweden and asked for parliamentary assistance in building a unified program. His general appeal aroused only antiministerial reactions. The Storting listened, but took no steps to make effective any of Hagerup's wishes, and its coldness to his pleas might be easily explained. *Venstre* had decided, in its three-day caucus prior to Hagerup's Storting appearance, to operate independently. *Venstre* speeches, reduced to a simple statement, said: Norway would have her own consular system in spite of all obstacles and consequences.[5]

In the cabinet Hagerup sought to create a policy on which all parties could agree. His statement proved too weak for most cabinet members, however; three of the six present shifted their preferences, and others plainly showed their disapproval of the prime minister's plan. In spite of Hagerup's gloomy predictions of Swedish aggression and of foreign intervention, a majority of the cabinet, although differing slightly on procedures, followed the Storting. In this session both Michelsen and Schøning disagreed with Hagerup and Ibsen, and the same day Michelsen quietly began plans for a new cabinet of which he would be chief.

Partially aware of these Norwegian projects, and determined to avoid a severance of negotiations if he could, Crown Prince Gustaf arrived in Oslo to attempt revival of joint discussions. Acting as regent during his father's illness, Gustaf received a chilly reception by cabinet, Storting, press, and Norwegian peo-

---

[5] Note that only two votes were cast in this meeting against Johan Castberg's motion that the present session of the Storting pass a consular law and frame a budget for the foreign service. Castberg, *Dagbøker*, I, 191-193.

ple, for it was rumored that he came "to speak Swedish to the Norwegians." Tales like these conveyed the impression that he came to convince them of Swedish superiority in the union and of the futility of appointing consuls who would not be accredited by foreign powers. Certainly the most misunderstood man of the year, the crown prince sought to make the union more elastic, to give Norway freedom of action, and to preserve a common monarchy and a Scandinavian defense pact. Only a frank discussion, he believed, would make it possible for the two peoples to continue an association protecting and extending their mutual interests. In spite of the crown prince's utterances and actions, Norwegians maintained their aversion to him, placing the worst interpretations on his speeches and efforts to mend the union's sorely strained ties. *Venstre* hastened its deliberations on policy and increased the pace toward a crisis, fearing that the crown prince might secure Conservative support for his program.

During the first week of his visit, Gustaf met with ministers and Storting members, and his two Swedish advisers followed suit. The three were warned repeatedly that Swedish obstinacy would result in an appointment of a *Venstre* ministry. The crown prince did not oppose such a cabinet, but he preferred that a new government be formed only after Storting elections in 1906. Hagerup's pessimistic warnings on the seriousness of the crisis failed to alarm Gustaf, who persisted in his efforts to reach more solid ground for negotiations and calmly accepted the thought of *Venstre* dominance in Norway.

Several trends indicated the futility of Gustaf's hopes. Arctic explorer Fridtjof Nansen, in an article entitled *Veien* ("The Way") which appeared in *Verdens Gang* (February 12), urged achievement of national sovereignty over both Swedish opposition and Norwegian minority protests. The Storting, he felt, should pass an act establishing a consular system and take the consequences. Under Nansen's influence, and in cooperation with other intellectuals, Norwegian writers published articles in German, Danish, and English newspapers while Nansen continued his series in *Verdens Gang* and his speeches in *Studentersamfund*. The total effect of Nansen's efforts, ably assisted by many prominent persons, was to push *Venstre* Storting members into public notice. Striving to keep ahead of the crest of popular pressure, as expressed by these men and meetings, the Storting went further than its majority often would have liked.

From another quarter, the editors of *Morgenbladet*, voices of the Conservative party, wrote of their distrust of the prime minister and of their wish for a positive program. Both Michelsen and Schøning expressed their reluctance to remain in Hagerup's ministry which daily was losing its parliamentary support. Benjamin Vogt, prominent lawyer and Conservative leader, also wrote Hagerup of his opposition to prevailing policies of their party. Vogt's defection augmented Hagerup's animosity against Michelsen, who was blamed for much of the ground swell against the ministry. On February 20 the prime minister directly challenged Michelsen to abandon his mask of indecision, only to receive the surprising reply that "he would not refuse to accept his parliamentary duty to form a new government, but that he did not know if it[6] would be successful."[7] Ibsen attempted also to desert Hagerup, for he was convinced that a majority of the Storting and cabinet favored immediate action. As he enigmatically remarked to his father-in-law, Bjørnson, his resignation from the cabinet would make him a free man.[8] But the final coup given Hagerup was by a caucus of his own party which approved a plan of cooperation with *Venstre* tantamount to full acceptance of the more radical program. The formation of the Special Committee added an extra blow, if such were indeed needed. Openly hostile to Hagerup, the committee seized the initiative in formulation of policy and retained control during the next four months. Power passed without dissent out of Hagerup's hands into those outstretched by the committee.

At its first meeting on February 21 the Special Committee debated two alternatives.[9] Both were *Venstre* proposals, and final

---

[6] Formation of a new ministry.   [7] Hagerup, *Dagbok*, 109.

[8] Bjørnson Mss., University Library, Oslo.

[9] Among the committee's nineteen members were eight Conservatives, eight *Venstre*, two moderates, and a Social Democrat. On sessions of the Special Committee three main sources have been used: Castberg's *Dagbøker*; Bothner's *Dagbøker (Diaries)*, deposited in *Riksarkivet*, Oslo; and Vinje Mss. *Riksarkivet*, Oslo.

choice narrowed to either the "short law line" whereby the king's veto of a law would be followed by a crisis, or to the passage of a resolution declaring the union dissolved. After two days of inconclusive policy discussions, the committee summoned a series of cabinet ministers and defense officials to appear and to testify on the extent of Norway's preparedness for a crisis. Because of the antagonism between Hagerup, Michelsen, and Schøning, virtually nothing was heard of government policies. Hagerup and Ibsen revealed the ministerial conflict in their reports and, at the same time, warned the committee of dangers accompanying an action policy. Hagerup's words came obviously from his speech to the Conservative party caucus, and he could hardly have erred more in repeating them to the Special Committee. Its members were in no mood to ask Hagerup any questions, but Castberg examined Ibsen closely on the possibility of war with Sweden if Norway carried through her program. Ibsen was quite optimistic in his opinion that both foreign and domestic considerations forced the Swedes to shun aggression. Ibsen's counsel, and information from other sources upholding his view, remained an important and constant factor in plans of the Special Committee and the Norwegian government during the ensuing months.

Minister of Defense O. S. J. Strugstad faced a severe examination, as several committee members opposed the Hagerup defense policy. In his review of Norwegian defenses, Strugstad admitted that the Swedish army was superior in numbers (about 80,000 versus 25,000), but insisted that Norwegian advantages in supplies, equipment, and morale more than compensated for numbers. The minister reiterated his gloomy predictions on the necessity of a large foreign loan. He withheld his estimates on costs of approximately nine million *kroner* ($2,250,000) per month and his opinion that foreign loans might cause Norwegian obligations to be called for payment, thus making foreign bondholders panicky. Neither did he mention the supply problem in the event of war: Norwegian munitions factories could not even furnish the necessary small arms ammunition, and artillery shells would have to be purchased abroad. Strugstad's failure to report this information to the Special Committee caused government officials considerable trouble during the summer. The Special Committee's doubts of the minister of defense were entirely justified, even if his fence-straddling under sharp questioning aroused unconscious sympathy. A naval report balanced Strugstad's statements on the army. The navy, so its spokesman said, was ready for action and, comparatively speaking, was better equipped and better prepared for hostilities than Swedish naval forces. Defenses of the Oslo fjord were in good condition, and its narrow entrance could easily be defended from attack.

During its several days of conferences the Special Committee gradually built up knowledge of the political and military picture, and slowly its members modified their views. Its leadership came to center in three persons: Konow, Castberg, and Berner. These three *Venstre*, the first two from the party's radical wing, gained an initial advantage in having a clear and appealing policy and a united party behind them. In contrast, Conservatives and moderates were disorganized, uncertain, and virtually leaderless. In addition, Konow, through correspondence with Wilhelm Christophersen, the Norwegian-Swedish consul general in Brussels, possessed detailed and skillful advice on the nature, propositions, and form of a consular law.[10] Under such conditions two Conservative members accepted the *Venstre* program for immediate action. Sophus Arctander, one of the oldest members of the committee and influential in *Venstre* circles, finally met the Konow-Castberg challenge and reluctantly agreed to support his party's program. Querulously, however, he stated his belief that the crown prince or Oscar II might sanction the consular law to avoid a Norwegian-Swedish conflict. The Swedish foreign minister, who accompanied the crown prince during his Oslo visit, likewise wrote in the same vein to Boström, advising compliance with Norwegian aims and modification of Swedish opposition to a separate consular system. So Arctander's vague hope seemed not very far from reality.[11]

10 Cf. Konow Mss., University Library, Oslo.

11 The absence of Boström from Oslo during this visit of Gustaf becomes conspicuous. He refrained from imposing his abhorred visage upon the Norwegians, knowing too well that their obstinacy would go up several notches if he appeared. During these conferences he kept closely in touch with

The growing unity within the Storting and Special Committee was matched in Sweden by increasing advocacy of peaceful solutions for the union's controversies. A Swedish delegation of Liberals, headed by Karl Staaff, a lawyer and later prime minister, visited Oslo and told the Norwegians of their pessimism over future relations of the two countries. Although Swedish newspapers minimized the effect of the visit and questioned the Liberal party's national power, these extensive conversations greatly influenced Storting members who perceived a Swedish political schism in this Liberal eagerness to seek peace or, if negotiations proved impossible, to dissolve the union. The delegation's report to a subsequent Liberal party meeting in Stockholm stressed Norwegian unanimity and determination which boded ill for the prospect of negotiations. In Stockholm the Social Democratic party's annual congress heard a clear exposé by Norwegian visitors of prevailing opinions in Norway, with a plea to their Swedish colleagues for aid to achieve Norwegian "independence." The Swedish party responded officially by a resolution supporting the Norwegians either in negotiations or by fulfillment of a program of separation.

These generous expressions of good will made the Special Committee decide to refuse all efforts to renew talks with the Swedish ministers. It summoned Hagerup to appear a second time and his vague and indecisive replies to sharp questioning turned the Special Committee to discussions of a new ministry. When the crown prince, who had been all but ignored these two weeks, published a letter to the committee asking for negotiations, it resolved again to force a change of government. A *Verdens Gang* editorial of February 26 asking for such a policy seemed to confirm the committee's determined belief. That editorial, and demands of political maneuvering, brought forth the resignations of Michelsen and Schøning and forced Hagerup from office.

On the morning of February 28, when Hagerup arrived at his office, he found on his desk letters from his two ministers

---

the crown prince and Swedish ministers, but evidently the advice of his informants effected no changes in his attitudes.

terminating their appointments. Schøning was responsible for these letters, and for the sequence of events in the cabinet that made them necessary. Convinced of his uneasy position and certain that his departure from the cabinet could not by itself jolt Hagerup from office, he cajoled, urged, and literally forced Michelsen to join with him in resigning. Schøning, on his way to work on the morning of February 28, called on Michelsen, who was sick in bed, and found him perusing a draft of a resignation letter. Schøning eagerly grasped it, thanked Michelsen profusely for his decision, wrote out his own, and hurried to the prime minister's office where he deposited the two resignations.[12] Without the respect of the Special Committee or the confidence of his own colleagues, Hagerup could not possibly continue in office. If he had expected to use the crown prince to hold office, he was disappointed by Gustaf's calm acceptance of political facts. It is more likely, however, that Hagerup entertained no such hope, for in retiring from office he advised the crown prince to appoint Michelsen.

The same day the prime minister and some of his colleagues appeared again before the Special Committee to report on changes in government policy. Neither Ibsen nor Benjamin Vogt added any information, although members of the Special Committee expectantly waited for Vogt's opinions. Should he persist in his previous view that a crisis ought to be postponed until after Storting elections in 1906, three committee members were poised with a barrage of questions. Hagerup's announcement of the resignations of Michelsen and Schøning came as an anticlimax, for the committee kept itself fully informed on the cabinet's schisms. Cabinet proposals, which he reported, varied from the committee's propositions and were given only casual attention. Naturally Hagerup kept the subject matter of his talks with Gustaf to himself. Schøning, for his part, laid great weight on two premises: Sweden's policy of seeking peace would not be suddenly altered, and the king would not sanction a consular law. Michelsen appeared later, but, weakened by his

---

[12] Cf. Schøning's report of the meeting of the cabinet on February 27, and the description above, *Dagbøker*, 310-313.

illness, he gave only a brief résumé of Norwegian finances. As head of the department of commerce he had been charged with the task of raising a loan for "eventualities."[13]

Norwegians neared their moment of decision. Although six weeks had passed since the rejection of Swedish conditions, leaders and parties moved slowly forward. More important than drama and color was the achievement of unanimity among all parties and sections of the Norwegian people. And most important of all, a national coalition gradually emerged, prepared for leadership during the storms of crisis. The slow maneuvering produced its results in a series of meetings of the Conservatives wherein the party submitted to *Venstre* demands and, on March 4, agreed to support its program for immediate action.[14] On the same date the Special Committee voted on adopting proposals for either the resolution or the "short law line." But the vote was so close that the committee approved Konow's compromise motion tabling the entire problem until formation of a new ministry. Two days later, however, the committee passed a consular law in accord with Carl Berner's suggestion, accepting with it the strategy of a crisis sometime in the summer or fall of 1905. The measure allowed a new cabinet to decide on whether a resolution or a crisis would dissolve the union. Indirectly, the probable adjournment of the Riksdag helped to determine the timing of the crisis.

In a closed meeting the Storting passed the Special Committee's proposition with approximately 100 members favoring an immediate crisis through passage of a consular law which would go into effect on April 1, 1906. Berner, Arctander, Konow, and Castberg, all *Venstre*, spoke in its behalf, but few representatives, even those with real doubts about its advisability, arose to speak. Some questioned if Norway were prepared for a crisis; some argued that this was not the best course; some preferred negotiations rather than a crisis which would irreparably damage the

---

[13] Arctander mentions this loan as having been partly placed at *Stockholms enskilda bank*. Arctander Mss., University Library, Oslo.

[14] Arctander estimated the vote to be 41 or 42 to 7, with 11 to 12 not voting. *Idem.*

good relations of the two peoples. But in the face of aggressive tactics of the four *Venstre* leaders, the timid retreated, and accepted their will. No member, however, wished retention of the union in its present form. Extensive modifications of the *Riksakt* in Norway's favor would have to be proposed and agreed upon by Sweden before even the most ardent friend of the union would be satisfied.

During the first fortnight of March, attention of government circles and public centered upon selection of a new ministry. No candidate for prime minister other than Michelsen was mentioned, and he began on March 1 to discuss probable candidates for cabinet posts. At least twenty prospective members received mention and careful screening on the basis of their stand on dissolution. The new coalition must prove Norwegian unanimity by its composition and must be prepared to stand the rigorous test of the crisis which would follow a veto of a consular law. Gustaf asked Michelsen directly on March 3 whether or not he would accept office. When Michelsen answered in the affirmative, the crown prince wanted to know whether the consular law would be ready before the Riksdag adjourned in May. Michelsen again replied yes, but actually the date for submission of the law to the king had not been set. Later the Special Committee and cabinet decided upon postponement until after adjournment of the Riksdag in order to take advantage of the "more favorable weather."

Michelsen's efforts to procure a cabinet composed of strong party leaders met with some difficulties from *Venstre* entrenched interests. Castberg, when asked to join, insisted upon inclusion of both Georg Stang and Konow, both of whom were known as "radicals." Michelsen's conversations with Castberg raised another tough problem, for he wanted a post either in Stockholm or in the department of commerce, which would involve a social reform policy distasteful to moderates and Conservatives. When Michelsen refused appointments for Stang and Konow, Castberg declined a post. Schøning bowed himself out on March 8 when it appeared that Michelsen had four Conservatives and would need four "pure" *Venstre* to match. His presence in the cabinet would have been construed as a sign of weakness. Instead, Michelsen, avoiding both Schøning and Castberg, turned to Harald Bothner and completed the cabinet list. Castberg, having been urged by Arctander and Berner to reconsider, changed his mind and telephoned Michelsen, only to find that he was too late. On March 11 the ministerial list was presented to the crown prince and was accepted.[15]

In spite of some doubts on the "purity" of the four *Venstre*, reactions favored the new ministry. Castberg wrote in his diary of his satisfaction, even though he had missed his chance, if the ministry proceeded directly to act on the consular law. Press comments in Norway lauded the coalition cabinet with general recognition of its unity and purpose. Swedish press views were subdued, but both Liberal and Conservative papers accepted the ministry and its stated aims calmly, with clear understanding of events in Norway. No one dissented from the crown prince's approval of the ministerial list since it was a constitutional question for only Norwegian consideration. But newspapers expressed some doubts regarding the way in which a consular law might be achieved; if completed without Sweden's consent and participation, then obviously the *Riksakt* would be violated.

Norway's great decision passed quietly, almost without the notice of those most concerned. The Special Committee's achievement of virtual unanimity on a consular law on March 6 and the Storting vote of 100 to 17 for the principle of dissolution were the first steps. The final decisive act was Michelsen's appointment as prime minister, with his policies reflecting the views of the Special Committee, Storting, and the Norwegian people. The clear decision for separation had been made, and a cabinet appointed to lead Norway in the coming conflict with Sweden over dissolution of the union.

[15] In the cabinet were the four Conservatives—K. D. Lehmkuhl, Edvard Hagerup Bull, Christopher Knudsen, and Christian W. E. B. Olssøn; and four *Venstre*—Harald Bothner, Gunnar Knudsen, Sophus Arctander, and Jørgen Løvland; with Michelsen and A. J. Vinje representing the moderates.

◇◇

CHAPTER VIII

THE UNION IS BROKEN

◇◇

THE decision to end the union received its formal and ceremonial recognition when Michelsen and his cabinet accepted office. Crown Prince Gustaf hesitated to assent to their policies, but he could only indicate his personal wishes, and those of the Swedish people, for a peaceful settlement preserving the union. As advisers to the king, the Norwegian cabinet officers must be partially hypocritical. They could give only partial information, since they must not reveal the full extent of their plans. Gustaf, even if he wished to do so, could not accept their advice. On the other side of the peninsula the Swedish government and Riksdag leaders refused to initiate any endeavors to preserve the union.

For its part the Michelsen ministry accepted the leadership of the Storting committee and, until June 7, depended largely upon that body. During his appearance before the Special Committee on March 16, Michelsen said little on matters of policy, but promised resolute fulfillment of the Storting program. He guaranteed to inform all citizens of the seriousness of the crisis and to prepare for all "eventualities." Military forces must be equipped and plans made for action in the event of a Swedish invasion of Norway. These rough outlines constituted the proposed process for "liberation of Norway from servitude to Sweden."

In order to make Norway's position in the union clear, representatives were sent abroad to talk with political leaders and to influence the press of other countries. At the same time, with both the consent and backing of the government, a private information committee solicited funds and personnel for such work. Leading publicists and academic figures[1] joined in this task of en-

---

[1] Dr. Hans Reusch was chairman of the committee and directed such persons as Fridtjof Nansen, W. C. Brøgger, the geologist, A. C. Drolsum, librarian, Benjamin Vogt, prominent Conservative lawyer, and Axel Heiberg, who later published the official documentary collection on 1905. In Paris Arne

lightenment. During April and May they collected some 25,000 *kroner* which paid for costs of publication of pamphlets and books, expenses of persons sent abroad, and for dinners and other inducements assuring favorable press relations. Fridtjof Nansen received government sponsorship for his London trip, and the committee gave him money for the translation, publication, and distribution of his writings on the union.

The Arctic explorer's purposes in London were threefold: to give a series of lectures, which would also be the occasion for the British public to become acquainted with a renowned Norwegian; to publish articles and letters in England; and to discuss with British parliamentary and government leaders some aspects of the conflict which might affect English interests. Nansen drew a good attendance for his lecture before the Royal Geographic Society on his polar expeditions in the *Fram*, and even the Swedish minister attended. But his articles in the *London Times* on the Norwegian-Swedish crisis and a series of interviews with Arthur Balfour, Sir Edward Grey, and Lord Lansdowne actually hit closer to the reasons for his trip to England. Grey, Nansen found, knew so little about the controversy that he believed Norway could secure her rights within the union. The British foreign secretary, on the other hand, sympathized with the Norwegians and knew much about the union, although he could only state that Britain would remain neutral in the impending crisis.[2]

With some assistance from Norwegians in London, Nansen sought out editors, reporters, and commentators of various British newspapers. He found the *Times* "fair-minded," and his letters appeared in its columns. The Swedes retaliated by using the celebrated explorer Sven Hedin, whose prominence matched Nansen's. The bitter verbal exchanges of Nansen and Hedin in

Hammar was the intermediary with the French press, just as H. T. R. Diesen in Finland, Andreas Urbye in Berlin, and Vogt in Germany labored strenuously in Norway's behalf.

[2] Sir James Rennell Rodd, the new British minister to Norway-Sweden, in his report of Nansen's interview with Lansdowne, assured the Swedish foreign office of this neutrality and of the foreign secretary's refusal to commit himself or England to any pro-Norwegian policy. Rodd to Count Gyldenstolpe, April 9, 4Mlb. *Utrikesdepartmentet Arkiv* (Swedish foreign office Archives). Hereafter cited *UDS*.

the *Times* left the British public bewildered by what the paper called a "tempest in a teapot." Nansen's *Times* article of March 26 was vigorously rebutted by Hedin on April 1; Nansen replied on April 12; Hedin refuted Nansen on April 18, and the inky battle continued into May and June. Hedin's answers indicated an awakened Swedish awareness of Norwegian schemes, even if Swedes only guessed at Nansen's official capacity. Both *Svenska Dagbladet and Stockholms Dagblad* (March 27 and 31) drew attention to Nansen's London visit and immediately reported his call at the British Foreign Office.

The Michelsen cabinet proposed also the dispatch of agents to the United States to influence Norwegian-Americans in general and President Theodore Roosevelt in particular. Nansen was first slated for this mission, but went instead to England, and only in the late spring was a Norwegian representative sent to America. The editor of *Verdens Gang* initiated a casual correspondence with Knute Nelson, the Norwegian-American senator from Minnesota, hoping to secure his support. To the dismay of the Norwegian cabinet, Senator Nelson disapproved of the dissolution of the union, and strongly urged that Norway try to attain her political objectives by convincing the Swedes of the rectitude of the Norwegian cause. Vigorous efforts failed to enlist the senator's support; throughout the crisis of 1905 he maintained an attitude of friendly neutrality.

But to the Norwegian cabinet the most important problem was Norway's defense. Minister of Justice Edvard Hagerup Bull visited Stockholm and he relayed to Oslo warnings about the prospect of war. Later, others corroborated his reports, and the Riksdag formation of a committee for secret debate seemingly confirmed the Swedish belligerent attitude. Minister of Defense Christian W. E. B. Olssøn, appearing before the Special Committee, testified on the state of Norwegian defenses and future armament needs "for any eventuality." He accepted his predecessor's figures and data, so added little to Strugstad's February report to the committee. But that agency persisted in its work and item by item went over defense needs of the country, including rye, oats, coal, and horseshoes on its list. It estimated that

half the required ammunition could be supplied domestically,
but that the rest must be bought in England and Germany. The
navy needed approximately five and a half million *kroner* for
coal, ammunition, and provisions, while the army would use
slightly less than five million. A total of nearly twelve million for
foreign supplies must be expended and an earlier loan of ten
million was nearly exhausted.

Neither the Special Committee nor the cabinet seriously expected that military operations would be undertaken by Sweden.
Preparations seemed justified even without relation to a possible
Swedish attack, for a strong defense would increase Norway's
bargaining power. The Swedish minister of defense and chief of
staff both assured Norwegian visitors to Stockholm of their country's peaceful intentions. General Axel Rappe, commanding
Sweden's army, said that "not a single soldier would be sent
against Norway, except if Norway should begin war by an attack
on Sweden . . . or if the king or crown prince were involved in
personal attacks in Norway."[3] Even some *Venstre*, who in 1895
most feared an invasion, felt reassured by changes in Swedish
opinion.

The fears that affected some Norwegians originated primarily
in the creation of a Swedish Extraordinary Committee. The unusual character of the committee was historically emphasized by
its use only in times of crisis. In 1855 and again in 1895-1896 it
had functioned and, in the latter case, had debated a possible
invasion of Norway. Norwegians watched its deliberations for
informative signs, although its Liberal members were some reassurance since they would not permit an armed invasion of Norway. News of the first meeting of the committee, which reached
the government and Special Committee through Hagerup,
caused some bitterness. Norwegians especially resented Gustaf's
chairmanship of the session, for they visualized a union officer
presiding over a Swedish committee plotting injury to Norway.
Gustaf's cogent résumé of the state of affairs presented an accurate picture and predicted closely the course which Norway
ultimately pursued. His stress on immediate preparation of plans

3 Bothner, *op.cit.*, May 20.

for every eventuality, ominous to Norwegians and their cause, resulted in a government project for negotiations on a consular system and a reform of the basis of union, which was never presented to the Riksdag.[4] Contrary to Norwegian alarms, the committee's debates and proposals indicated extensive modifications in Swedish opinion. In the committee Karl Staaff advocated negotiations with Norway and, backed by the Liberals, he attempted to arouse Swedish leaders to the obvious dangers of sitting idly by while Norway acted. But, by circumstances, Sweden was forced to await a Norwegian request for collaboration.

Election of the Extraordinary Committee was strongly opposed by the Swedish Liberal and socialist press. *Dagens Nyheter* (March 19) editorialized on its historical meaning, blaming Boström and anti-Norwegian motives for its formation. The secrecy of the committee's sessions seemingly proved that it plotted an attack on Norway. The Conservative press criticized the appointment of Karl Staaff and other Liberals because they generally believed their party to be the only political group capable of truly representing the country.

Norwegian public reactions to the committee's formation, in view of the existence of their own similar body, showed a comic violence. *Verdens Gang* (March 24) likened it to a body suited to Russia, Turkey, or some medieval state, and entirely consonant with Swedish chauvinism. Castberg saw in it the same character and same program as its predecessor in 1895. Norwegian leaders publicly displayed anger and resentment, but in private they discounted the committee's abilities and power.

Norwegians proceeded without qualms to write a consular law. Castberg and Konow presented their draft to the Special Committee on March 22. Debate was understandably brief, for plans in February revealed its major provisions, and the only cause of dispute was a technical and minor problem on the date at which a separate consular service would begin operation. After some talk on the timing of a crisis, advantages in postponement of war,

---

[4] Arne Wåhlstrand, *1905 års ministärkriser* (Uppsala, 1941), 37, and Appendix, 340-342.

and other hypothetical and frightening possibilities, the committee eventually agreed on a date—April 1, 1906—for the inauguration of the new consular system. Approval of the law by Oscar II was considered improbable, but Michelsen, in order to influence the king, deliberately gave misleading information on Norwegian expectations of its sanction.[5] Detailed discussion of the law is unnecessary, for it never went into operation and served only as partial groundwork for a later law applicable to the entire foreign office. In reality it was merely a means to produce a crisis dissolving the union.

In an effort to counter Norwegian measures the Swedes responded with a move which placed the Norwegian members of the joint council[6] in an embarrassing position. From the Extraordinary Committee's earlier plan, Gustaf proposed a "broad new basis" for negotiations in which all union problems would be involved.[7] The Norwegian councilors rejected none of his proposals, but insisted on delay until royal acceptance of consular legislation. The thoughts of the ministers, as they read Gustaf's project, must have been jumbled and confused. They assumed that he sought to split the Norwegian people and their government and to shift attention from the consular law, if not to stall its passage entirely. They surmised, also, that he attempted to unite Sweden's political leaders and her people against Norway and to create defenses for the monarchy in the event of a crisis. When Gustaf asked their agreement to publication of the plan, the three ministers refused point-blank, knowing that their

[5] The German consul general at Oslo sent a report on the expected sanction which reached the Swedes. Faber du Faur to the foreign office, April 18, *Aus. Amt*, 2956, *Utenriksdepartmentet Arkiv* (Norwegian foreign office Archives). Hereafter cited: *UDN*. These documents are photostats of captured documents from the German file on Norway.

[6] Harald Bothner, Jørgen Løvland, and Edvard Hagerup Bull.

[7] The proposals began with an official confirmation of equality between the two kingdoms. Gustaf then offered the old proposition of a joint foreign minister, either Norwegian or Swede, responsible to some joint union agency. Separate consuls for both kingdoms would be administratively subject to the union officer. An achievement of some means to solve all union problems by study and agreement on a friendly basis concluded his program. On Norwegian reactions see *Statsråd Edvard Hagerup Bulls dagbøker fra 1905* (Oslo, 1957), 12-14. Hereafter cited: *Hagerup Bull*.

consent would give it a semblance of authority, and, perhaps, even their tacit approval.

The crown prince's five-point program appeared in the newspapers on April 6. The Norwegian cabinet ignored it completely, not even discussing it. When forced to an answer, the cabinet refused unanimously to embark on new negotiations. Norwegian press comments ran either toward an ardent opposition, or, as in the case of *Aftenposten*, toward acceptance, if the consular bill were first sanctioned. Any conditional "clasp of the brother's hand" was unthinkable to Swedes who, of course, accepted Gustaf's plan to win time or to check passage of a law. Even the crown prince held out small hope for his proposals, and most moderate and Conservative leaders shared his pessimism.

Gustaf's "broad, new basis for negotiations" effected immediate changes in Sweden which furnished sensational news on April 7. Boström resigned. The press immediately loosed an anti-Norwegian barrage as *Vårt Land, Nya Dagligt Allehanda,* and *Svenska Dagbladet* denounced the intrusion of Norwegian influence in Swedish politics. *Vårt Land* spewed its indignation over several columns and exhumed ancient differences to prove its contention that Norway and Norwegians possessed a voice in Swedish domestic affairs. Actually, Boström's resignation was a matter of practical politics. If Gustaf's plan was to succeed, the Conservative leader would have to be replaced by someone less repugnant to the Norwegians, for over the years he had become to them a symbol of the despicable in union politics. They believed that he had blocked negotiations in the first place and plotted the series of incidents of the past ten years. Swedish Liberals had argued for his dismissal long before his resignation, and the Extraordinary Committee voted in favor of confirmation of his departure from the government. Even Gustaf and Boström themselves, though close personal friends, disagreed on the former's plan and the prince favored the prime minister's resignation.[8]

[8] Note the sudden cessation of correspondence between the crown prince and Boström in April, Boström Mss., RAS, and *Bernadotte Arkiv.* Cf. Circular of April 10, 4A14, *UDS.* On the general background and influence of Norwegians in the ministerial crisis see Wåhlstrand, *1905,* 4-16, and Billing, *Anteckningar,* 274.

With Boström's resignation in hand, the crown prince resumed his conversations with the Norwegian councilors. But this "broad, new basis," even with the archfiend some distance removed, was so familiar to Norwegians that they could quote entire passages of arguments against it from the speeches of the last twenty years. And, to make matters worse, the crown prince now coupled his plan with an inconceivable postponement of the consular law. The ministers, needing no reflection, answered as before with an emphatic negative. Gustaf, with his temper ruffled by comments of the ministers and their summary dismissal of his plan, began to argue, but the Norwegians refused to listen. The next day he complained peevishly about their hostility and their churlish treatment of him.

Neither Gustaf nor most Swedes understood entirely the Norwegian legend surrounding the crown prince. He symbolized everything which Norwegians deemed immoral and unethical in the Swedish character. Supposedly in 1895 he offered peace while furtively drawing a dagger to plunge into Norway's back. The myth of his hatred for Norway formed a substantial part of every Norwegian's estimate of relations with the neighbor, and now in 1905 he purportedly inspired the Swedish "ultras" in their wish to force Norway to kneel in humble submission. Although Gustaf now wholeheartedly desired peaceful maintenance of the union and coequal status for the two countries, most Norwegians could not visualize him in his new role.

The crown prince's program did, however, force the Norwegians to some minor actions. The Special Committee discussed enactment of a law prior to the Easter vacation to prevent Norwegian reflection on Gustaf's proposals. After some debate, however, the committee postponed action until after Easter, because Defense Minister Olssøn's strategic commitments depended on a later date for a crisis. Castberg's motion for an immediate answer to the crown prince raised another issue. Michelsen's tactic was to circumvent the monarchy and to negotiate with the Swedish parliament and government, thereby avoiding offense to supporters of the royal family and drawing attention to the popular nature of the controversy. The cabinet drafted three answers in which the central theme was agreement to negotiate only after establishment of a separate consular system. But the Special Committee, dominated by the Konow-Castberg coterie, opposed all three. Castberg even blamed Michelsen for originating the idea of negotiations. Prospects of success for new *pourparlers* alarmed the radical *Venstre* into adopting a more stubborn stand on the necessity of dissolving the union. This debate ended with a decision to recess for the Easter vacation (April 15 to May 1) and thus an opportunity to achieve some solution to the union's problems was ignored.

Resolution of the Swedish ministerial crisis, which Boström's resignation precipitated and the crown prince's program deepened, came only after many persons refused the thankless task of leading Sweden in her most difficult year.[9] A secondary decision, after selection of a new ministry, involved formulation of a policy on Gustaf's plan and on negotiations with the Norwegians. The new ministry was an obvious compromise, for the monarchy, avoiding strength, selected an administrative cabinet with Johan Ramstedt as prime minister. Its composition displayed moderate principles and some political leadership; certainly some of its members were not the nonentities suggested in press criticism. Its two "ultra" members, as defined on the basis of their attitudes on the union question, advocated the use of force against Norway, but both eventually agreed to a peace program, and their presence in the cabinet could not be construed as a reflection of "die-hard" anti-Norwegian sentiments. The ministerial crisis, and the new cabinet's selection, revealed how fully Swedish leaders deemed the union beyond the possibility of being salvaged. Choice of Ramstedt, no matter how capable he or his colleagues might be, thrust a solution of the union crisis squarely on the monarchy. If the Swedes wished to maintain the union, a much stronger cabinet would have been the only choice.

The Swedish press gave the new ministry a cool reception, although some expressed satisfaction with its attitude on the union question. Neither Conservatives nor Liberals would be wholly content with a ministry which would not solve the press-

9 For full details see Wåhlstrand, *1905*, 17-24.

ing questions of franchise reform and tariff revision. Conservatives especially voiced their disgust with the new cabinet's proposals on both reform and union issues and criticized the new ministry as offering no program.

The Ramstedt ministry was simply "old wine in old bottles" to the Norwegians. Boström's shadow, they assumed, fell over the cabinet, and he supposedly dictated details of the "new, broad basis of negotiations" of which the crown prince spoke so urgently. Although Boström did not participate in cabinet deliberations, and exercised no influence upon its decisions, he might well have been present, so far as Norwegians were concerned. No matter what kind of cabinet was appointed, even if entirely of Liberals, the Norwegians would have been suspicious of its intentions and would not have retreated one inch from their program to attain a separate consular service.

Indicative of the Storting attitude was its approval of a forty million *kroner* foreign loan before it recessed for Easter. The Special Committee urged its placement with the French *Crédit lyonnais*; although protesting, Michelsen yielded to the committee's wishes and negotiated with that foreign bank. On April 18 the Norwegian council in Stockholm brought the proposal for a loan to the crown prince-regent for his sanction. Gustaf inquired first about the prospects for negotiations but, after the ministers attempted to prove that negotiations were impossible, he approved their request without opposition. Later in the month, at Oslo, Gustaf talked with Michelsen about the loan. In answering the crown prince's question as to its purposes, the Norwegian prime minister listed purchases of long-needed grain, provisions, and other supplies for the military forces. The crown prince expressed his wonderment at these exceptional and unusual purchases in peace time, adding some queries on rumored mobilization of Norwegian troops for service in the frontier forts. Michelsen's explanation that army maneuvers in May were entirely normal was not questioned by Gustaf. But both the Norwegian *Social-Demokraten* and the Swedish *Nya Dagligt Allehanda* deplored the probable effect of this "war fund."

Gustaf's calm sanction of the loan was partially explained by endeavors of the Swedish foreign office to have the French government balk its acceptance by the *Crédit lyonnais*. French Foreign Minister Théophile Delcassé, however, informed the Swedish envoy that the bank opposed the government and had on occasion delighted in refusing cabinet requests of a similar nature, even though ordinarily the government refrained from intervention in private manipulations.[10] Norway's loan did cause the Riksdag in July to appropriate 100 million *kronor* for "special purposes." Both "war loans" or "war credits" remained unexpended, although large purchases of matériel in England, Germany, and other countries nearly consumed the Norwegian loan. By an irony of diplomacy and international banking, *Stockholms enskilda bank* bought part of the loan, as it had the one before it, and thus Swedes contributed directly to Norwegian defense.

The effects of the loan, military operations and the general air of tension could be seen personally by those Storting members who visited Stockholm during the Easter vacation. A state supper, given by the Norwegian ministerial council, furnished the occasion for a social meeting with leading Swedish Liberals. The speeches, naturally, were copiously larded with proper sentiments of amity and accord, and of good wishes for solution of the consular problem, but Norwegians said little about acquiescence to any Swedish or royal plan of negotiations. Other Norwegians sought to use the meeting of the Scandinavian section of the Peace Society to sound out Swedish friends. Innumerable private conferences between Storting members and leading Liberals, among them Karl Staaff, earnestly but fruitlessly endeavored to find equitable bases of agreement. It seemed clear to the Norwegians, however, that Swedish Liberals opposed any resort to arms and that many of their number favored dissolution as a means of ending the union's quarrels.

The Easter vacation passed without incident, and at its close Gustaf went to Oslo for firsthand impressions of the impending crisis and for details of the proposed consular law. In a cabinet session on April 25 the crown prince avoided an answer to a

[10] Akerman to Gyldenstolpe, May 18, 4A14, *UDS*.

direct query on possible sanction of the law, although he might then have outlined the consequences of both veto and sanction on either side of the peninsula. Both Conservatives and *Venstre* warned him of the probable repercussions of a veto and insisted that the Norwegian council alone was involved. But, the crown prince interjected, would not the union's future course and the results of either veto or sanction be important to Sweden? He requested a copy of the proposed law, and, although Hagerup Bull wished otherwise, one was found.[11]

The consular law received the approval of the Special Committee and passed to the Storting in the second week in May. At the same time the cabinet drafted a plan of action for the ministerial council whose three members were to return to Stockholm on May 19. No one expected the king to sanction the law, and instructions for the council were based on his veto: when the king or crown prince orally announced his formal rejection, the councilors were to offer their resignations; they must leave Sweden after a couple of days, giving the impression of a leisurely departure; they could not sign any protocol of the council meeting; and they received firm orders not to discuss the ministerial crisis.[12] Later, on the train traveling to Stockholm, Løvland, Bothner, and Hagerup Bull completed details of this outline.

This action on the consular law coincided with the celebration of Norway's Constitution Day on May 17. This *Syttende mai* was like no other: speeches rang with fervor; parades shone with an unprecedented glimmer; anticipation was rife that the next year's celebration would see Norway independent. Every Storting member spoke from a rostrum that day and all Norwegians, of whatever age, marched, sang, danced, and celebrated. Editorials in all newspapers from *Aftenposten* and *Morgenbladet* to *Social-Demokraten* saluted the "country's honor and fortune." At the prime minister's dinner that evening toasts were drunk to the men of Eidsvoll and silent wishes were prayerfully offered up for a free and independent Norway.

11 *Hagerup Bull*, 28. The discussions of this period were fully circulated, both in Norway and Sweden, and even reported in Berlin. Cf. Leyden to Bülow, May 8, *Aus. Amt*, 2956, *UDN*.
12 Cf. draft in Arctander Mss., University Library, Oslo.

It was in an almost hysterical state of patriotism that Storting members returned to parliament on May 18. Debate on the consular law was limited by the Special Committee, and strict discipline imposed on party members. Only Hagerup showed the temerity to request its postponement until the next year. His motion caused several brief speeches of some repressed oratorical fervor, but eventually his motion lost by 82 to 6. These results measure fairly accurately the vote by members of the Storting on the consular law which passed by acclamation. Rigid party discipline, years of debate, and unanimity of opinion, both in and out of parliament, made a rapid and summary disposition of the act quite easy.

News of its passage immediately reached the Norwegian ministers in Stockholm and they arranged with Gustaf for consideration of the law at a time when Oscar II would be present. At frequent intervals for the past decade, the king's illnesses had forced him to turn over governmental duties to Gustaf. But in this decisive question it was considered best for the king to take personal charge since Gustaf might antagonize the Norwegians. The crown prince had planned to be in Germany, but he postponed the date of his trip in order to be present. Newspapers restricted themselves to a relatively few mild words on the impending crisis as if reserving their choicest comments for the event itself. Norwegian ministers in Stockholm wagered a bottle of champagne on the chance of a veto or sanction, with Hagerup Bull betting on sanction and Løvland and Bothner on a veto.[13]

The Stockholm council meeting to consider the consular law began in an atmosphere of expectation. The three Norwegian councilors, the crown prince, Oscar II, and the secretaries were the only persons present. With only bare preliminaries the king stated his objections to the legislation and refused his sanction. Quietly the ministers presented their prepared, written resignations. The king asked for a ministerial countersignature on the proceedings of the session to confirm the veto, but the Norwegian ministers refused. He then requested a signature by the delegation's secretary, but Løvland stepped forward to block him from

[13] Cf. *Hagerup Bull*, 36, and his "Fra 1905," *Samtiden*, XXXVII (1926), 388.

moving to obey the old monarch. During the subsequent brief exchange of words, Bothner aroused the excitable king by defending the Norwegian refusal on grounds of loyalty to their mother country. Oscar II indignantly exploded: "I am as good a Norwegian as you." At this point Gustaf intervened to restore peace. Tactfully and discreetly he interposed himself between the councilors and his father's anger. When Oscar II was on the point of refusing the ministers' resignations Gustaf urged him to comply: "Yes, father, that you must do." A brief statement was written out, with a request for time to form a government: "Since it is clear to me that no other government can be formed now, so I do not agree to accept the resignations of the council members."[14] The king's exit concluded this most important and fateful last meeting of Oscar II, Gustaf, and their Norwegian ministers.[15]

This memorable session was followed by a long meeting of the Norwegian ministers with Ramstedt and Gyldenstolpe. Both revealed their uneasiness and their chagrin at the failure of Oscar II to consult with them prior to his veto. Nothing could be done, however, because action must yet be taken by the Storting or Norwegian government. Officially the ministers could say that, since they had resigned, solution of the crisis rested with the Storting. In Swedish and Norwegian papers, and in private conversations, these resignations were viewed as a step toward deadlock but not necessarily the union's end. That night guests attending a supper at the Norwegian ministerial residence drank toasts to a free, sovereign, and independent Norway and to the future, which, at the moment, appeared to be so bright.

Departure of the Norwegian ministers from Stockholm was quiet and uneventful with only a few friends coming to the station to see them leave. An inquiry as to whether the king wished to see them was answered by his giving them permission to go. On Monday, May 29, the ministers' train left Stockholm

14 Heiberg, op.cit., 195.
15 For details see Løvland, Menn og minner fra 1905 (Oslo, 1929), 109-114; Bothner, op.cit., May 26 and 27, Hagerup Bull, 39-43.

without anticipated incident and without apparent evidence of Swedish interest.

Swedish Conservative papers, however, expressed themselves with virulence. *Nya Dagligt Allehanda*, in its furious support of the king's veto, warned the Norwegians about embarking on the "revolutionary path." *Social-Demokraten* (May 29) began an editorial, written by Branting, with the words: "Norway out of your hands, king!" In the same paper another column announced the death of the ninety-one-year-old union and its impending interment. In Norway the press was restrained by the government and restricted itself to straight reportage on events in Stockholm with pictures and statements from the various ministers involved in the historic sessions.[16]

The news of the veto and resignations arrived in Oslo at noon while the Storting was yet in session. Castberg enthusiastically recorded in his diary a description of the jubilant parliament and its members.[17] The session was adjourned for the day, and afternoon Oslo newspapers carried banner headlines on the veto and resignations. Conversations on streets and in hotels and restaurants revolved around this historic conference and its probable meaning for Norway.

When the ministers arrived in Oslo, they were given a joyous reception. Storting members and spectators crowded the railroad station to receive them and escorted them to the Storting building amidst hurrahs and shouts. Their account of the last council meeting was naturally filled with anecdotes on attitudes of king, crown prince, and Swedish cabinet ministers. Storting members clamored for news and greeted each new bit of information with glee, except, as Hagerup noted, for some Conservatives who accepted the situation with fatalistic calm.[18] May 30, except for a cabinet session, was a holiday, and even early the next morning revelers filled Oslo's streets celebrating the break with the king.

For the cabinet and Special Committee this joyous atmosphere

[16] *Verdens Gang* did criticize Gustaf's trip abroad, because, it stated, he might procure assistance from the foreign powers for an attack on Norway.

[17] Castberg, *Dagbøker*, I, 327-329.

[18] Hagerup, *Dagbok*, 155.

was quickly replaced by days of intensive work. In its session on June 1 the cabinet studied the entire situation and agreed on a future plan of action. The first topic of discussion concerned the handling of the crown prince or Oscar II, should either come to Oslo. No plan was made, but someone facetiously remarked that the king or crown prince should be put on the train for Stockholm since neither now held office in Norway. The presence of any member of the royal family would have been extremely embarrassing, for an incident might easily have begun hostilities between the two countries. After some debate, the cabinet decided that the three ministers would not return to Stockholm and that a resolution would be sent to the king. Berner drafted one from his several years of experience in the art, and it formed the basis for the eventual document which was sent. In this move the cabinet chose the quicker crisis according to the plan evolved in March.

Through a conference with Francis Hagerup on June 2, Michelsen added a new element to the plan. The former prime minister, who was asked to go to Berlin, suggested the possibility of either a Bernadotte or a Danish prince on the Norwegian throne.[19] He assumed that Norway would retain a monarchical form of government and stressed the effect upon Swedes and others of an invitation to Oscar II to nominate a son for the Norwegian throne. It would make quite clear Norwegian affection for the royal family and Norway's singular purpose in seeking freedom from the union. After his conference with Hagerup, Michelsen argued with *Venstre* cabinet members in favor of the invitation, mentioning the reasons evolved in his conference with Hagerup and adding a comment about England's favorable reaction. In the evening the cabinet debated the invitation and,

---

[19] Cf. Jacob Worm-Müller, "Prins Carl blir konge i Norge," *Håkon 7* (Oslo, 1947), 79-91, on thoughts of the Bernadotte invitation. Worm-Müller emphasizes the role of Sigurd Ibsen and his influence on Hagerup. Cf. also his "1905," *Samtiden*, XLII (1931), 158-159, and Edvard Hagerup Bull, "Fra 1905," *Samtiden*, XXXVII (1926), 394-395. Note especially Worm-Müller's statement that Gunnar Knudsen presented the plan to the cabinet which is inconsistent with Knudsen's objections to a monarchical form of government, as later shown in his resignation.

since no one dissented, it was decided to have the Special Committee consider it.

That body demonstrated its power by refusing to accept either Berner's resolution or the advice of the cabinet. Under ordinary circumstances a ministerial crisis might have ensued, but the times demanded that there be no constitutional or parliamentary conflicts. Rather the cabinet drafted new plans which it offered to the Special Committee on June 5. Haste seemed imperative because the crown prince might come to Oslo after his return from Germany, possibly on June 10. In his report to the Special Committee Olssøn added a bright prospect for Norwegian military defense, but he refused to call up Norwegian reserves until mobilization of Swedish forces. To this Michelsen added that war would be postponed as long as possible, even beyond reasonable limits, for a conflict between the two countries would be suicidal. The prime minister depended upon numerous statements from the king and crown prince, from Swedish Liberals, and from Norwegians avowing Swedish determination to prevent war. To a Social Democratic query about the invitation to Oscar II to nominate a son for the Norwegian throne, Michelsen answered that the scheme had been dropped.

But the next day both cabinet and Special Committee debated the Bernadotte issue. Cabinet arguments all favored it for a number of reasons, both internal and external. Since it involved no change in form of government, the initial insecurity attendant upon any major change would be minimized. Even more important, Norway would avoid a constitutional controversy arising simultaneously with a crisis with Sweden. Moreover, this evidence of Norwegian respect for the Bernadottes would have favorable effects in Sweden and other countries, which in turn might facilitate recognition of Norway. Finally, it would prevent a scramble among foreign candidates for the Norwegian throne. The elaborate reasons evolved in cabinet debate were not only multitudinous but sound and, since there were no constitutional barriers or even strong objections, the cabinet again accepted the plan for the Bernadotte invitation.

In the Special Committee the resurrection of the question,

however, stirred the radicals to protests. Dr. Alfred Eriksen, a Social Democrat and also a pastor, vehemently opposed it, both because he disliked monarchy and because he believed such an invitation would have a binding effect on a future form of government. Castberg agreed with Eriksen, not so much on constitutional grounds as out of dislike of the Bernadottes who, if elected to rule in Norway, would only represent the old order. Konow voiced some truth as to the motives of both cabinet and Special Committee proponents of the invitation in his sarcastic aphorism that it was "not necessary for Norway's sake, but perhaps necessary for our Conservatives' sake." He also remarked that a "kingdom is a truth with a lie on top."[20] Two other important motives were involved. By accepting the plan to invite a Bernadotte, the government would indeed, as Eriksen had predicted, bind itself to a program of constitutional monarchy. On the other hand, its acceptance would lead foreign countries, impressed by the Norwegian love of the Bernadottes, to reason that this was no "revolution." Michelsen remarked facetiously on a "fagforening" (princes' union) which would approve highly of the invitation. The session of the Special Committee closed its debate early to permit the Storting to convene.

Storting debate on the Bernadotte invitation continued on the same lines as in the Special Committee. Michelsen first placed the government's propositions before the body and he, Hagerup, and members of the cabinet dominated the first hour's speeches. Not until later did Eriksen have a chance to raise his objections, which both Konow and Castberg supported. Upon the latter's request for a vote, Michelsen stated his opposition to a ballot of any sort, except on the whole government policy, and insisted on treating the matter as a cabinet question. Castberg, he said, was guilty of disloyalty. In spite of threats of a cabinet crisis, Castberg continued to argue the absence of a mandate to bind future generations of Norwegians as to their form of government. Eriksen, thinking perhaps of Social Democrats in Sweden, urged Storting members to weigh their actions carefully, for the Berna-

---

20 *De stenografiske referater fra de hemmelige møter i Stortinget i 1905* (Oslo, 1951), 60. Hereafter cited: *Hemmelige møter.*

dotte invitation would antagonize Swedes. To dethrone one member of the family and to ask another to become the ruler of Norway would be an insult. Hagerup, perhaps most responsible for the invitation, reversed himself to stand with Eriksen and, in contradiction, to argue:[21] "It will awaken a storm that might conceivably work against the royal house and, therefore, in my opinion, in an exaggerated form will diminish the prospect of solution of the crisis by this [peaceful] means that I also consider to be the easiest and best method." But Eriksen went further and touched on a point which the cabinet realized it must resist at all costs. He assumed that the dissolution of the union nullified the constitution and required the holding of a convention, not only to decide on a form of government but to write a new constitution.[22] In other words, the action proposed—in effect deposing the king—was a constitutional revision and required changes beyond the competence of the present Storting. Hagerup Bull, minister of justice in the Michelsen cabinet and a leading jurist, agreed with Eriksen's legal arguments and advocated a new government after the passage of a resolution by the Storting. Michelsen and other cabinet officers turned on their colleague and rushed to defend the competence of the Storting and government.

In spite of arguments, which lasted until after midnight of June 6, the session finally closed with a decision to meet the next day. On the next morning, after some sleepless hours and feverish preparations, Michelsen read the proposed address to the king before a closed meeting of the Storting. Eriksen protested the Bernadotte invitation and insisted that in open session he would not only vote against the government's proposal but would also offer a protest against it. After a private conference with Michelsen, however, Eriksen announced that he would limit his opposition to the Bernadotte invitation: he would vote against it but would refrain from offering a formal protest. The address was then accepted.

[21] *Hemmelige møter*, 11.

[22] Cf. Steen's comments on the new constitution of November, 1814, and compare the juridical basis of Eriksen's position. If Steen is correct, then Eriksen was entirely justified in arguing as he did. Steen, *1814*, 281.

The plenary session of the Storting was minutes long. Visitors sat quietly to hear Michelsen read the address to the king and to listen to members answer *aye* on the roll call. The resolution to Oscar II ranks with the Eidsvoll constitution as a memorable document:[23] "When the ministerial council's members have resigned their functions, When His Majesty the King has declared himself unable to form a new government for the country, When the constitutional royal powers thus have ceased to function, The Storting authorizes the members of the resigned ministry to continue until further as the Norwegian Government and to administer the authority granted to the King in agreement with the Royal Norwegian Constitution and applicable laws, with the alterations that are necessary thereto, and that the union with Sweden under one king is dissolved in consequence of the king's ceasing to function as King of Norway." Members voted unanimously for this proposal, and on the Bernadotte invitation only the five Social Democrats dissented. The president of the Storting then closed the historic session with the words: "God preserve our fatherland!"

Spectators in the galleries and those waiting outside heard the clock striking eleven as the doors of the Storting opened. When the session closed, few reflected on the "revolution" that had taken place in these few moments. For them on that day and night it was sufficient to think only of the glorious fact that Norway was finally freed of her bonds of union and that over five hundred years of subjugation to Denmark and Sweden had ceased. The remainder of the day was taken up with a long and gay celebration. Crowds accompanied many of the Storting and government leaders to their homes. Even the appearance of one of these persons was sufficient to set large crowds to roaring. *Ja, vi elsker*, the national anthem with Bjørnson's memorable words, was sung hundreds of times by thousands of voices. Toasts were drunk in profusion to the "New Norway." At five o'clock the next morning the streets were still swarming with people, dancing and singing in their celebration of the birth of a new European nation. Even today many Norwegians recall June 7 with the strongest emotion and for them it is a symbol of freedom.

[23] Heiberg, *op.cit.*, 206.

CHAPTER IX

SWEDISH CONDITIONS AND NORWEGIAN REACTIONS

THE Norwegian act of singlehanded dissolution of the union on June 7 shocked Sweden. The news reached Stockholm late in the evening of June 7, and many Stockholmers left their homes to read the sheets posted before newspaper offices and the Swedish news bureau. Rumors of the event spread rapidly throughout the capital, but only the next morning could all Swedes learn complete details of what had taken place in Oslo. Although government and Riksdag leaders knew the consequences of a veto of the consular bill, Swedes generally had given little thought to its potential results. Thus the storm of indignation displayed by most Swedes astonished the Norwegians, who anticipated some anger but not to the degree shown on these days following publication of their resolution. Swedes felt deeply this "insult" to their king and this severance of union ties without consideration of their place in the association. They had never expected the Norwegians to dare such a stubborn and courageous act. In the past Swedes had either ignored Norwegian threats or considered them meaningless.

Reactions of the Swedish cabinet, which met during the evening of June 7, were much as the Norwegians expected. Some ministers blustered about war against Norway, but all eventually agreed on peace as the best objective to seek. The cabinet decided to order the army and navy to ready themselves for action, but to use neither force unless Sweden were provoked or attacked. In the cabinet the ministers of war and marine argued for immediate military operations against a defenseless Norway, but received no support from their colleagues or from Oscar II and Gustaf. Debate centered mainly on framing an appropriate action program for the Riksdag.

The next day party leaders of parliament met to consider future policies. They posed several questions. Should Norway be hindered from achieving recognition and independence? Should the government agree to nominate a Bernadotte for the Norwegian throne? At what time should the special session of the Riksdag be called? Gyldenstolpe, the foreign minister, partially answered the first query through a circular sent to Swedish ministers that instructed them to inform the powers of the Norwegian "revolution" and to request them not to recognize the illegal government thus created. Swedish officials, the circular continued, must abstain from any relations with Norwegians or the new regime, either in writing or in private conversation.[1] The Bernadotte invitation remained unanswered and in the ensuing weeks it became, as Folke Lindberg calls it, a "trump card" in Swedish hands. The third question, on convocation of the Riksdag, was extensively debated, but a special session was postponed until the cabinet prepared its propositions for consideration. In these hours of speeches, no leader favored an armed attack on Norway; but, as one Conservative stated, war could not be entirely ruled out, for Sweden must, whatever the results, resist aggression by Norway.

Three cabinet ministers reported at this session of party leaders, and their statements exerted major influence on these men sitting in the conference room. For his part Ramstedt insisted on a peaceful course, and, with additions by Gyldenstolpe, explored all aspects of the situation. From his hearers came explosive words like "suicidal," "criminal," "hazardous," and "dangerous," but their minds turned constantly to two crucial questions: first, what would be the results of an attack on Norway? And second, a most important question, what would the powers do if Sweden attempted to maintain the union by force? As if in answer to their own questions, the ministers agreed that Sweden could achieve a military victory, but the destroyed union could be replaced only by an unendurable terroristic regime. They agreed on three further points: the European powers would never permit Sweden

[1] Cf. copy in Konow Mss., University Library, Oslo, sent by Christophersen to Konow.

to attack Norway; Sweden was isolated and could expect no foreign aid; Scandinavia must never become a "Balkan peninsula."

In view of Germany's importance in Swedish foreign policy the cabinet awaited with suspense her answers to direct queries. On June 9 reports from the Swedish minister at Berlin and from Gustaf, upon his return from Germany, gave precise details on the attitude of the German government. Later reports from Swedish ministers in London, Paris, Copenhagen, St. Petersburg, and elsewhere gave substantially the same discomfiting reply. Germany and the other powers would not recognize Norway prior to Sweden's acceptance of the new regime; armed force neither could nor should be used, and, therefore, the conflict must be terminated quickly. If it were prolonged, these powers would be under no obligation to refrain from recognizing the Norwegian government. The German imperial family wished especially the nomination of a younger Bernadotte prince for the Norwegian throne to prevent any European scramble for it and to check any undue foreign influence in Scandinavian affairs. If the Swedish government and royal family barred a Bernadotte from accepting the throne, a Danish prince ought to be selected. Gustaf, in arguing for these same ideas in the cabinet, added that Sweden could expect neither sympathy nor aid from Europe, especially if the crisis were extended, and insisted upon immediate action in complete support of the ministerial propositions which were now nearly formulated. As a consequence the crown prince and cabinet forced through the date of June 20 for the opening of the special session of the Riksdag against the will of many Conservatives who wished a month's delay before its summoning.[2]

Outside these secret government sessions, the people of Stockholm and the entire country grew restless. News of the Norwegian "revolution" spread rapidly. In the evening a crowd, estimated to number between four and eight thousand, marched

[2] Gustaf's attitude arose from his conversations with the Kaiser and Bülow whose statements surprised the Swedish crown prince. In England later, he talked with Edward VII, Lansdowne, and Balfour and received the same shock. His letters to both his father and cabinet ministers grew so insistent that Oscar II wrote to plead with, and then to order, his son to do nothing. *Bernadotte Arkiv*, Stockholm.

to the palace at Djurgården to display their faith in the king. A much larger and better organized demonstration on June 8, with considerable newspaper publicity, wended its way along Strandvägen to Djurgården where the entire royal family, with the exception of Gustaf, assembled to receive the ovation of the crowd. Telegrams by the thousands poured into the palace from all sections of the country, offering individual services, testifying to the popularity of the old monarch, and pouring out Swedish ire at the Norwegian "insult" to the king. This popular support of the monarchy was deeply appreciated and even more needed. When demands for positive action arose in the Riksdag later in the month, the government used this early demonstration as evidence of the crown's strength.

Any cries for action came mainly from Swedish newspapers, which, except for the few Social Democratic journals, wholeheartedly condemned the Norwegian "revolution." They called it a "coup d'etat offensive to the monarchy" and disrespectful of "constitutional forms or Swedish legal rights." They warned Norway that she could not dissolve the union without Swedish consent, but even the most Conservative papers refrained from demanding the use of force against Norway. The majority of the press urged immediate solution of the crisis. Even *Vårt Land* (June 8) wrote that the union was devoid of value for Sweden and, therefore, the use of force was unthinkable. The paper concluded with typical venom, accusing the Norwegians of using "brutal and harsh" methods in dissolving the union.[3] The first evidence of a change in feeling came with *Vårt Land's* report on Norwegian mobilization on June 15, which was followed by a request for "compensation" and for "punishment" of Norway. Later it expressed fears of "Jameson raids" out of Norway against bridges, depots, and other vulnerable Swedish military points.

Swedish individuals expressed much the same sentiments as the newspapers they read. Conservative leader and soon-to-be prime minister Christian Lundeberg wrote about the difficulty

[3] On newspapers see especially *Svenska Dagbladet*, June 8, 9; cf. the *Verdens Gang* (June 8) comment from Norway that even the most anti-Norwegian papers preserved a quiet tone.

of collecting one's thoughts and about his sympathy for the old king. But he laid the blame for the crisis on the wavering policy of both government and monarchy as well as on Swedish Liberal pacifism and irresponsibility. Even in private, Lundeberg refrained from advising the use of armed force. In his conversations with Gustaf at Warnemünde in Germany, where Lundeberg had been vacationing, he agreed with the crown prince that war must be avoided to prevent Europe's intervention in Scandinavian affairs.

Contrasting somewhat with these views, the opinions of Harald Hjärne, published in *Svenska Dagbladet* (June 19 and 20), showed a moderate spirit, tinged with some nationalism. "We know now that Norway is led by a revolutionary and senseless military faction—and we must govern ourselves, therefore, so we can have an assured future in our hands." Most Norwegians were unionist, he thought, and Michelsen the leader of a minority government. Sweden's policy should be to defend herself in case of attack, but neither war nor troop concentrations on the frontier should be permitted. As to future policy, he wanted "as strong guarantees as we can [secure]" and a Norwegian government with a full popular mandate from Norwegian citizens. Hjärne's guarantees formed the nucleus for the "conditions" which in July the Riksdag asked the Norwegians to accept and, in turn, these were based primarily upon Hjärne's proposals earlier in the year.[4]

Entirely different opinions were expressed fully and publicly by Hjalmar Branting, leader of the Social Democrats and editor of *Social-Demokraten*. Like the crown prince, Branting hoped for an immediate recognition of Norway to be followed by negotiations on the best terms for dissolution of the union. For probably the first time in its history *Social-Demokraten* praised the monarch and his speech from the throne at the opening of the Riksdag when he urged these same principles. Branting converted his peace program into action by taking some twenty thousand workers into Stockholm's streets to demonstrate against war. "Down with War," "Up with Peace," "Norway Independent," "Workers

[4] Cf. Chapter VII.

for Peace" on placards carried on June 16 were echoes of Branting's advice to workers that, if war came, they must strike against the government. The activities of Branting and Swedish workers during the summer, while psychologically reassuring to Norwegian leaders, irritated Swedish Conservatives beyond reason and resulted in some arrests.

What these people pondered was the perplexing question of what to do next. In vague terms the cabinet touched on proposals for a Swedish agreement to a dissolution of the union. Debate in the two weeks before the opening of the Riksdag and during its entire session revolved around an acceptable list of conditions which the Norwegians would have to fulfill before Sweden recognized the new country and nullified the *Riksakt*. These conditions, as suggested by various leaders, parties, and newspapers, ran from the extreme of a military invasion of Norway to maintain the union to a proposal for her unconditional recognition. An elaborate and lengthy debate cleared the way for an acceptable list which the Riksdag approved and which was eventually presented to the Norwegian government. Such items as the destruction of forts along the Norwegian-Swedish border, the signature of an arbitration treaty, a neutral zone covering the boundary, and many others appeared on the final composite set. In the heated discussion of these conditions most Swedes had something to offer. As a consequence Riksdag members studied laboriously more than a hundred suggestions before settling upon eight. The main theme of this debate was that Norway could not be freed of her obligations unless she made concessions and guarantees assuring Sweden of some compensation for an agreement to end the union.

In a meeting of Riksdag party leaders on June 14 these opinions were freely aired. Conservative Carl Säve spoke openly for war, and others, like Arvid Lindman, advocated the use of threats of war, either to preserve the union or to secure conditions favorable to Sweden from the dissolution. Lindman's position, both in the Riksdag and subsequently in the Lundeberg-Wachtmeister cabinet, raised the stature of his views to a level of high importance. He wished force to be displayed, if the dissolution were accepted, in order to gain Swedish objectives and he urged that there be no arbitration treaty and no immediate recognition.

Party leaders, having seized the initiative, continued to plunder government prerogatives. They summoned Ramstedt and others for consultation, and the prime minister stoutly defended the cabinet program in an atmosphere of cold hostility. He fumbled his answers to questions concerning Swedish defense and state finances, thus confirming a belief in his ministerial incompetence. The result of the meeting was that parliamentary leaders were convinced of their right to refuse full powers for the cabinet handling of negotiations with the Norwegians.

Riksdag members, especially the Liberals, and cabinet officers ascertained without difficulty Norway's wishes on what ought to be done. Norwegians residing in Stockholm, or sent there to tell the Swedes of their desires, attempted to persuade their Swedish friends to adopt their views. Among the main agents sent to Sweden, three went with official approval and a fourth needed no backing. Benjamin Vogt, on Michelsen's request, went to Stockholm on June 11 and talked with Boström, Lagerheim, Ramstedt, and Staaff. Norwegian aversion to razing the border forts, even in combination with an arbitration treaty, was undoubtedly conveyed to those with whom Vogt talked. He failed to achieve an immediate recognition of Norway, which was his main objective, and returned disconsolately to Oslo for further instructions. After conferring with his own cabinet he traveled back to Stockholm to urge again the wisdom of recognition, but failed again. Ramstedt told him that "the first thing the Riksdag must do was to annul the resolution of June 7."[5] These conferences gave Swedish leaders information on Norwegian wishes for peace, but, unfortunately, later caused many Riksdag members to suspect the cabinet of private arrangements with Vogt for the program it presented on June 20 and 21. Although the adverse effects of Vogt's mission on the cabinet's strength were important, they should not be exaggerated, for the majority of

[5] *Hagerup Bull*, 63.

the Riksdag had long before decided that Ramstedt and his colleagues must be dismissed.[6]

Where Vogt's mission completely failed, Frederik Wedel Jarlsberg's private trip did clarify the prevailing confusion. Wedel, as a former member of the union foreign service, was greeted with vehement, personal reproach by Oscar II when the two met. The king listened with obvious displeasure to what Wedel said, but agreed on a peace program. Wedel's most difficult task was to defend the Bernadotte invitation which the king condemned as the purest hypocrisy. As Oscar phrased it: "Why ask for a Bernadotte for the Norwegian throne when you have deposed me?" Wedel left Oscar II in the definite belief that the king would not permit a Bernadotte to accept the Norwegian throne. In subsequent talks with Prince Carl, the king's third son, Wedel, like Vogt, found the prince unwilling to shoulder the burden of ruling a people who would regard him only as a "Swedish king."[7] From Stockholm Wedel embarked on a "swing around the circle" which took him to Copenhagen, to London, and back to Oslo. In Copenhagen he initiated his campaign for Danish Prince Carl for the Norwegian throne. In England he saw Lansdowne, Balfour, and other leaders; talked with Bildt, the Swedish minister to England; and studied British views on the Scandinavian crisis. He spoke of British recognition for Norway, of her policies, of proposals for solutions of the crisis, and of the Norwegian throne which both England and Denmark wished Prince Carl to have if no Swedish prince were elected. Without the consent or knowledge of the Norwegian government, Wedel launched his scheme of securing a king for Norway before either the union was dissolved or the Swedish government or king made known their attitude on the Bernadotte candidature.

The third agent, Halvdan Koht, sought to learn the attitudes of leading Social Democrats and Liberals. As a Norwegian historian, intellectual, and Social Democrat he was well qualified

[6] On this mission, see Vogt, *Indtil 1910* (Oslo, 1941), 80-87.

[7] Wedel naturally talked with Ramstedt and friends in the foreign office. In doing so he partly duplicated Vogt's mission and the two exchanged words on the proper extent of their operations. Cf. Wedel, *1905*, 28-29, and Vogt, *Indtil 1910*, 84. Cf. also *Hagerup Bull*, 57-58.

for his task. In Stockholm from June 14 to 19 he saw various Liberals and Social Democrats, including Branting and Staaff. He participated in the Social Democratic parade of June 16 where over twenty thousand workers demonstrated against their government's policy toward Norway, assisted in the preparation of a protest against Swedish conditions which was signed by Swedish writers, artists, and intellectuals, and busily went about Norway's affairs. He learned from Branting of his pessimism and of his distrust of Swedish Conservatives and their future activities. He listened to Staaff's wishes for peace and his hopes that the Norwegian government would present some "outstretched hand which Sweden could grasp." Others informed Koht of the Swedish resolve not to use force. He returned to Norway, spoke to the cabinet of his findings, and successfully completed the mission for which he was selected.[8]

The fourth member of the quartet was W. C. Brøgger, an outstanding geologist and scientist, who for some years was professor at *Stockholms högskola*. Although unofficially asked by Arctander, Brøgger knew his selection was approved by the Norwegian cabinet. He, like the others, was in Stockholm during the week end of June 14-19, and, like them, saw his friends. Through them he came to meet Staaff, and the conversation turned to the subject of an "outstretched hand" gesture by the Norwegian Storting. Several Swedes had proposed it to Vogt and the Swedish cabinet accepted the idea in principle. A Storting address to the Riksdag had even been drafted. On June 18, when Brøgger returned from Sweden, he filed a copy of a draft, written by Staaff, with the several versions already in the hands of the cabinet. Staaff's draft was accepted with delight by the government, for it showed Swedish views. In its translations some modifications crept in which caused Staaff to complain later, for he had insisted that it not be altered, except for necessary editorial revisions required by translation. On June 19 the address, now a government proposal, was given to the Special Committee where Konow, Castberg, and the radical minority attacked its weak and

[8] Cf. Koht, "Da den norsk-svenske unionen vart sprengt," *Historisk tidsskrift* (Norwegian), XXXIV (1947), 285-320.

timid tone.[9] After a brief debate it was accepted, redrafted, and hurried to a waiting train for its dispatch to Sweden.[10]

In addition to these four official agents, a host of Norwegians sought to influence their Swedish friends. Norwegians in intellectual and academic circles, especially, arranged for dinners, private conversations, and group meetings and reported frequently to the Norwegian cabinet about what they heard. Their only influence, however, was upon Swedes already convinced of the need for a peaceful dissolution of the union. For their part, Swedes made no efforts to travel to Oslo or to see Norwegians in Stockholm, which was not surprising in view of the nature of the trouble between the two peoples.

Swedes watched more carefully the opening of the special session of the Riksdag on June 20. Its debate began in an atmosphere most unfavorable to compromise. Newspapers, speeches, letters, and private conversations had said or written much about the proper course for the Riksdag. Men in both houses of parliament had publicly stated that Sweden should avenge Norwegian "insults" by an immediate invasion, while others were willing to approve such a policy if a large majority of the First Chamber favored it. These extremist views in both chambers made immediate decisions impossible, yet the task facing the Riksdag was to resolve these differences and agree on a policy which would unite Sweden, not necessarily against Norway, but in favor of a future security without a union. Some Conservatives and moderates, while favoring amicable, bloodless solution of the crisis, extended their pacific tendencies neither to the cabinet nor to pro-Norwegian Swedes. Those in favor of war were forced to reflect on various alternatives confronting them. Some belligerent Conservatives demanded "compensation" or "punishment"; some favored stalemate by proposing conditions unacceptable to Norwegians; some wished postponement of a settlement until the following year, ostensibly on the pretext that a year of "cooling

[9] Castberg, Dagbøker, I, 411-412.
[10] For details of the entire mission of Brøgger, see Jacob S. Worm-Müller, "Karl Staaff, W. C. Brøgger og Stortingets adresse av 19de juni 1905," Historisk tidsskrift (Norwegian), XXXV (1953), 644-650.

off" would make negotiations easier, but actually to prevent the issues from ever being resolved. Liberals, while determined to settle the crisis quickly and amicably, were unwilling to promote extensive compromises with Norwegians. Alterations in Norwegian attitudes, even though difficult, must be forthcoming to check the Conservatives, especially the "saber rattlers," and Staaff and the Liberals corresponded and talked with Norwegians to prevail upon them not to provoke a Swedish nationalist attack. Liberals were Swedes, Scandinavians, and pacifists, in that order, which sometimes meant the subordination of Norwegian interests and reactions to more important politic considerations. Opportunism became, therefore, the primary Liberal policy and in that the Norwegian government joined them after June 19. Its success depended upon the wisdom with which Liberals in Sweden and Michelsen and the Norwegian cabinet managed affairs.

Presentation of the government's propositions to the Riksdag on June 21 opened to public debate the question of what should be done with Norway. The cabinet simply proposed recognition of Norway and a grant of full powers from the Riksdag for negotiations with the union partner. Boström and the moderates defended the cabinet, and G. L. de Geer, a Liberal leader, moved acceptance of its proposals. Conservatives protested and, outside the Riksdag, their press joined their vigorous opposition. *Vårt Land*, during the last week in June, opened all stops in its rabble rousing: the cabinet's program was a shameful, socialistic capitulation; Sweden must mobilize immediately; Ramstedt and his spineless cohorts must be dismissed at once; the Norwegian army plotted a surprise attack; Swedish "honor" was being deliberately and traitorously surrendered. Debates and party conferences, common in Swedish parliamentary practice, soon diminished the clamor of extremists, and more moderate views slowly emerged.

The crucial decision on policy came on June 27 in the selection of a special committee for preparation of a program and on the definition of its scope of activities. The usual political maneuvers occupied the attention of the Riksdag. In the First Chamber, moderates emerged victorious over the "ultras," although two of the latter were kept from the committee only by sacrificing two former Conservatives whom the party wanted punished. The divergent character of First Chamber representatives might also be ascribed partly to Conservative opposition to Boström, his policies, and his support of the cabinet. Concessions granted to the moderates tended to secure their agreement to punish Boström and made First Chamber delegates favor a peaceful solution of the crisis. In the Second Chamber, by agreement, Liberals received five seats; the Conservative-Farmer party five; Moderate Reform Friends, one; and Independents, one. Among these appeared several future ministers. Through political maneuvering the reform party selected Harald Hjärne. Of the committee's total of twenty-four members the majority favored a moderate program and Conservative, but not "ultra," views.

In its initial meeting on June 28, the Extraordinary Committee established the usual machinery and settled into preliminary consideration of Swedish conditions to be asked of Norway. Then, before launching a fuller study, it decided to examine the state of Swedish defenses. A military report by General Axel Rappe showed an army of over 40,000 with approximately 500 rounds of ammunition per man. Naval vessels had three torpedoes per tube. In comparison with estimates of Norwegian military and naval forces, Swedish defenses seemed to be in excellent condition, except for the navy's need of newer ships. The data, in its details on Norwegian preparations, bore a remarkable resemblance to Olssøn's report of March, although Rappe did exaggerate the size of the Norwegian field army.

Rappe's statement mollified Conservatives and reassured the timid. The committee, with minds free of qualms about Sweden's capacity to defend herself, turned to basic issues of principles, improvement of Swedish defenses, and foreign relations. It could be further assured of the European powers' willingness to postpone recognition of Norway, despite their implied threat to do so if the crisis were not settled quickly. In the debate on principles, Riksdag and government proposals served as bases of argument. Only two of the cabinet's conditions became major questions—a ten kilometer neutral zone on both sides of the Norwegian-Swedish frontier and a guarantee for the Lapps in their annual migrations between the two countries. The committee analyzed at length perhaps forty conditions but never seriously accepted the idea of presentation of so large a number. Debate on the use of armed force or delay in negotiations showed them to be hypothetically applicable only as threats against Norway.

The main issue, to which debate returned again and again, centered on the frontier forts. Their thin line of guns and masonry walls pointed directly into Sweden from the sea on the south to almost the sixty-first parallel north of Hamar. They barred Swedish armies from a direct attack on Oslo and could be breached only by fierce fighting and heavy losses of men. If taken, or bypassed, they would be a liability to the Norwegians themselves for their own garrisons could neither escape attack nor effectively utilize their stores of munitions and provisions. In winter they often stood unmanned since army strategy shunned winter operations where ten feet or more of soft, fluffy masses of snow could engulf guns, men and horses. But to Norwegians the destruction of these forts, a symbol of their sole defense against Sweden, would be a shameful and dangerous act denuding Norway of her protective eastern shell. The Riksdag committee, however, considered their destruction as of the first order and also assumed that the cabinet included them in the neutral zone which extended to the sixty-first parallel. But a cabinet memorandum invalidated that assumption. The committee then added the neutral zone to its list and adopted the principle of razing the many frontier forts. But there still remained the question of whether this condition could be an item for negotiation at an eventual Norwegian-Swedish conference. Staaff argued for negotiation, but the committee overruled him and agreed eventually on a compromise by which new additions to the forts would be razed and the neutral zone might be created if the Norwegians wished. When the Riksdag later debated the proposal, the Second Chamber refused to accept Staaff's motion to permit negotiations on the demolition of the forts and approved the committee's recommendation.

The manner by which the Norwegians should indicate their desire to leave the union, since the committee refused to acknowledge the resolution of June 7, furnished the only other question of much interest. Choices narrowed finally to two: a new Storting vote or a plebiscite. The latter won most support and its chief proponent, Sigfrid Wieselgren, undoubtedly based his case on Norwegian preference for the latter course.[11] In a later debate the Second Chamber argued long enough to cause a compromise. A choice between a plebiscite and an appropriation of 100 million *kronor* was opposed to the election of a new Storting. The "war grant" or "war fund" was for use in case of military operations, but a new cabinet might find other ends for it to serve. Staaff favored only fifty million *kronor* and its control by the king. In the end the choice of a plebiscite or a new Storting was made by Norway, and the entire 100 million *kronor* was placed in the hands of the Riksdag. On July 22 the parliament approved this compromise which opened the way to the dissolution of the union.

These conditions, of which the public learned on July 25, incorporated four main introductory points. First, Sweden protested against the Norwegian unilateral dissolution of the union and demanded a request from the Storting for negotiations. Second, the Norwegian people by a plebiscite or a vote on a new Storting were to express their views and to give legal standing to the Michelsen cabinet. A conference for a final settlement, upon Norwegian request, and a promise to fulfill agreements reached by that body completed the basic demands. A series of specific requests, subject to minor changes through negotiations, included the razing of the frontier forts, the Lapp agreement, guarantee of equal rights for transit and for access to transfrontier water courses, creation of a neutral zone, and a future arbitration treaty.

These five questions actually constituted the core of the later

11 Cf. mention of letters from G. W. W. Gram to Wieselgren and Wieselgren to Gram, *Hagerup Bull*, 79-80; cf. also Gunnar Knudsen, "Folkeavstemningene 1905," *Samtiden*, XXXVI (1925), 534-539; also Arne Rygh, "Statsminister Gram og norsk unionspolitikk," *Samtiden*, XLI (1930), 606-616.

conference between Norwegians and Swedes. In deciding on the destruction of the forts, the Swedes had in mind the end of tensions resulting from military appropriations and operations on the frontier. They asked the razing of the new additions only, leaving the historic sections of Kongsvinger and Fredrikssten as monuments of the past. As compensation to the Norwegians, a neutral zone would blanket the area once covered by the forts where military operations would be forbidden, thus eliminating one hazard in pacific relations between the two countries.

The Lapp agreement, as everyone knew, would not involve concessions or conflict, for treaties and agreements covering their migrations went back to the seventeenth century. These colorful migrants maintained a winter residence in Sweden, but also needed the summer grazing grounds in the Norwegian mountains for their reindeer, which furnished food, clothing, and shelter as did the buffalo for the American Indian. The depredations of the reindeer in a settled community seemed to be the only complaint lodged by Norwegians against the Lapp migration into Norway, although problems concerning their poverty, disease, and assimilation later plagued both Norwegian and Swedish governments.

No one expected the provision for a guarantee of equal rights for transit and for access to water courses to cause any difficulties. The chief concern was the two or three railroads which linked Norway and Sweden, such as the *Ofotenbanen* and the Oslo-Stockholm line. Since these railroads were vital for both countries Norway certainly would not object to reciprocal rights affecting transit of goods on them. The main problem regarding waterways, from the Swedish point of view, was the danger that Norway might divert or diminish the annual spring flow in the rivers and thus prevent the floating of timber to mills from the mountains along the border.

The arbitration treaty, likewise, seemed to be no serious question, for both countries advocated pacific settlement of disputes. The Swedes wished to secure one which would not endanger their national sovereign rights. It constituted a concession to Swedish Liberals which the Conservatives were willing to grant if they were given support on the neutral zone issue and on the razing of the forts.

These conditions appear to be dictated by a sense of proportion and a willingness to be fair. The reactions of the Swedish press and political leaders varied according to party opinions. The Extraordinary Committee's careful collaboration with both houses of the Riksdag laid the ground for an easy acceptance, and the conditions passed by acclamation in the Second Chamber and without debate in the First. The Liberal party meeting of July 25 and 26 agreed on the fair nature of the propositions, even if the possibility of war and the personnel of the new cabinet, not yet created, made the future uncertain. Objections to the 100 million *kronor* appropriation stemmed basically from fear of the unknown, while other conditions, such as razing the forts, were approved almost without question. Both Branting and Staaff accepted the principle of demolition of the forts, believing it to be an assurance of future peace, although Staaff recognized the absence of reciprocity for the Norwegians. On that score Lindblad thought the lifting of economic burdens to be reciprocity enough. The First Chamber and most Conservatives considered the conditions as favorable to Sweden and as the ultimate to be attained in view of the great need for compromise.

Dagens Nyheter, Social-Demokraten (with Branting writing the editorial) and other liberal papers favored the conditions, although Branting took violent exception to the 100 million *kronor* "war grant." Conservative papers said little, except for comments regarding the political complexion of the new cabinet which would carry them out. Most echoed *Dagens Nyheter's* words, "the Riksdag has spoken," and went on to amplify the need for upholding what the Riksdag said.

During the Riksdag debate, in spite of rabid articles in Swedish papers, the Norwegian government and press maintained outwardly a discreet calm. The silence of the Norwegian press was not entirely voluntary, for the cabinet kept a firm hand on expressions of anti-Swedish sentiments. After a brief trial, however, the government ceased to impose any controls. Telephone and telegraph messages, the latter observed for approximately two weeks, also revealed nothing of import, and surveillance was stopped.[12] The cabinet did discuss foreign public opinion and dispatched several new agents to Paris, London, Berlin, and Copenhagen. They planned to send three persons to the United States, but after Nansen's withdrawal sent only Nils Irgens. Upon his arrival he learned that a note had been written to the United States government requesting recognition of Norway. The Department of State delayed an answer until late in the fall, and then announced that the United States would await European action. Fridtjof Nansen, Norway's unofficial ambassador to England, turned up again in London for a series of lectures on his Arctic explorations and their meaning for science. Other prominent Norwegians appeared in Copenhagen, Berlin, and Paris. The cabinet sent Brøgger to Stockholm a second time on July 18 to discuss Swedish conditions with Liberals, especially Staaff, and to express Norwegian willingness to hold a plebiscite. He failed to achieve any success, but the fight in the Riksdag over the plebiscite owed something to Brøgger's efforts.[13]

These schemes and endeavors were initiated because reports from Sweden aroused the apprehensions of the Norwegian cabinet. These reports, circulated widely by the Swedes, rumored of mobilization in Norway, spies, fleet maneuvers, mining of bridges, and other hostile preparations. The cabinet, in its meeting on June 24, listened to reports on the serious military imbalance and heard that Swedish troop concentrations made it impossible for Norway to defend herself from attack. Olssøn's report led to cabinet discussions on June 26 and 27 and, on the latter day, the Hedemark and Smaalene battalions, and other detachments, were ordered to reinforce the frontier forts. The cabinet also decided to purchase ammunition in Germany, for only 325 rounds per man were available at the front. Cabinet officers realized the effects of their action on Sweden, but were determined to defend Norway at all costs.[14]

---

[12] *Hagerup Bull*, 74.

[13] Cf. Jacob S. Worm-Müller, "Karl Staaff, W. C. Brøgger og Stortingets adresse av 19de juni 1905," *Historisk tidsskrift* (Norwegian), xxxv (1952), 650-662; Bothner, *op.cit.*, July 20; *Hagerup Bull*, 88-92.

[14] On the defense situation see Bothner, *op.cit.*, June 27, and *Hagerup Bull*, 66-70.

In Sweden the Riksdag settlement of the conditions made the Ramstedt ministry's position most untenable. Realizing his weakness Ramstedt agreed to resign when the Extraordinary Committee and Riksdag completed their work. As early as June, Conservative papers initiated attacks on Ramstedt with *Vårt Land* in the lead while *Dagens Nyheter* and other liberal papers called for a coalition government. The press in July generally concentrated on two names, Lundeberg and Wachtmeister, and in doing so indirectly urged creation of a coalition ministry. Both Lundeberg and Wachtmeister accepted the invitation to form a ministry and conferred with the king. On July 27 they circulated a tentative ministerial list of moderates and Conservatives. Evidently their list was not broad enough and Lundeberg, the next day, went to Staaff to inquire if he would sit in a ministry under his leadership. In this move Lundeberg received the backing of the monarchy, some Liberals and the Liberal press, but disapproval from his own Conservative party. After receiving the consent of a Liberal meeting, Staaff agreed to join the ministry and with him went J. Elof Biesèrt.

By July 30 most cabinet offices were filled. On that day Staaff gave a pledge to Lundeberg to maintain secrecy on cabinet discussions. The request, although somewhat unusual, originated in rumors about the Liberal leader's secret conversations with Norwegians. He, in turn, asked Lundeberg for a no-war pledge, but the prime minister refused to tie Swedish hands in this fashion. Staaff subsequently assumed, as part of his share of responsibility in the cabinet, the direction of Swedish information work abroad—an assignment which kept him in correspondence with some eight agents in France, Germany, England, and elsewhere.

On August 2 the cabinet went to the palace for formal reception by the king, and that evening newspapers carried a list of its members. Naturally *Vårt Land* and *Nya Dagligt Allehanda* wanted a Conservative ministry and would be satisfied with nothing less. *Dagens Nyheter* and other Liberal papers expressed pleasure, while *Svenska Dagbladet* and *Stockholms-tidningen* not only noted their satisfaction but commented on the elimination of fears of internal and foreign difficulties. Branting attacked the ministry for its Conservative majority and its possible attitude on social reform and domestic questions.[15] On the whole, recognition of the temporary and special nature of the cabinet was widespread. The September elections and the end of the union would see changes in the ministry.[16]

The new cabinet's sole task was the solution of the union question on the basis of the conditions laid down by the Extraordinary Committee and Riksdag. Lundeberg had chaired the former, and eight of his cabinet associates served as leaders of their parties in the First and Second Chambers. Thus political strength and Swedish unity were achieved by the sacrifice of action on domestic reforms. Most Conservatives regretted the inclusion of Liberals but they did not regard Staaff's appointment as any bar to a settlement with Norway. Quite the contrary, the cabinet's truly national character, which assured the execution of the Riksdag's wishes, produced general relief and satisfaction with this solution of the parliamentary crisis.

The Lundeberg-Wachtmeister ministry (Branting persisted in calling it the Lundeberg-Staaff coalition) stands as an historical landmark in Swedish parliamentary practice. It was the first cabinet since 1809 with a complete change in personnel (only one person, Hjalmar Hammarskjöld, had served as a member in an earlier cabinet). It contained the first lawyer, the first *bonde*, and the first Liberal. It included eight party leaders, four from each of the two chambers, a fact which signified a new stature of parliamentary equality for First and Second Chambers. It was the first national coalition cabinet, as it may properly be called, in Swedish history. In 1905 Swedish democracy began a new life when the union crisis forced an acknowledgement of the subordination of party interest to national strength. The first steps toward a modern state administration and parliamentary responsibility date from August 2, or from November when Staaff formed the first Liberal ministry.

With their own house in order the Swedish people could now accept the union crisis without fear of war or violence. The par-

---

[15] *Social-Demokraten*, July 28.
[16] Cf. newspapers for August 2 and 3, and Wåhlstrand, *1905*, 225-227.

liament and its leaders finished their task of setting conditions for Norway to fulfill before ending the union. Few Swedes dissented from these prerequisites and approved wholeheartedly of their guarantee of a peaceful and stable future. The country could expect the new cabinet to stand firm on these conditions and, because of the new ministry's coalition strength, could rest secure in the knowledge that Norway would pay for her offense in attempting to dissolve the union by herself. It was a well unified and fortified Sweden that asked the Norwegians to act on the conditions proposed for the end of the union.

◇◇

CHAPTER X

NORWAY AND SWEDISH CONDITIONS

◇◇

WHILE the Swedes relaxed in their security and their new cabinet accustomed themselves to the routine of office, Norwegians began their attempts to set their own house in order. From the missions of Vogt and others, the cabinet possessed full information on what to expect. Throughout, Norwegians assiduously studied formulas which would permit them to have their "face" and the Swedes their conditions. It was not an easy task, however, when rumors of war and troop mobilization affronted and alarmed both Norwegians and such widely disparate Swedes as Branting and Bishop Billing. In July rumors exaggerated the true situation so grossly that newspapers in both countries, not to mention the foreign press, wrote openly of war preparations. *Verdens Gang*, for its part, accused Sweden of manufacturing reasons for mobilization. The editor also charged the Swedish general staff with planning an attack on Norway when the crisis reached its height.

As *Verdens Gang* fired its salvo, *Vårt Land* compared the union crisis with the political and military scene in the United States prior to the Civil War, ending in unflattering comparisons of Norway with the South and noting the inevitable result of Swedish strength. Sweden must not follow Lincoln's example, continued the paper, but she must have the same right to use force, not to preserve the union but to guarantee the future security of the motherland and of Scandinavia. *Vårt Land* could not refrain from a rhetorical question: Would preservation of the Scandinavian union lead to a similar growth in stature and domestic strength? But it continued in rage against Norwegian fifth columnists in Sweden: Social Democrats, radicals, *Dagens Nyheter*, and Liberals: "Shame upon those who dishonor Sweden!" "Tourists" flocked into Sweden by the hundreds to spy upon military installations; a Swedish "tourist" (*Vårt Land* permitted no doubts of his innocence in visiting the Norwegian fortress of Ørje) reported indignantly on the Norwegian army officers' bitterness against Sweden.

Reports in other Swedish and Norwegian papers bordered on hysteria. *Aftonbladet* and *Svenska Dagbladet* in their advocacy of greater military expenditures and their attacks on "pacifists" verged on a demand for war.[1] *Nya Dagligt Allehanda* (July 13) wrote in assumed anger that the "Norwegian revolution was certainly well planned and its development to now [has] met no single difficulty." Its readers deduced the obvious moral lesson that Swedish leaders must halt this successful venture, which, after all, was an "infernal revolution," hatched in secrecy, with chauvinism and "Regent" Michelsen as archdevils. Rising belligerency in both countries, however, approached the ridiculous when *Vårt Land* on July 16 reported Lloyd's of London betting on a Scandinavian war.

With such verbal barrages from left and right the governments and presses of neither country could be expected to resist demands for action. Defense Minister Olssøn asked the Norwegian cabinet to increase supply purchases, especially of heavy artillery shells, for the Rødfoss factory could produce only 40,000 per day, or approximately enough for three hours of actual firing. In Sweden Lars Tingsten requested and got Lundeberg to place controls on export of all war materials, partly to halt shipments to Norway, and to retain under arms the three conscript classes on duty in 1905. Tingsten also complained about the absence of common-sense border checks against Norwegians spying on Swedish military installations.[2]

Revival of an earlier rumor of a Norwegian purchase of armored light cruisers abroad sent the Swedes on a world-wide search for the elusive vessels. The Swedish minister at London, Baron Carl Bildt, reported on Norwegian purchases of ammunition, but no ships, from Armstrongs; and, according to his in-

[1] Cf. *Svenska Dagbladet*, July 4, 5, 11; *Aftonbladet*, July 4, 13.
[2] Douglas wrote to Lundeberg to indicate his displeasure with Swedish defenses. Cf. Tingsten to Lundeberg, July 7, and Douglas to Lundeberg, July 7, Lundeberg Mss., Uppsala University Library.

formant, there was "not much" even of ammunition.[3] An alleged offer by the Chilean and Argentine governments to procure some naval vessels through an English commission house Bildt claimed to be untrue.[4] Reports on artillery bought from Armstrongs by a von der Lippe contained the surprising news that this same gentleman was acting in Norway's behalf in negotiations for an Argentine cruiser. Bildt, possibly with tongue in cheek, suggested to Foreign Minister Gyldenstolpe that the Swedes purchase both ships and artillery and thus keep Norway from securing either.[5] During July telegrams and letters tracing these rumors were sent to Montevideo, Buenos Aires, Valparaiso, Shanghai, Australia, and London. Lansdowne alarmed the Swedish foreign office further by denying any possibility or intent of stopping Norwegian purchases of war materials in England.[6]

Beset by these rumors and threats of war, Norwegians studied the Swedish conditions. Castberg, who bravely orated, "not one stone of the forts will be removed," refused doggedly to accept them. These "harsh" terms not only annulled the July 7 resolution, he wrote, but they made rubble of Norwegian border defenses. Upon hearing of Michelsen's tentative acceptance of conditions he charged that the government was composed of negotiation men of 1903, was faltering and compromising, impotent and unworthy. His only hope, he continued, was in the rural press and in *Venstre*, if he and Konow could arouse them to positive action. Michelsen answered a direct query from Castberg on the forts with the statement: "we fail to see that we [can] not immediately condemn some of the proposed conditions." But then the prime minister later called the razing of the forts a "bagatelle" and a "formality." Within *Venstre*, as Castberg found out, fears of war caused a majority of its members to urge calmness and deliberation. Berner, vested with the authority of a Storting president, accepted the idea of a plebiscite which Castberg in his turn called a Swedish ultimatum making the June 7 resolution a "comedy." The fiery radical saw looming a

---

[3] The informant was Sexton Noble. 4M1C, *UDS*.
[4] Bildt to foreign office, July 17, 4M1C, *UDS*.
[5] July 11 and 26, 4M1C, *UDS*.
[6] Bildt to Gyldenstolpe, June 29, 4M1C, *UDS*.

possibility of a repetition of 1895 when Norway had so meekly submitted to Swedish threats.

The cabinet quickly agreed on the plebiscite, although it did nullify the June 7 resolution. Even before seeing the complete list of conditions, it unofficially informed the Swedish government of its agreement to a plebiscite. By July 20, nearly a week before formal Riksdag approval of the conditions, it cleared the necessary legal and technical aspects for holding a vote. On July 28 a government proposal on its details was brought to a secret session of the Storting.[7] Michelsen explained the cabinet's position, which radicals attacked without hesitation. Their bitterness stirred the Storting by its stress on a Norwegian capitulation in accepting the conditions.[8] Michelsen accused Castberg, both openly and in cabinet, of disloyalty to the government, although Bothner defended motives of both leaders of his party. Even Castberg recognized, however, that a government victory was a foregone conclusion, and in the public Storting session the radicals accepted the plebiscite.

The favorable opinion in the Storting toward the conditions came from an acknowledgment of their moderation in not demanding more and the great harm their rejection would bring to Scandinavia. Cabinet officers, and a majority in the Storting expressed their satisfaction with Swedish forbearance, although some privately agreed with the radicals on razing the forts. But, as hopes for modifications in the Swedish terms remained, they continued to expect alterations; even razing the forts might be avoided if handled with tact and moderation.

The Norwegians could hardly refrain from an attempt to modify Swedish conditions. One possible escape was to secure the intervention of the powers, or at least their support for a scheme which carries the various labels of the Trolle-Wedel, the Gustaf-Bernstorff, and the Gustaf plan. Norwegian efforts in its behalf began at Copenhagen in June with Wedel's efforts to secure a king for Norway. Long before his trip to Denmark, and even before the Storting resolution of June 7, rumors circulated of a

7 *Hemmelige møter*, 114-142.
8 Cf. Castberg, *Dagbøker*, I, 431-432.

possible choice of Prince Carl of Denmark for the Norwegian throne, when and if it became vacant.[9]

In a report to the Norwegian cabinet Wedel summarized his negotiations and labeled his proposals as the Wedel plan. It contained all the merits of thought and of possible attainment. Its basic components, to which additions were made later, included a maneuver for the election of Prince Carl of Denmark, if Oscar II and the Swedes refused to permit a Bernadotte to accept the Norwegian throne. Both British and Danish favor would be won by Prince Carl's election; Edward VII would give his eager support since his daughter was the wife of the prince. Germany might approve, even if her Kaiser and government wished selection of a candidate less pro-British, such as a Bernadotte. After publication of the Swedish conditions, still another item added itself to the list of reasons why Wedel should go to Copenhagen to persuade Prince Carl to accept the throne: If he did accept, then might not England and Denmark recognize Norway prior to negotiations with the Swedes? Michelsen's acceptance of the plan was followed by a conference with Løvland on whose fears of republicanism Wedel proceeded to play. A republic, so Wedel stated, would cause political strife; it would be frowned upon by the European powers; and monarchy carried to the Norwegian people echoes of King Haakon's good old times. Under this persuasion, Wedel wrote, "the old national spirit arose" in Løvland and he willingly approved the scheme.

As an unofficial Norwegian envoy, Wedel pursued his plan both at Copenhagen and at London. He first saw Danish Count Mogen Frijs, who could open palace doors, and from him extracted a promise to convey full details of the Wedel plan to the crown prince, the king, and Prince Carl. Others shared in the execution of the project, although Count F. C. O. Raben-Levent-

---

[9] Cf. Gude's report of April 13, 4M1b, *UDS*. In reference to the policy of the powers, especially England, see Folke Lindberg, *Kunglig utrikespolitik*, 196-230, and Wedel, *1905*, 42-201. Note also a report of a conference between Gustaf and von Richtofen where the former stated that no Swedish prince would ever sit on the Norwegian throne, to which the German secretary of state replied that Germany would oppose only a candidate favored by England. *Aide-mémoire* of von Richtofen, June 10, *Aus. Amt*, 2956, *UDN*.

zau, the Danish foreign minister, handled later details.[10] For a brief time Wedel continued his diplomatic efforts in London where his inexhaustible energy and his many friends aided him. Through an old friend, private secretary to Lord Lansdowne, he arranged to meet the British foreign secretary. With him on June 20 Wedel was most successful. Although the cautious British foreign secretary stressed the unofficial and provisional nature of his comments, he did express the government's wish for a rapid settlement of the crisis, its satisfaction with the Bernadotte invitation, and, if that failed, its approval of the selection of Prince Carl of Denmark as king of Norway. Lansdowne even added the thought that the Swedish government might favor Prince Carl because of his Bernadotte mother.

Upon his return to Oslo, Wedel reported to Løvland and Michelsen. Their jubilation increased his own and Wedel wrote: "All is in order . . . the king of England gives his approval . . . *We no longer stand alone.*"[11]

What the Norwegian government did not know, however, was that Gustaf, when in Germany and England, had proceeded to discuss a similar plan. He not only secured German and British approval for it, but he persuaded his father and the Swedish cabinet to accept the Danish prince as the only candidate. The Swedes, while consenting to this arrangement, would not approve his election before solution of the crisis and a rejection of the Bernadotte invitation. Until the announcement of Swedish conditions on July 25, the two plans ran a parallel course and both received the support of Danish, Norwegian, and Swedish governments as well as that of the European powers.

Back again at Copenhagen, Wedel busily continued his diplomacy. On June 28 he visited the Danish foreign minister and later in the day he talked with the British chargé d'affaires with whom he arranged for a meeting with the Danish crown prince. Late that same evening, at eleven o'clock, Wedel received a surprise visit from a cyclist. With Prince Carl, who so calmly arrived

10 Of this diplomacy, Bothner complained, the cabinet had not heard or given its consent. Bothner, *op.cit.*, June 19.

11 Wedel, *1905*, 61, 62. The italics are Wedel's.

in this unroyal fashion, Wedel settled details of the civil list, protocol, ceremonial, and even the names to be assumed by the prospective king and crown prince. Because of the historic symbol of the last two kings of Norway in the 14th century, Prince Carl thought Haakon and Olav rang with tradition and bore the mark of authenticity. The next day Wedel wrote to the British minister in Stockholm to urge Edward VII's personal intervention for his son-in-law's election. At the same time, the Danish crown prince wrote to Oscar II to ask his approval of the election of his son and received a reply on July 2 stating that no Bernadotte would occupy the Norwegian throne, unless the Riksdag insisted, but requesting delay until a final settlement of the union question.[12] In the course of the next few days Wedel saw most of his plan finished.

The energetic Norwegian envoy then reported on all these details, in person, to Løvland and Michelsen.[13] Envoys at Copenhagen, so Wedel reported, seemed to approve; the French minister to Denmark, with Gallic wit, dismissed fears of an infectious spread of the French disease of republicanism by saying it "is not an export article." Michelsen added a new ingredient to the election of Prince Carl by suggesting its use to hasten Sweden's snail pace in working out suitable conditions.[14] The new addition simply requested Norwegian recognition by the powers, if Swedish conditions were not immediately forthcoming, for which Prince Carl's election to the Norwegian throne would be a payment. Danish Count Raben became the intermediary with the powers and he stressed Norwegian disquiet and alarm over the Riksdag's delaying tactics and the Swedish royal family's refusal to nullify the Bernadotte invitation openly. Norway could hardly wait much longer to have her independence acknowledged by Sweden, Raben reported, and, in addition, the Danish king fav-

---

[12] 4M1a, *UDS*.

[13] Løvland confirmed Wedel's report by a letter of Count Frijs of July 4. The count asked for an immediate private binding agreement regarding Carl's election in preparation for emergencies. Sweden would be irate, the Count continued, but the risk more than justified itself in the better prospects for the welfare of Denmark, Norway, and Scandinavia.

[14] Wedel's and Michelsen's words were repeated in Schoen's dispatch to Bülow on July 11.

ored the election of his grandson to the Norwegian throne. The "could not wait" theme entered into Wedel's letter to the British minister at Stockholm, and even Oscar II used it in a Swedish cabinet meeting on July 12.[15]

The utility of the Bernadotte invitation in checking Norwegian impetuousness was now illustrated fully in Sweden's negotiations with the powers. The Swedish king, crown prince, and cabinet made good use of it with the German Kaiser at Gävle when Wilhelm visited that small Baltic port in July. Both Danes and Norwegians watched uneasily the leisurely progress of the *Hohenzollern* northward along the Swedish coast. The meeting of the Kaiser, Oscar II, and Gustaf on board the imperial yacht on July 12 and 13 raised flurries of rumors.[16] In their meeting with Wilhelm II, Oscar and Gustaf emphasized Swedish requests to withhold recognition of Norway until dissolution of the union, and their desire to find a quick and peaceful solution if Norway permitted. The Kaiser stressed the need for speed[17] and pressed Oscar to nominate one of his own sons to the Norwegian throne to avoid a European scramble for it. If such a nomination were impossible, then the Kaiser wished personally for Danish Prince Waldemar to have the crown. The Kaiser commended the prince for his lovely wife (who was not British), two fine children, cosmopolitan background, and, in contrast to Prince Carl, whom he

---

[15] Cf. Copy of Oscar's statement in the *Bernadotte Arkiv*, Stockholm.

[16] To dissipate Norwegian fears Bülow asked Schoen to inform Wedel of the friendly interest of Germany and of the meaning of the Gävle meeting. Faber du Faur, the German consul general at Oslo, gave Michelsen the same report. Bülow to Schoen and to Faber du Faur. July 17, *Aus. Amt*, 2956, *UDN*; also in Bothner, *op.cit.*, July 13-14. Norwegian and Swedish newspapers carried profuse details of the meeting but none of its meat. Cf. *Aftenposten*, July 12-15; *Nya Dagligt Allehanda*, *Vårt Land*, and other Swedish papers for the same dates. Notice also the articles in *Morgenbladet* on Prince Carl's candidature which started the rumor mill on contenders for the Norwegian throne as a trial balloon.

[17] Cf. Lundeberg *Anteckningar*, Uppsala University Library; Müller to Bülow, July 13, *Aus. Amt*, 2956, *UDN*; Taube to Gyldenstolpe, July 27, 4A15, *UDS*. German foreign office reports of the Gävle meeting are in Müller's letters to Bülow and a long report by the Kaiser to the German Chancellor, *Aus. Amt*, July 15, 2956, *UDN*; *Die grosse Politik des europäischens Kabinette, 1871-1914*, eds., Johannes Lepsius, Albrecht Mendelssohn Bartholdy, Friedrich Thimme (40 vols. in 54, Berlin, 1922-1927). XIX, pt. 2, 461. Hereafter cited: *G.P.*; Tschirschky to Bülow, July 17, *Aus. Amt*, 2956, *UDN*.

considered lazy and unskilled, his energy and training for the post.[18]

In spite of exaggerations and misconceptions Swedish and German policies remained as they were prior to the Kaiser's visit to Gävle. Wilhelm wanted a speedy solution of the Scandinavian crisis and nomination of a Bernadotte or Prince Waldemar, and agreed to withhold recognition of Norway. The latter was the major, almost the sole, objective of the Swedish king. Later reports of these conversations at Gävle distressed the Swedish government. Public naming of the meeting as a "new Tangier" annoyed the Swedes by its misinterpretation of their honest effort to avoid European entanglement and possible intervention in Scandinavian affairs.

As a result of Gävle, Germany increased her pressure for selection of a king for Norway less favorable to, and less influenced by, England. Instructions to support Waldemar went to various German envoys on July 16. Both the German consul general at Oslo and the German minister at Copenhagen reported complete failure when they sought to convince the Norwegians of the virtues of Waldemar. Christian IX preferred Carl to Waldemar, and the Norwegian government (Wedel) refused to accept a prince with a Catholic wife. The Oslo report confirmed this view and remarked on the ruffled and upset feelings of Michelsen, who refused to consider Prince Waldemar and asked the reasons for this sudden shift in German neutrality. But it should have been clear to Michelsen that Germany would seek to check England at any point, but especially at this one. The election of Prince Carl and his English wife to the throne would extend British influence in the North and thus affect both Russian and German interests in the Baltic.[19]

[18] Re the pressure of the Kaiser see Lindberg, *Kunglig utrikespolitik*, 206-207, where he identifies it with diminishing German fears of Russia which permitted the Kaiser to recommend a prince married to a Russian and dominated by Russian influences. However, Lindberg's identification of the Waldemar candidature with the later Björkö meeting between Wilhelm and Czar Nicholas II does not agree with the documents.

[19] Cf. Faber du Faur to *Aus. Amt*, July 19 (telegram), 2956, *UDN*; Wedel, *1905*, 110-111; Bülow to Oslo and Copenhagen, July 20, *Aus. Amt*, 2956, *UDN*. The Kaiser's failure to influence the Norwegians caused him to withdraw his

The Kaiser's diplomacy and rumors of widespread Norwegian republicanism (carefully nurtured by Raben and Wedel in Copenhagen) caused Lansdowne to ask Johnstone's assistance for Prince Carl's candidacy. But the British foreign secretary later stated that England would not recognize Carl until after Sweden did so.[20] The lengths to which the British government and King Edward would support Prince Carl gradually took shape during these crucial days in August when the Norwegian government sought escape from the Swedish conditions.

The first steps toward such a plan originated from rumors of an early announcement by Oscar on the Bernadotte invitation.[21] Instructions from Løvland to Wedel contained in their five points the essence of the "Wedel-Trolle" or the "Gustaf-Bernstorff" plan. After holding a plebiscite on the dissolution, the Norwegians would inform the Swedish government of its results and Oscar would refuse the throne. Prince Carl would then be elected king, and Norway would formally accept the Swedish conditions as a basis for negotiations, "with other questions raised from the Norwegian side." Løvland's basic point was predicated on the existence of a complete Norwegian government, including a king, before negotiations began.[22]

In Copenhagen Wedel took these instructions and swung immediately into action. He expressed his confidence of English, Danish, and even Swedish approval. In another direction he benefited by the Kaiser's arrival in Copenhagen, for he, too, approved of Prince Carl's election, although he would prefer Waldemar. Wedel received full support from the British and Danish governments, but for days he struggled unavailingly against the

---

favor. But his visit to Copenhagen in August, and conversations with the Danish royal family, convinced him that both Danish and Norwegian governments stubbornly insisted on Prince Carl.

20 Cf. Lindberg, Kunglig utrikespolitik, 218; cf. also his essay in Historiska studier tillägnade Nils Ahnlund, "Englands nordiska politik sommaren 1905," 304-324, which has footnotes.

21 Cf. Castberg, Dagbøker, I, 418-420. Løvland and Michelsen framed a plan to be sent Wedel. By coincidence the same day as the instructions to Wedel received their final wording the Danish cabinet decided to refuse permisson for Prince Carl to go to Norway until after Swedish action.

22 Løvland to Wedel, July 28, P8A, 3/23, UDN.

stubbornness of Christian IX who refused to permit his grandson to assume the Norwegian throne until Sweden recognized the new state. Speed was essential, as Wedel knew and as Løvland kept telling him in his orders. The Norwegian foreign minister wished especially firm commitments on British and Danish recognition of Norway once Carl became king. The only promise Wedel could extract from the Danes was permission for Prince Carl's leadership of Norway in her negotiations with Sweden after nullification of the Bernadotte candidature and Prince Carl's election by a plebiscite.[23] The British envoy in Stockholm, Sir James Rennell Rodd, served as Wedel's intermediary with Gustaf to gain Sweden's consent to the plan. But the crown prince added the unpleasant modification that Carl could not go to Norway until after signature of a Norwegian-Swedish agreement. Both Wedel and Raben rejected this alteration, for Norwegians must have Carl to lead the negotiations.

In England this Wedel-Løvland-Gustaf-Raben project, which Lansdowne received from Rodd, was laid by the British foreign secretary before the Swedish minister to England. But Bildt, unaware of Gustaf's share in it, turned it down unhesitatingly.[24] Trolle, immediately upon his arrival in Copenhagen as the new Swedish minister, was buttonholed by Raben and questioned. Trolle wired Stockholm for instructions. Even after Trolle gave the Swedish government's emphatic rejection, Raben persisted in urging compliance with the plan and even added threats of Danish impatience with delays. Possibly Norway should have been added to the list of impatient sufferers.

The Swedish cabinet naturally resented this furtive diplomacy and also grew anxious. In a session on August 2 it decided to send Gustaf to Copenhagen to insist upon Danish fulfillment of their promises.[25] The crown prince's mission, as he personally carried it out, varied somewhat from the Swedish cabinet's expectations. He readily fell in with the Norwegian plan, and even enlisted

[23] Løvland to Wedel, August 1; Wedel to Løvland, August 2, P8A, 3/23, UDN.

[24] Bildt to Gyldenstolpe, August 2, 4A15, UDS.

[25] Cf. Berg's notes, Arne Wåhlstrand, Karlstadkonferensen 1905 (Stockholm, 1953), 296.

Trolle's aid in its behalf. Gustaf defended the proposal on three grounds: it would allay fears of a republic in Norway; it would have English and Danish support; and it would be a strengthened guarantee of a peaceful solution of the crisis. He suggested two additions to the proposal, however: that Carl's election be provisional, and that Gustaf's own personal influence with the Swedish government be used to persuade it to accept the plan. The crown prince sadly overestimated his powers. When he returned to Stockholm with a copy of Wedel's memorandum, the cabinet ordered a severe reprimand of Trolle and studiously ignored Gustaf's statements.

Oblivious of deepening Swedish antagonism, Wedel and his friends persevered. Michelsen asked Wedel to procure British and Danish aid for the Norwegians in securing freedom to elect Carl. "If Sweden answers no, we propose to the Storting to elect Prince Carl of Denmark who must have previously declared himself willing and have secured England's and Denmark's recognition. Do you [Wedel] think England and the Danish government [will be] agreeable thereto?"[26] Conscious of Germany's importance, Wedel again asked Schoen, the German minister to Denmark, if his government would use its good offices at Stockholm in behalf of the plan. Although Schoen replied cautiously that Germany would remain as neutral as England, he stated flatly in a letter to his own foreign office that England would recognize Carl with or without the consent of Sweden.[27] Certain of English and Danish support, Wedel telegraphed via Johnstone to beg Edward VII's intervention with the Swedish government to approve Prince Carl's election and his appearance in Norway prior to negotiations, with the proviso that if the Swedes refused Prince Carl would go anyway. If the British accepted the plan, they would be serving in the capacity of gullible intermediaries, for it lacked any benefits for England.

The indirect approach through Edward VII resulted in his writing to Gustaf to urge Swedish approval of Carl's election. The

---

[26] Michelsen to Wedel, August 11, P8A, 3/23, *UDN.*

[27] August 11, *Aus. Amt*, 2956, *UDN.* Later to Bülow, Schoen added that Norway wished recognition if she proceeded with the plan. August 13, *ibid.*

reasons for his doing so were based on British wishes for peaceful and stable negotiations which, Edward claimed, would be impossible without a Norwegian king to head the government. Once burned by his sincere efforts at Copenhagen, Gustaf used the cabinet's aid in composing a reply, even though the answer was the same. The Bernadotte candidature would not be declared nullified until after conclusion of negotiations; no Bernadotte would be seated on the Norwegian throne; and the entire royal family looked with favor upon Prince Carl.[28]

Unaware of the results of Edward's letter, which could not have been known in Oslo earlier than August 20, Nansen informed the Norwegian cabinet that England would recognize Norway and her king in the event of the prince's election, even if Sweden refused to nullify the Bernadotte invitation. Optimistic in this direction, Nansen then mentioned objections of the Danish royal family and government and Wedel's request for help in Copenhagen.[29] Løvland instructed Wedel to continue his negotiations and told him that the Storting, when it met on August 21, would be asked to elect Carl immediately after the withdrawal of the Bernadotte invitation. He stressed the major problem as procurement of English recognition.[30] Prince Carl, wanting more positive proof of Norwegian policy, asked for confirmation of Wedel's plan and received full approval.[31]

In Copenhagen the Danish cabinet opened debate on the diplomacy of the Norwegian crown. Trolle, chastened by his reprimand at an earlier stage, threatened Raben with the possibility of war if Denmark meddled in Norwegian-Swedish affairs. Although Wedel scorned the threat, the Danish cabinet accepted it in all seriousness and decided that the support of the powers was necessary before anything could be done. Raben, Wedel, and Nansen could create no new scheme, and Gustaf's letter to Edward produced a British retreat. On August 20 the bad tidings

[28] Cf. original of Edward's letter and three copies of Gustaf's reply in *Bernadotte Arkiv*; cf. also Widén's notes, Wåhlstrand, *Karlstadkonferensen*, 344.

[29] Bothner, *op.cit.*, August 14.

[30] Løvland to Wedel, P8A, 3/23, *UDN*.

[31] Cf. Nansen to Løvland, August 16, P8A, 3/23, *UDN*.

of England's withdrawal came to Copenhagen, and the same day Wachtmeister informed the Swedish cabinet of Christian's refusal to approve the Wedel plan. Both Nansen and Wedel then left for Oslo to report their disheartening failure.

The two envoys clarified the entire foreign situation for the Norwegian cabinet. Britain agreed to recognize a Norwegian government under Prince Carl only if Denmark did so.[32] Denmark and Christian IX refused permission to let Carl sail to Norway before the end of negotiations and Oscar's final proclamation. But the spectre of republicanism had been banished, for Norway bound herself morally to accept Prince Carl and a monarchical form of government. If commitments were nullified it would be a "slap in the face of England, Denmark, and all Europe."[33] The British government applied even more pressure by asking Nansen and Wedel to convince Norwegian leaders of the need for settling with Sweden before taking any further steps.[34] The British fleet, scheduled for maneuvers off the Norwegian coast during the latter part of August or early September, received orders to hold them in less political waters. The Norwegian cabinet had now no alternative except to abandon its efforts to escape the Swedish strangle hold. It was clear now that Norway must face her opponent at the conference table without a formal government or king and without European recognition. Only then did the Norwegians recognize the strategic error of issuing the Bernadotte invitation and the use to which Sweden could put it.

What was the rationale of Norwegian policy in this month of diplomatic maneuvering? The cabinet's main objective had been to present the Swedes with a *fait accompli*. A Norwegian king supported by the powers, or, if that failed, a provisional election of Prince Carl and his recognition by the powers, would have placed Norway in a strong position. At the coming conference

[32] This was later changed to three governments, Britain, Denmark, and a third, *British Documents on the Origins of the War, 1898-1914*, eds. George P. Gooch and Harold W. V. Temperley (11 vols., London, 1926-1938), VIII, 84. Hereafter cited: *B.D.*

[33] Wedel, *1905*, 191.

[34] See Johnstone's letter of August 12, *B.D.*, VIII, 84.

she would then have had leeway for compromise, because with a recognized government she could withdraw and depend upon the powers to support her. At the same time Norwegian diplomacy at Copenhagen, involving three nations and two disputants, pointed out their obvious distaste with Swedish conditions. Most could be accepted with equanimity, but destruction of the frontier forts, with consequent opening of the road to Oslo, was more than Norwegians could bear. Cabinet officers feared Storting and popular reactions and, in spite of Castberg's harsh condemnation of him, on this point Michelsen refused to bow humbly before the Swedish delegation or to submit to the conditions without compromise. Norwegians at a conference in such a guise could not negotiate but merely capitulate. Wedel's policy of scaring Raben, Johnstone, and others with a republican bogey and with rumors of war and mobilization attempted to retrieve some Norwegian prestige with the aid of the powers and Denmark. But Swedish intransigence, and especially the firmness of the new cabinet, prevented the Norwegian plan from succeeding.

At the same time as this secret diplomacy attempted great things, most Norwegians prepared busily for the plebiscite on August 13. Government proclamations informed the public about polling places, voting procedures, and other specifications, while newspapers converted the plebiscite into a national prestige matter. Norwegian women were beseeched to organize information clubs, even if they did not have the franchise, and women's groups campaigned throughout the country for an affirmative vote. The National Railways offered free transportation to all voters, only requiring the name and polling place of the passenger in lieu of a ticket. Storting members and cabinet officers stumped the country to make August 13 both a festival and an expression of Norwegian unanimity. Even that day's clear weather favored the Norwegian cause and thousands of cheerful, rejoicing voters, who might have stayed home if it had rained, thronged the countryside. Women went to the polls or their votes were solicited at home by boys and girls to show feminine opinions on separation from Sweden. Over two hundred thousand women added their ballots unofficially to the men who voted in favor of dissolution. Instances of irregularities and pressures did occur, but excessive charges of violence and brutalities by *Nya Dagligt Allehanda, Vårt Land,* and other Swedish Conservative papers merely expressed their biliousness and dimmed very slightly the plebiscite's patriotic meaning. The vote in favor of separation was nearly unanimous: 367,149 yeas and 184 noes.[35]

But, as Castberg wrote in his diary two days later, Swedish conditions remained unacceptable. Pressures from the Storting and from the Castberg-Konow faction persisted and cabinet members began to lose their confidence. Desperate and unwilling to procrastinate further, they begged Michelsen to do something. The need for more precise information on Swedish conditions furnished him with a pretext for sending an envoy to Stockholm, but his real purpose was to test the new Swedish cabinet and, most important, to procure some concessions on the forts.

Again Benjamin Vogt was selected as the best qualified person for this mission. He stepped off the train in Stockholm on August 16 and went to meet the four members chosen by the Swedish cabinet: Lundeberg, Wachtmeister, Hammarskjöld, and Staaff. These four were also delegates to the Norwegian-Swedish conference and, therefore, could best inform Vogt of Swedish policies. Their first session with Vogt dealt primarily with minor preliminaries: selection of Karlstad as the site of the conference; an agreement, at Staaff's suggestion, for a formal Norwegian request for negotiations; and the tentative time of the meeting. When Vogt tried to extend the scope of his discussions, he gained nothing and his real purpose—to secure concessions on razing the forts—completely failed.

Back once again in Oslo, Vogt reported to the cabinet on Swedish tenacity and unity, pointing to Staaff's presence on the committee that talked with him. Unless Norway accepted the conditions, Vogt continued, Sweden would mobilize at the risk of war. Lundeberg had stated that any arbitration on the question of the forts was out of the question. The Swedish ministers

<hr />

[35] For descriptions of the day see *Aftenposten* and *Verdens Gang* for August 14, 15, 16; Castberg, *Dagbøker,* I, 441-443; Bernt Nissen, *1905* (Oslo, 1930), 147-148; S. C. Hammer, *Det merkelige aar* (Oslo, 1930), 206-208.

wished to avoid war and asked Norway to put up no opposition which might lead to hostilities. The entire Swedish cabinet stood behind the conditions, but other Swedish leaders with whom Vogt talked advised the Norwegians to seek compromises on razing the forts. Everyone urged Norway not to seek foreign intervention; Staaff, who might be expected to be friendly, agreed most strongly with his colleagues on this request. Vogt's report surprised the cabinet. Until he spoke its members expected some Swedish concessions, but he offered no hope. Because of the cabinet's refusal to believe what he told them, Vogt was asked to return to Stockholm in a direct effort to secure some modification of the Swedish stand on the forts. He returned, therefore, on August 18 to assail Swedish stubbornness, but the cabinet worded its refusal to compromise even more strongly than before. Reports on movements of Norwegian troops and naval stores and on increases in frontier defenses stimulated Swedish fears of war, even among the Liberals, and Vogt's mission was completely unsuccessful.[36]

Vogt's failure arose in part from convictions of the Swedish ministers that the conditions were reasonable and fair. An article by Castberg in *Dagbladet* on August 18, in which he stressed the impossibility of negotiations on the basis of the Swedish conditions, made the Swedes realize, too, that they must stand firm, or grounds for settlement of the crisis would dissolve under their feet. Castberg's article, in its relation to Norway, sought to force the Storting to resist acceptance of the Swedish proposals, but it resulted in an opposite effect both in Norway and in Sweden.

The Norwegian cabinet faced both domestic resistance and a notable succession of failures. They suffered from Castberg's attacks on themselves for their "spineless" acceptance of the Swedish conditions. They failed completely to secure foreign support for Prince Carl's election. Vogt's mission revealed Swedish solidarity behind the conditions. Thus, in the Storting, the cabinet faced the most stubborn opposition when they sought affirmation

[36] For details on Vogt's mission see his *Indtil 1910*, 89-91; Christian Lundeberg's and Widéns notes in Wåhlstrand, *Karlstadkonferensen*, 281-284, 341-345.

of both government propositions on the plebiscite and a grant of
full powers for the delegation at Karlstad. The Storting sessions
of August 21 and 22 rated among the stormiest that body experienced in 1905. Because of its secrecy the session's deliberations[37] did not reveal to the Swedish government the strength
of the minority around Konow and Castberg. If they had known,
their irritation might have been increased, but their fears lessened. The debate quickly exposed a major weakness of the radicals in their lack of a parliamentary leader to cope with Michelsen's consummate skill. The prime minister blunted their
charges by comparing them with Swedish First Chamber na-
tionalists who desired war. He was hardly fair to the radicals,
but he succeeded where, perhaps, gentler methods would have
failed. He claimed both governments to be equal and sovereign,
which could not be officially stated because it would give "wind
for the sails of 'Swedish chauvinists.'" Michelsen implied that
those who would demand such a statement were in the same
category. He played up the influences of Norwegian actions on
Swedish elections in September and the dangers to Norway if
she refused to negotiate. Although the debate on acceptance of
negotiations had no time limit, Michelsen shrewdly made it appear as if the Swedes wished an immediate answer. In more
drastic language, he implied that a Swedish ultimatum stood
behind the government propositions. When the contestants
showed signs of weariness at eight-thirty, the Storting agreed to
a postponement until the following day when debate would be
finished.

The session on August 22 resounded with diplomatic repartee
and parliamentary exchanges fit to delight the heart of a politician. Someone raised the question of a vote of no confidence,
which cabinet officers furiously attacked as an overt threat. No
cabinet crisis could be permitted during this period, but a few
stragglers, still striving to assemble their wits and votes, were
frightened into joining the government's side. Despite fears
and alarms the outcome was ridiculously tame. The final vote
of 104 to 11 favored full powers for the government and a formal

37 Report of the debate is in *Hemmelige møter*, 143-248.

notice to Sweden. The eleven radicals stuck to the last to their insistence on rejection of the Swedish conditions regardless of the consequences and without offering alternative solutions. Shortly after six o'clock on August 22 the government report on the plebiscite and a request for negotiations and full powers for a Norwegian delegation were hastily assembled and hurried to the train for Stockholm.

A few details remained to be arranged. The date of the Norwegian-Swedish conference at Karlstad was set for August 31. The Norwegian cabinet wrestled with the thorny question of the choice of delegates; the main issue in their debate was whether Carl Berner, president of the Storting, could go.[38] When Berner was approved, the other three candidates fell into order with Michelsen heading the delegation. Løvland and Benjamin Vogt completed the list.

But these delegates could not leave Oslo until some agreements were made on defense preparations and some plan of action devised in case of a sudden disruption of negotiations. Olssøn reported both increases in Swedish forces, effected by retaining recruits past their normal tour of duty, and decreases in Norwegian troops at the front because defense chiefs were not duplicating the Swedish action.[39] Olssøn's complaints on Norwegian military weakness, and his insistence on calling reserves, forced Michelsen to promise the cabinet that a crisis at Karlstad would be postponed by an adjournment. If military leaders found mobilization imperative, Michelsen pledged himself to support a call for the reserves. In such an event, the cabinet decided, the first step would be to move military depots from the western coast to Drammen and troops up to a line on the Glommen River some fifteen or twenty kilometers west of the border. Olssøn gloomily reported that Norway's military position was hopeless and that everything depended upon negotiations. Michelsen's facetious, yet meaningful, comment was that Norway

[38] Cf. the debate in the Storting secret session on approval of Berner, *Hemmelige møter*, 255-274. Castberg and Konow, too late, decided to block his selection.

[39] Olssøn reported that Fredrikssten's garrison totalled only 49 men of a complement of 517; at Ørje 57 were left of 384, and at Urskog only 10 of 242.

would mobilize King Edward, a remark that grew in fame as legends encrusted the story of 1905.

The press naturally offered advice for the delegates to the conference. *Svenska Dagbladet* approved of the conditions and of delegates who "know and think Swedish" and would remain firm so "no Norwegian lawyer can get by." *Verdens Gang* stressed the peaceful intent of the conference and the policy of realism which both delegations would follow. The Norwegian negotiators, the paper continued, went with the good wishes of the entire nation. These sentiments were backed by an overwhelming majority of both peoples, but neither wished a "capitulation" or a "surrender" through negotiations. Tensions developed by three months of public and press debate, however, could hardly be dispelled in an instant.

CHAPTER XI

◇◇

THE KARLSTAD CONFERENCE

◇◇

THE meeting of the eight Norwegian and Swedish delegates at Karlstad on August 31 contained great historical and symbolic meaning for Scandinavia. A successful conference would ensure peace in the North; its failure would mean war's ravages and foreign intervention. If the delegates arose from the conference table in anger, the Baltic might be converted into that blood bath of which Axel Oxenstierna spoke in the seventeenth century. Now, after three months of suspense, they sat down to a table in Karlstad's Masonic Hall at one o'clock to initiate diplomatic talks for an acceptable agreement to end the union.

The Norwegian representatives faced the more difficult task. As chief of the delegation Michelsen displayed a calm willingness to recognize realities, and his insistence upon avoiding war with the Swedes marked him as the leading man of the eight at the conference. Tall, handsome, and bearded, the frock-coated Michelsen made his presence felt soon after the opening of this assembly. Løvland, whose short, squat figure and square-bearded face resembled a dour troll peering over spectacles, knew the Swedes from two decades of antagonism and keenest enmity Carl Berner shared Løvland's *Venstre* political views and more directly faced a dependence upon the Storting and party colleagues. In his twenty years or more of Storting experience, he, too, had seen the Swedes threaten and bluster, flatter and cajole, and had passed through all these phases with calm resolution. The last of the four Norwegian delegates, Benjamin Vogt, was a relative newcomer to Norwegian politics, even though a leader among Conservatives and a member of an influential family. A lawyer by profession, he was slated for the knotty legal questions involved in the various agreements to be drafted. His several missions to Stockholm and talks with Swedish ministers during the past months qualified him well for his task.

The Swedish delegation was headed by Christian Lundeberg whose limited experience in government did not detract from his powerful position as leader of the Conservatives in the Riksdag. Lundeberg possessed as cool a head as Michelsen and as sound an understanding of the prerequisites of his task at Karlstad. With a businessman's eye he saw the issues clearly and recognized the need for standing firm on the conditions which he had helped frame. Wachtmeister, with whom Lundeberg shared responsibility in the cabinet, was a moderate with excellent experience in government. Determined to find a road to improved relations with the Norwegians, he knew that neither they nor the Swedes must quit the conference table as vanquished or victor. Firmness and clear-minded resolution were his cardinal characteristics and his influence with his colleagues allowed him often to put in a soothing word. Hjalmar Hammarskjöld, like Vogt an expert on international law, was chosen to argue with the Norwegians on the legal aspects of the agreements. Prominent in Swedish politics and governmental circles, and eventually a leading figure in the League, Hammarskjöld bore a name which his son, Dag, was later to make world renowned as Secretary-General of the United Nations. At Karlstad he resisted concessions to the Norwegians, who regarded him as the person most responsible for their failure to attain more favorable conditions. The most controversial and important of the four Swedish delegates was the Liberal Karl Staaff. He had been reluctantly admitted to the cabinet because of the need for Liberal support. Distrusted because of his advocacy of a mild policy toward the Norwegians, he had, through conversations over the past month, come to an understanding of the need for determination. His lawyer-mind grasped the elements of a dispute quickly and he often summarized an hour or more of debate in succinct phrases. He possessed power in Swedish politics, and neither his colleagues nor the Norwegians wished to make an enemy of him. An enigma to the Norwegians for his willingness to listen during July and August, he proved to be the hidden obstacle upon which their hopes for concessions floundered. Staaff, more than any other member of the Swedish delegation, was the first Norwegian target and, when he refused to yield, they turned their sarcasms upon him. Yet, through it all, he maintained equilibrium even if his sense of humor sometimes failed him.

These delegates had been preceded at Karlstad by fifty to sixty correspondents from Scandinavia and foreign countries. Hugh Blakiston of the *London Times*; Franz Jessen, free-lance writer with the Danish *Politiken*, and his colleague, the historian and professor, Aage Friis; representatives of the German, French, and British news services; and members of the Associated Press came prepared to report the conference to the world. But these journalists found themselves thwarted by the stringent secrecy surrounding the conference. They consumed as much space as they could on Karlstad's quaint scenic beauties, impressions picked up at the hotel, press comments from Norway and Sweden, and other trivia. By September 4 most of the correspondents left Karlstad for Scandinavian tours or the trip home. Only the Norwegian and Swedish reporters stayed to the end. Their papers, failing to make headlines with conference news, amplified reports of troop movements, mobilization, and spy stories, to the annoyance of the delegates, who read every news item relating to the work of the conference.

The conditions put before the Norwegians in July formed the basis for the deliberations of the two delegations. Thus, they faced debate on the Lapp question, the transit on rivers and waterways, a neutral zone, an arbitration treaty and, most important of all, the destruction of the border forts. Separate agreements were to be drafted for each of these questions, which eventually came to be known as the Karlstad Convention. In their first two-hour meeting the delegates settled formalities of the conference and waded directly into the most difficult problem on the agenda. No stenographic report was kept, although digests of the proceedings were exchanged and approved each day. The chairmanship of the sessions rotated daily between the heads of delegations. Michelsen, with good parliamentary and diplomatic sense, nominated Lundeberg as the first presiding officer. Then they started into the main task, with the Swedes insisting upon the destruction of the border forts, especially those monuments of Norwegian resistance—Kongsvinger and Fredrikssten.

In debate the Swedes continuously hammered on the offensive uses to which the forts could be put. They asked for the demolition of only the new portions of Kongsvinger and Fredrikssten, so Michelsen wrote Arctander, acting prime minister in Oslo, but both Ørje and Dingsrud would have to be completely destroyed. Michelsen's cogent rebuttal of Swedish opinions was answered by a general summary by Lundeberg. The Swedes intended to avoid insulting the Norwegians, as could be discerned in their permission for retention of the old sections of the two historic forts which had become symbols of Norwegian nationalism. At the same time the necessity for good relations between the two countries depended upon an open, undefended frontier.[1]

In spite of Hammarskjöld's emphasis upon the benefits of a neutral zone the Norwegian delegates could not be satisfied. Vogt insisted that these forts neither menaced Sweden nor violated international law and added that their destruction would arouse Norwegian opposition. Staaff posed two alternatives: either the neutral zone and no military frontier defenses, or a deepening enmity between the two peoples and the impairment of Scandinavian peace. No servitude on Norway's part was intended in the Swedish demand, the Swedish Liberal continued, for equality and reciprocity were implicit in the neutral zone. But Staaff directed at the Norwegians his chief argument that the removal of the forts would eradicate friction and guarantee future harmony. His strong defense of the Swedish proposals struck a severe blow to Norwegian hopes, for all four delegates expected his support for their side, even though he had clearly informed Vogt in August that he backed this condition to the limit. For a moment the Norwegians remained silent. Then Michelsen embarked upon a long, superfluous summary of the history of Norwegian-Swedish quarrels. The Swedes were both irritated and

[1] Cf. Johannes Hellner, "La conférence de Carlstad d'aôut-septembre 1905," Le Nord, III (1940), 30-32. Hereafter cited: Hellner. Cf. also Hellner's notes in Wåhlstrand, Karlstadkonferensen, 24-86. Hellner was the secretary of the Swedish delegation.

slightly amused by his confusing the past with the dispute on the table before them. Michelsen concluded by repeating the servitude argument and the untenable and unreasonable nature of the Swedish condition. Lundeberg stressed anew the distinction in the proposal between the old and new portions of Kongsvinger and Fredrikssten.[2] Vogt, either to confuse the issue or out of genuine distress, proposed that the European powers be guarantors of the neutral zone, either in lieu of razing the forts, or as a security for Norway if the forts were destroyed. Hammarskjöld, speaking for the Swedish delegation, asked for a chance to study this new proposal.

Berner opened the session on September 2 with a report on the defensive nature of the forts. Unfortunately, Storting debates in 1901 had emphasized the opposite view in the event of military operations against Sweden. No matter how adroitly the Norwegians asserted their claims, the Swedes could stop their arguments with their own words.[3] Stalemated on the fort question, the conference dropped it to take up the less controversial subject of the Lapps.

Both Lundeberg and Michelsen made much of the difficulties in a humanitarian solution of the exceptional problem of the Lapps, their reindeer, and their migrations. Norwegians stressed damages done by migratory Lapps to both forests and crops, but actually much of the discussion revolved around legal aspects of agreements ranging from 1751 to 1905. Michelsen did set forth, however, the unequal and nonreciprocal burden of the Lapp convention on Norway, since she would receive more Lapps than she sent to Sweden. The Swedes left both points pass uncontested. When Michelsen proposed a ten-year agreement, with an arbitration of outstanding problems at its conclusion, some argument ensued over the Riksdag demand for an agreement in perpetuity, but it appeared that a project treaty could easily be drafted.

[2] Emphasis must be placed on this point for Vogt, in his *Indtil 1910*, and contemporary sources and reports insist that the Swedes asked for razing of all sections, whether old or new.

[3] Hellner, 34-40; Wåhlstrand, *Karlstadkonferensen*, 40-41, 107-108.

On Sunday the conference rested. Johannes Hellner, secretary of the Swedish delegation, wrote, however, of his use of much midnight oil in a study of the transit problem, scheduled for Monday. His associates went to the theater and relaxed. On Monday, September 4, agreement on reciprocity in transportation and communication met no obstacles. The conference voted to draft a proposal and, in addition, to delegate Løvland and Hammarskjöld to frame an arbitration treaty. The afternoon session, therefore, dealt with details of both transit and arbitration conventions. The nature of the arbitration agreement caught most of the conference's interest, for Løvland and Vogt wished one unlimited in scope, similar to the Dutch-Danish treaty. That convention exempted no cases from jurisdiction of the arbitration process, not even those of "national interests" or "national sovereignty." Staaff, to the surprise of the Norwegians, argued against such a treaty on the grounds that it risked being treated with disrespect and being ignored in solutions of conflicts. "Vital interests" and "national honor" were the two main categories which the Swedes demanded for reservation as nonarbitral.[4] In two days of informal conversations between Løvland and Hammarskjöld a clearer picture of the proposed arbitration treaty and neutral zone appeared. The penciled notes of Arctander, acting head of the cabinet in Oslo, indicate that "the Swedes finally agreed on the neutral zone, *if each country by itself* would seek great powers' guarantee of its neutrality."[5]

The conference, on Tuesday, passed to the topic of river transport, with Lundeberg reading the main Swedish requirements. The Norwegians raised no objections to a grant of full reciprocity and full access to those streams essential for timbering operations. After only an hour's session the conference adjourned for the day after agreeing to accept in principle a convention on transit. Michelsen's main comment was a compliment to the framer of the proposal for its fairness.

During September 6 and 7 delegates wearied of their burden

[4] Hellner, 42; Wåhlstrand, *Karlstadkonferensen*, 45-51, 129-136; Michelsen to Arctander, September 4, P8A, *UDN*.

[5] Cf. Michelsen to Arctander, September 5, P8A, *UDN*; Wåhlstrand, *Karlstadkonferensen*, 221.

of talk and debate. On these days they returned to the tough and bitter argument on the neutral zone and the forts. Hammarskjöld began with a report on his and Løvland's study of an arbitration agreement, which, he cautioned, was entirely preliminary. Hellner, in his comments on this exchange, points to Hammarskjöld's irritation with Løvland for his many interruptions and equivocations, but the Swedish secretary also noted that tempers of all delegates were short, as if they "had awakened on the wrong ear."[6] The arbitration treaty suited both Norwegian and Swedish delegates, even if they argued mildly on its form and on the Swedish request for reservations on "vital interests."

But their assault on the fort issue threw them immediately into deep difficulties. Michelsen started by dogmatically insisting that Norway would not accept the razing of Kongsvinger and Fredrikssten. For Ørje and Dingsrud, a neutral zone would be enough compensation, if it were completely neutral; "a zone which," in Michelsen's words, "could not be used as a theater of war operations or as an assembly point for military operations, and in which there must not be troops or [military] depots." Lundeberg, while offering no complaint on the principle of the neutral zone, did object to the unreserved nature of Michelsen's proposal and stubbornly refused to discuss a great-power guarantee. Either country, he said, could later secure its own assurances, but the Swedish government sought to prevent European intervention. He asked for a memorandum of the Norwegian proposal. A long, involved, and repetitious dispute on the forts ensued. Michelsen, Hellner says, was magnificent in his oratory, his ability to clarify details of the questions, and his moderation. In the afternoon session, Lundeberg, having been handed a Norwegian memorandum, stated that it lacked detail and expressed the unanimous dissent of the Swedish delegation of any form of great power guarantee or international sponsorship.[7]

September 7 was the most crucial day in the first half of the conference. The two delegations stood, as one writer expressed

6 Wåhlstrand, *Karlstadkonferensen*, 54.
7 Hellner, 43-44.

it, face to face as mountain to mountain. A Norwegian memorandum on the forts conceded much: inclusion of Kongsvinger and Dingsrud in the neutral zone; razing of Ørje and the forts of Hjelmenkollen; preservation of Fredrikssten, Gyldenløve, and Overbjerget; an international guarantee of the neutral zone by each state after the conference. These concessions had to be approved by the Storting. After some preliminary remarks Lundeberg requested an adjournment and, after a long conference with his colleagues, asked to see Michelsen. Evidently nothing was gained by their talks and at four o'clock the Norwegians received a Swedish statement which insisted on destruction of the forts, and demanded an acceptance by Saturday, September 9. Michelsen described it[8] as a twenty-four hour ultimatum with further "dramatic scenes and spectacles" to follow.

The Swedish note was indeed an ultimatum. It placed the Norwegian delegation in the embarrassing position of either acceptance or rejection without allowing them to soften its harsh demands. In addition the note proposed an adjournment only until Saturday. Michelsen countered with a request for the interval's extension to a week in order to consult Storting and cabinet members. Apparently Lundeberg had intended conferences only with ministerial colleagues and might have wished to exclude the Storting where he thought the Norwegian stand on the forts would be supported. Michelsen and Lundeberg both became excited and the Swedish prime minister, somewhat angrily, pushed his personal views. Both delegates conferred with their colleagues and returned for a brief private conference. Lundeberg then repeated his ultimatum demanding a two-day recess and an immediate answer.

The Norwegian delegation could not act unless the Storting could participate in discussions during the recess. Although Lundeberg could hardly have been expected to realize it, this Storting meeting was vital to the success of the Karlstad negotiations. Without it the Norwegian cabinet could only refuse to act. Fortunately Michelsen persuaded Lundeberg to yield and

8 Michelsen to Arctander, P8A, *UDN*; Wåhlstrand, *Karlstadkonferensen*, 221.

he won a longer adjournment to September 13. Michelsen did promise, on behalf of his colleagues and his government, to refrain from mobilization of the Norwegian army. Lundeberg's fears of military preparations originated, so Michelsen said, in the recent rotation of three battalions on frontier duty. The last moments of the session were friendly, with Lundeberg commenting on his respect for the Norwegian delegates and on his trust in their maintenance of the greatest secrecy. Whether or not he had in mind the Storting may be doubted; he obviously had in mind other "leaks" which might involve the Norwegian public or foreign powers. The two delegations left that evening for their respective capitals, after handing the press a brief and frustrating communiqué on the need for conferences with colleagues and cabinets.[9]

The adjournment from September 7 to 13 caused much public comment. Speculation centered on the vexatious problem of the forts and their destruction. The two delegations had solved most of the other negotiable conditions either in principle or in actuality and the great obstacle was whether the Swedes would insist on their earlier stand on the forts. The need for concessions was most crucial, for if neither side yielded, the conference could only be disbanded. Both Norwegian and Swedish papers said a great deal on the recess. *Nya Dagligt Allehanda*, like other Swedish papers, carried maps of the frontier with the Norwegian forts and the proposed neutral zone clearly marked. The Swedish press naturally blamed the Norwegians for disruption of negotiations and taunted them with having to consult their colleagues and the Storting. *Vårt Land* (September 9) even suggested that the Norwegians might refuse to resume negotiations.

During those days when Norwegian delegates at Karlstad sought a settlement with Sweden the cabinet in Oslo faced a troublesome interpellation from Konow on two questions. What was the truth in the rumors of Swedish mobilization? What ac-

[9] Wåhlstrand, *Karlstadkonferensen*, 60-65, 157-163, 386-390; Michelsen to Arctander, September 7, P8A, *UDN*. The historical argument over responsibility for adjournment hardly needs comment after Wåhlstrand's publication of the documents, but it might be noted that the Swedes came prepared to adjourn and first presented the suggestion to the conference.

tion, if any, had been taken by the minister of defense to prepare for an attack? In his speech Konow estimated the number of Swedish troops at sixty to eighty thousand and reminded his audience of the possibility of an invasion. The government's case, presented by one of the Storting presidents, deplored the rumors and maintained that the cabinet knew best what course to take. Defense Minister Olssøn enigmatically proclaimed that the government knew of Swedish military operations and measures had been taken "that the situation demanded." Konow's reply, "That was certainly a very short answer," was an attempt to bait Olssøn, but neither he nor Castberg could goad the minister into revealing more.[10] Olssøn's colleagues refrained from defending him in order to stifle debate and to magnify the trivial nature of the interpellation.[11]

Privately, however, Olssøn's anxiety over military imbalance increased, but he feigned an outward calm to reassure his colleagues. Although troop movements from the west of Norway to reinforce the frontier forts were planned, these soldiers could not be moved without causing a decline in Norwegian morale and arousing Swedish fears. Even the few troops sent to the border nearly caused Lundeberg to precipitate a crisis on September 7 and motivated his demand for a promise from Michelsen not to mobilize further Norwegian units.[12] Both Bothner and Arctander, after vague remarks from Olssøn, came close to panic. In desperation Arctander ordered a cabinet meeting to discuss the movement of western troops and depots eastward. They were saved from rash action by Michelsen's telegram from Karlstad informing them of the recess.

In Sweden the public and government officials remained quiet and undisturbed. The cabinet held daily meetings, discussed the latest news, and waded through departmental routine as if

---

[10] *Hemmelige møter*, 275-287.
[11] Wåhlstrand, *Karlstadkonferensen*, 379-380, 424-425.
[12] Wåhlstrand, *Karlstadkonferensen*, 389-390, 424, 426, 434-435. Michelsen's statement to Lundeberg that three battalions were being rotated was not truthful, but what could he do when Lundeberg was so angry? The three battalions were additions to forces already at the front, not replacements; Olssøn reported later in September after partial mobilization that Norwegian forces totaled only 22,563, including the navy.

Karlstad were an ordinary matter.[13] Branting's repetition of his threat of a general strike if the Swedish army mobilized caused some caustic comments and slightly reassured the Norwegian cabinet.[14] Swedish newspapers stayed relatively quiet. *Vårt Land* by its grumbling explained why: secrecy at Karlstad. *Svenska Dagbladet* (September 3) warned the Norwegians against holding foolish expectations from deliberations at Karlstad and added the peculiar suggestion that, naturally, with the road to Oslo opened by razing the forts, Norwegians would realize the sincerity of Sweden's love of peace.

These forts composed the hard problem for the Swedish delegation in its report to the several ministerial meetings during the five days of recess. Lundeberg's résumé to the cabinet virtually duplicated the summary that Michelsen was simultaneously giving his colleagues in Oslo. Lundeberg pointed out the wide range of agreement between the delegations and he praised the Norwegians for their ability and friendliness. The main problems, Lundeberg continued, were the neutral zone and the forts, where only a minimum of understanding had been attained and about which both cabinet and delegates agreed there should be no compromise. The Swedes had rejected a Norwegian proposal permitting Kongsvinger to be outside the neutral zone. After Lundeberg's report the cabinet posed and discussed a hypothetical war with Norway, but they arrived at the unanimous conclusion that peace was the better solution.[15] On the following day both Tingsten and Lundeberg showed signs of wavering. Tingsten would permit Kongsvinger to be outside the neutral

[13] Lindman, acting foreign minister in Wachtmeister's absence, relayed two minor bits of information to Karlstad, one on the forts which the Swedish general staff had prepared, and the other denying rumors of Norwegian purchases of naval vessels. The latter, as Lindman expressed it, was a "witch hunt." Lindman Mss., RAS. The staff report was a map with two alternative lines for the neutral zone. One line swung west to incorporate Kongsvinger, the other did not. Amusingly, the map, marked secret, was one published by Aschehoug in Oslo, available to anyone. Cf. Hellner's report in Wåhlstrand, *Karlstadkonferensen*, 56; also Lundeberg Mss., Uppsala University Library.

[14] Vilhelm Bjerknes, who passed this information to Hagerup Bull, had seen Lindhagen, Branting, and De Geer in Stockholm and had discussed the crisis fully with them. Cf. Hagerup Bull in Wåhlstrand, *op. cit.*, 426.

[15] Cf. Lindman Mss., RAS.

zone if its guns were turned away from Sweden, and Lundeberg would agree if Norway promised not to extend or improve its installations. Tingsten's study of the forts, which depreciated their military value, signaled the beginning of a Swedish retreat.[16]

On September 10 the ministers began to make real decisions for the delegates soon to return to Karlstad. Biesèrt, Widén, Alfred Petersson, and Staaff asked for the exclusion of Kongsvinger from the neutral zone if a crisis at Karlstad forced Swedish delegates to choose between its inclusion or war. Wachtmeister saw no value in war for Sweden in such an instance. The crown prince, who had favored peace from the first, suggested to the king that Kongsvinger, without its new installations, be left outside the neutral zone, but Oscar wished the forts completely destroyed. The cabinet meeting on September 12, before the return of the delegation to Karlstad, showed in summary that Sweden's military position could not be better[17] and that the country could be capable of launching an offensive war against Norway if exigencies at Karlstad demanded it. The cabinet, even at the last, remained divided on the fort question. As a result the delegates took no instructions with them to Karlstad. Lundeberg, Hammarskjöld, Lindman, Tingsten, and Albert Petersson favored razing all the forts except the old portions of Fredrikssten and Kongsvinger. Wachtmeister, Staaff, Biesèrt, Widén, and Alfred Petersson insisted on a compromise rather than stranding negotiations on the inclusion of Kongsvinger.[18]

Lacking knowledge of the choices or alternatives the Swedes were working out, the Norwegian delegates spent five arduous days. Michelsen summoned the cabinet for a session on September 8 and his long narrative gave his colleagues a fair and complete report.[19] He complimented the Swedes on their sincere de-

[16] Wåhlstrand, *Karlstadkonferensen*, 308-314, 359-372.

[17] Both Tingsten and Lindman reported on the excellent morale and fitness of the army and navy. Forty-two ships of the fleet lay at Strömstad not far from the Norwegian border ready to initiate a blockade of Norway or to fight.

[18] Wåhlstrand, *Karlstadkonferensen*, 312-314.

[19] Wåhlstrand, *op. cit.*, 386-390, 431-437.

sire for peace, but remarked that they wished their conditions fulfilled. The forts presented the major obstacle, for the Swedes saw only their offensive purpose. Other questions offered no difficulties. Study of an arbitration convention by Hammarskjöld and Løvland showed no major differences of opinion, although the Swedes stubbornly refused to permit European guarantees or intervention in Scandinavian affairs. The prime minister stressed the sincerity and seriousness of purpose of both delegations, despite the Swedish ultimatum on the last day before adjournment. Michelsen spoke of his certainty of hidden influences at work, for Wachtmeister, who stood close to the crown prince, had suddenly turned stubborn on September 7. Swedish firmness and tenacity, Michelsen concluded, forced Norway to accept Swedish conditions, for Norwegian troops could not be mobilized. In addition, he recommended adjournment of the Storting to prevent incidents when negotiations were resumed. He promised to confer with the German consul general in Oslo and to send Nansen to Copenhagen to secure great power intervention at Stockholm. At the same time the prime minister expressed doubts of any extensive changes in Swedish policy.

Since the military position of Norway demanded close attention in view of the choice of compromise or defiance on the razing of the forts, the cabinet spent much time with the military committee and generals. A majority in the committee gave the forts small place in Norwegian defensive strategy, but a schism developed within the general staff. In comparing the Norwegian and Swedish military picture, Commanding General Ole Hansson left no doubt of the outcome of war by his estimate of 28,000 Norwegian troops against a Swedish force of 80,000, and Olssøn corroborated both his figures and predictions of disaster. When the generals departed, the cabinet agreed to the demolition of the forts if accompanied by an arbitration treaty.[20]

The spirit of gloom deepened further in the cabinet session of September 11 which the Storting presidents attended. In a mood of despair a carte blanche was extended the delegates on condition that an arbitration treaty and a neutral zone would

[20] Wåhlstrand, op. cit., 390-391, 437-438.

become parts of the Karlstad agreements. Due probably to the presence of the Storting presidents, the cabinet agreed on a report to gain parliamentary support and to test its opinion.

Michelsen's speech to the Storting that evening after dinner displayed the prime minister's mastery of oratory and appeal. Sensible, calm, and moderate, he clearly explained the problems of the Karlstad delegates. He permitted himself some signs of pique in comments on Staaff's nervousness and the lack of influence of his party in Sweden. As Michelsen characterized it: "those that threaten and swing knives are not as dangerous as those [Liberals] who stand with knives hidden behind their back ready to strike."[21] An appeal to Staaff for his support on a compulsory and full arbitration treaty had been refused. A neutral zone would not be guaranteed by the powers because of Swedish opposition. But, at the same time, the Swedes had European support. Michelsen did express his confident opinion that they wished no war, even if their Karlstad delegation was hard pressed by public opinion.

The Storting session adjourned at eight o'clock to return at nine. During the interval Castberg and Konow held a hasty meeting in which they agreed to attack the government for its weak compliance with Swedish demands. As an alternative the two leaders would leave the forts standing and add to the arbitration and neutral zone agreements a Norwegian-Swedish defense alliance which would satisfy all but the Swedish extremists. In his speech Castberg charged that the Swedes hypocritically advocated peace because their demand on razing the forts showed them to be contemplating an attack on Norway. Razing the forts would be defense nihilism. Immediate war was preferable to delay or capitulation to Swedish ultimatums. Castberg received his answers from Michelsen who charged him with complete irresponsibility and denied any monopoly of patriotism by any special group or persons. Minister of Defense Olssøn argued his own policies on military preparations and minimized the role of the forts in defense strategy. Løvland's speech, supporting the government, was an admirable and capable summary

21 Castberg, *Dagbøker*, I, 477.

of its stand. He favored razing the forts and seeking compensation and security in the arbitration treaty and neutral zone. Otherwise, Sweden would refuse to recognize Norway, and the European powers would merely support that position. That would leave Sweden entirely free to wage war against Norway. If the Storting wished to break off negotiations at Karlstad, the delegates must be given a clear mandate and everyone must accept the consequences. Løvland's speech could not be effectively answered, unless Konow and Castberg wanted to recommend war.

After a pause, and as if in answer to that alternative implied by Konow and Castberg, Olssøn summarized Norwegian defenses. He spared his listeners no illusions on the gloomy military picture. Although his pessimism allowed the two radicals to attack the government for its lack of decision and foresight, in the end Olssøn emphasized, without saying so, the need for abandonment of the forts and for a realistic approach. Long past midnight the debate was concluded by Michelsen, who said that he wanted no mandate from the Storting but only its opinion. The government's full powers as previously granted gave them authority to go as far as was defensible. To Konow's question whether an arbitration treaty would precede recognition of Norway, Michelsen answered that none of the forts would be razed until acceptance of both an arbitration convention and a neutral zone. At two o'clock in the morning the weary men left the Storting building, depressed and confused by what they had heard and by their responsibilities. As for the ministers, especially the four Karlstad delegates, their office never weighed so heavily upon their shoulders. In a spirit of resignation they returned the next day to resume negotiations with Sweden.[22]

As Michelsen promised his colleagues, he energetically sought foreign intervention. To Wedel he telegraphed:[23]

Buy Colonel Nissen's map of eastern Norway. Show Denmark's foreign minister, together with the German and English ministers, our frontier forts, which are all small obstruction forts.

22 On the Storting meeting, which was not reported, see Hagerup, *Dagbok*, 182-187, as the best account.
23 Wedel, *1905*, 218-220.

The Swedes desire them all razed; we agree to raze Hjelm-kolden and Veden, together with Fredrikshald, Ørje, and possibly Dingsrud at Urskog, together with the establishment of a neutral zone entirely free in war or peace of 10 km. breadth in each kingdom. But we hold to Kongsvinger and Fredriks-sten, especially for their historic memories. Because of disagreement on these two forts it appears as if the negotiations will be disrupted, while there is hope for the solution of other problems. Ascertain how our standpoint is considered by the named persons and by their governments. Nansen comes tomorrow evening with further oral instructions.

Wedel immediately conferred with Raben, Prince Reuss, German chargé d'affaires, and Johnstone, and the four agreed that Norway had done enough. Nansen, when he arrived, added information on the threatening presence of 80,000 Swedish troops on the frontier and the Swedish "ultimatum" on the forts. Raben volunteered the suggestion that Germany, Russia, and England present a *démarche* at Stockholm to relieve pressure at Karl-stad.[24] At the British Foreign Office Johnstone's imploring note received critical and skeptical study. Sir Thomas Sanderson, British Under Secretary, understood the Norwegian plea as an effort to secure concessions through foreign intervention. Rodd wrote from Stockholm that the Swedes were not insisting upon the razing of the old portions of Kongsvinger and Fredrikssten, as the foreign press and Norwegians reported. Through an exchange of telegrams Bülow received similar intelligence and the German chancellor instructed representatives to stand aloof, while the consul general at Oslo was told to inform the Norwegian government of Germany's continued neutrality.[25]

[24] Cf. Wedel, *1905*, 218-219; Reuss to Bülow (telegram), September 9, *Aus. Amt*, 2956, *UDN; Fridtjof Nansen Dagbok fra 1905*, ed. Jacob S. Worm-Müller (Oslo, 1955), 10-13. Hereafter cited: *Nansen.*

[25] Richtofen to Bülow, September 9; Schoen to Bülow, September 11; Richtofen to Bülow, September 11, *Aus. Amt*, 2956, *UDN; Aus. Amt* to Faber du Faur, September 11, *ibid.*, Wåhlstrand, *Karlstadkonferensen*, 398-400, 440-442; *Nansen*, 32-47. Conrad Mohr, a personal friend of the Kaiser, went immediately to Germany, but Michelsen's fears of no results were confirmed by Mohr's letter to the Norwegian prime minister.

The Norwegian diplomacy of securing foreign pressure on the Swedes did, however, have some success. On September 13 the Russian and French ministers, probably after consultation with each other and not with their governments, presented a *démarche* stating their countries' interests in a peaceful and speedy solution of the Scandinavian crisis. Interesting speculation revolves around the hypothetical question of whether the Norwegian misstatement on the razing of the old portions of Kongsvinger and Fredrikssten had any effect in producing the Franco-Russian note.

By coincidence this note arrived as the conference reopened on September 13. Unaware of the *démarche*, the conferees immediately struck at the knotty fort question. The Norwegians repeated their requests, but made no progress over the refusal of the Swedes to budge from their position. In the midst of this stalemate came both the news of the Franco-Russian note in Stockholm[26] and copies of *Dagbladet* and *Intelligenssedler* in which appeared two articles by Castberg and Konow. The papers from Norway, which the Swedish delegation carefully read each day, produced a sensation among the four Norwegian delegates and aroused Swedish anger. Details in the articles, so Michelsen telegraphed Oslo, revealed Storting opinion as favoring acceptance of Swedish demands and, therefore, reduced Norwegian bargaining power, or, as Michelsen phrased it, "cut the ground from beneath their feet." The Swedes objected because the articles clearly showed that the promises of secrecy, exchanged on September 7, had been broken. Added to the astonishing news of the *démarche*, which likewise revealed Norwegian "perfidy"

[26] Lindman's forwarding of the notes was a matter of routine, for he discounted them and assumed that the Swedish delegation would do likewise. The Norwegian representatives, including Nansen and Wedel, assumed that the Swedish government would take a serious attitude toward the notes. The French minister, so Gyldenstolpe wrote Lindman, had no instructions from Paris and the French foreign minister was as much in the dark on the reasons for his action as were the Swedes. September 14, 4A15, *UDS*. The cabinet in Stockholm briefly considered the notes, but did nothing. Gustaf, Lindman, Oscar II, and the others knew that England would not intervene and that negotiations at Karlstad would have to proceed on the basis of razing the forts. Cf. Lindman's notes, Lindman Mss., RAS. Cf. Åkerman's notes in Wåhlstrand, *Karlstadkonferensen*, 189, which give the bitter reaction of the Swedish delegates to the *démarche*.

in appealing to the powers, the articles produced far more response than they warranted. But Lundeberg, and every member of the Swedish delegation, had cautioned the Norwegians not to appeal to the powers for intervention in Scandinavian affairs and had asked full secrecy. Any lingering sympathy for Norwegian hardships vanished completely. In Oslo a telegram from Michelsen was read to a special meeting of the Storting, reprimanding Konow and Castberg for their indiscretion, but the two were quite unrepentant.[27]

Of more consequence than these distresses at Karlstad were the mobilization orders which the Norwegian cabinet in Oslo blundered into giving. Frightened by rumors of Swedish troop concentrations and by a definite growth in their military strength due to continuous influx of recruits, Olssøn finally demanded partial Norwegian mobilization. He wished especially the strengthening of eastern defense and the movement of supply depots to Drammen where they could be reached by the navy without leaving the Oslo fjord. Arctander drafted and sent a telegram to Michelsen, noting the mobilization of the Telemark, Valders, and Hallingdal battalions and six defense, or home guard, units and the orders given the fleet to stand to sea and to guard the mouth of the Oslo fjord. Later Arctander talked with Michelsen on the phone and was told that responsibility for mobilization rested upon the cabinet alone.[28] The cabinet, with the exception of Gunnar Knudsen, favored mobilization; on the movement of the depots only Vinje dissented. Troops began to move on September 14 and somewhat calmed cabinet fears.

At Karlstad anything but quiet resulted when the Swedes heard

[27] Michelsen to Arctander, September 14, P8A, *UDN*; Bothner, *op.cit.*, September 14; Castberg, *Dagbøker*, I, 487-488; *Hemmelige møter*, 317. Castberg in his diary, and in a small book which was published later in Norway, insisted that the information in the two articles could not have damaged the Norwegian case. The documents in Wåhlstrand seem to justify his opinion, for the Norwegians had given way prior to the arrival of the papers in Karlstad. For Michelsen, however, their action was at least a means by which they could be blamed and some responsibility for Norwegian failure at Karlstad placed on their shoulders. Cf. Castberg, *Dagbøker*, I, 487-488; *Om begivenhederne i 1905* (Oslo, 1906), 29-30.

[28] Cf. Arctander's draft telegram in his Mss., University Library, Oslo; Wåhlstrand, *Karlstadkonferensen*, 400-403, 442-445.

rumors, and then confirmation, of Norwegian mobilization. The Norwegians found themselves caught in an awkward moment just as they were retreating on the fort issue. Lundeberg immediately demanded a private conference with Michelsen and in a stormy exchange of words they came near to breaking off negotiations.[29] In a resultant series of telephone calls by Lundeberg to Stockholm, and conversations with Lindman, Tingsten, the crown prince, and others, he demanded full powers and complete freedom in negotiations.[30] In other words, Lundeberg strategically seized the moment of apparent success at Karlstad to stop the Swedish cabinet from rash action against Norwegian mobilization. His vigorous response to opportunity, and to a querulous telegram from Gustaf, greatly modified the tone of a message drafted by the Swedish cabinet in response to his telephone calls. By a compromise, their cable message eventually read in part: "Our confidence in the delegation's circumspection is unchanged. We have not intended to limit [your] freedom to negotiate previously given you." That night (September 16) at twelve-thirty a message from Karlstad stated that the conference had apparently arrived in calm waters.

This byplay of Norwegians and Swedes at Karlstad, the mobilization of troops in Norway, and pressure on the Swedish cabinet seem almost synchronized. Lundeberg's near ultimatum on mobilization forced the Norwegians to retreat faster. His coercion of the Swedish cabinet, while ostensibly a response to their doubts of the delegation's firmness, was in reality designed to bolster a compromise offered by the Swedes at Karlstad to achieve a peaceful solution. Yet Lundeberg's strategy worked successfully both on his colleagues and on the Norwegians.

The Norwegian cabinet's fears were alleviated by news of the changed atmosphere at Karlstad. But its members remained unrepentant over their action in ordering mobilization. Løvland informed Oslo of the satisfactory arrangement of an arbitration treaty and asked government sanction for it, which was readily

[29] Hellner believed war to be imminent at this point, 48-50.
[30] Cf. Berg's notes, Wåhlstrand, *Karlstadkonferensen*, 319-323.

granted. At the same time the cabinet was told that the Swedish delegation accepted Norwegian proposals on the neutral zone. Olssøn subsequently expressed his reassurance and could say that "Swedish recruits would be sent home." Most of the cabinet, including Bothner, who held out the longest, swung to favor demolition of the forts.[31]

The issue of the forts, on which both Norwegians and Swedes yielded, had been stalled on the position of Kongsvinger. The Swedes finally permitted it to remain outside the neutral zone, its old portions still standing, but the new sections razed. The final agreement resembled fundamentally the Swedish original condition, except for the concessions on Kongsvinger and the inclusion of an arbitration treaty. On September 16, at eleven o'clock the two delegations agreed on a communiqué which appeared the following morning in both Norwegian and Swedish papers. "From Karlstad it is officially stated that there is every expectation that the negotiations in the near future would lead to a positive result."[32]

The following seven days were full of strenuous work but few surprises. Separate teams began their labors on the Lapp, transit, and water course conventions which extended over two days.[33] Clarification of details followed: the three languages (French, Norwegian, and Swedish) of the texts, measures for an approval of the agreements, a statement on the Bernadotte candidature, and Oscar's proclamation. A formal statement was drafted on the demolition of the forts and the procedures necessary to achieve it. On September 18 and 19 the delegates worked on agreements and held no formal sessions. However, Michelsen and Lundeberg conferred privately on disposition of military forces and Norwegian mobilization. Tingsten had threatened to resign

[31] Wåhlstrand, *Karlstadkonferensen*, 445-449.

[32] *Verdens Gang*, September 17.

[33] Løvland wired a request to have J. E. Sars, the Norwegian historian, write an article on arbitration which appeared in *Morgenbladet* on September 18. This article, its timing and contents, remains curious, for it appears from the historical context to have been written to prepare the Swedes for modifications in their conditions. Norwegians approved wholeheartedly of an arbitration treaty, including the "vital interests" section over which some difficulty had arisen.

unless Norwegian troop concentrations ceased and mobilization orders were canceled. Michelsen consented to have soldiers, then moving to the front, held at concentration points, but insisted that Lundeberg must order Tingsten to permit no new Swedish troop movements. The two prime ministers further agreed to withdraw troops and to keep them at least 1 kilometer from the border to avoid incidents.[34] The next day an official notice appeared in Norwegian Telegram Bureau dispatches canceling mobilization orders, thus carrying out Michelsen's promise. The bureau suffered some embarrassment, for three days previously, on orders from Oslo, it had denied Swedish reports of Norwegian mobilization.

In Stockholm the news alarmed the cabinet, and Tingsten, the crown prince, and the king now showed surprising signs of belligerency. Berg reported Tingsten to be hoping for a break in negotiations for he preferred an immediate war since the neutral zone was entirely unsatisfactory. Gustaf and Oscar II could hardly be restrained by their advisers from desperate action once the crisis was settled. In the cabinet meeting on September 20, both quieted down through diversion of their attention to discussions on the chances of the Karlstad agreements in the Riksdag.

Likewise, in Karlstad, the session of September 21, proceeding calmly to draft the five conventions, was suddenly thrown into confusion by a Swedish withdrawal of consent to the neutral zone.[35] Apparently, after some discussion, the Swedish delegation became alarmed over the possibility of Riksdag rejection of the arrangement, which differed slightly from specifications. Lundeberg yielded only when Michelsen threatened to take the Norwegian delegation home. Berner and Staaff, paired to work out a solution, returned to the September 7 agreement. By it the zone would be neutral both in war and peace, with the area free of military installations or troops. September 22 was a wearisome gantlet of translation, minute details, and petty debate. But the

---

[34] Cf. Tingsten, *Hågkomster* (Stockholm, 1938) 227-228; Wåhlstrand, *Karlstadkonferensen*, 325, 410; Lindman Mss., RAS.

[35] Cf. Berg's notes, Lundeberg's letter, and Michelsen's telegram, Wåhlstrand, *Karlstadkonferensen*, 229, 328-330.

next day in the final full session of the conference delegates approved the general introduction to the agreements, exchanged protocols of debates and discussions, and complimented each other for various merits displayed in conference sessions. Even at that, the concluding hour was postponed three times until after six o'clock when Lundeberg thanked the Norwegian delegation for their efforts and remarked on the sense of responsibility both delegations had shown in arriving at an agreement. Michelsen, in his answering speech, placed great emphasis on the future and minimized the views of contemporaries:[36]

"It is possible that many of us at present will hear harsh condemnation of what we have done. But over us stands future judgment. The future will recognize that what we have done has been in the interests of peace."

On September 24 both delegations arrived in their respective capitals, tired and distressed of mind, convinced of their accomplishments, but still uncertain as to future approval of the agreements. The Norwegian delegation and cabinet colleagues thankfully praised a settlement not nearly so painful as had been feared. Press comments in Norway and Sweden joined with them in approval of Karlstad. Even *Vårt Land* restrained its objections to mild disagreement with the arbitration treaty and the position of Kongsvinger outside the neutral zone. Liberal papers commended fully the Swedish delegation, and Branting wrote in *Social-Demokraten* that now the whole of Scandinavia could draw a free breath. The Norwegian press reacted in subdued tones, but a few days later Hagerup Bull, speaking of demobilization of troops, expressed Norwegian general sentiment when he wrote delightedly: "This is the way for civilized people to act."

The Karlstad Convention[37] consisted of an introduction and five articles covering an arbitration treaty, the neutral zone, the razing of the forts, the Lapps, and transit and water courses. The main convention left standing the two historic forts of Kongsvinger and Fredrikssten. Today both remain, Fredrikssten

---

[36] Hellner, in Wåhlstrand, *Karlstadkonferensen*, 85-86.
[37] See Heiberg, 647-672, for the formal agreements which were signed on October 26 in Stockholm.

guarding the southern sea approaches to Norway and Kongsvinger on its hill overlooking the railroad into Sweden, as monuments,
not to stubbornness, military prowess, or a victory of Swede over
Norwegian, but to a peace which has now endured more than
a half century.

◇◇◇

CHAPTER XII

THE AFTERMATH OF KARLSTAD

◇◇◇

THE Karlstad Convention was generally hailed with satisfaction in Norway and Sweden. Newspapers printed complete texts of the agreements and a majority of the editorials in Norwegian papers noted the alterations in Swedish conditions, expressing some approval of this evidence of retreat. Some newspapers, for example *Verdens Gang* (September 27 and 28), reprinted long columns of Swedish comment and stressed Norwegian gratification over the completion of the difficult negotiations. Only the agreement on the forts ought to be changed, the paper wrote, but even here the victory of democratic processes over the Swedish "ultras" and their nationalism was a good omen for the future. In Sweden the moderate and Social Democratic press jubilantly praised Karlstad and defended the delegates and government for their policies in the negotiations. That Kongsvinger's walls still stood, *Svenska Dagbladet* and *Stockholms Dagblad* (September 26) stated, did not conflict with the Riksdag conditions. Only the most Conservative and nationalistic papers like *Vårt Land* were offended by the Karlstad Convention.

Individual Norwegians strongly favored the agreements. The minority remained opposed to the razing of the forts, while most Norwegians genuinely hailed the peaceful solution of the crisis. A handful did share Jakob Schøning's reactions upon reading the texts in the offices of *Aftenposten*:[1] "I sat alone. Read and read. I had tears in my eyes and pains in my bosom. *Thus should 7 June end.* Such a defeat should overcome us. It is huckstering our dearest possession. And there arose in me such a deep gratefulness for the higher powers that spared me from being in this government."

The small coterie behind Konow and Castberg sought also to

[1] Schøning, *Dagbøker*, 409.

oppose the ministry. Like Schøning they saw only humiliating defeat in the results of Karlstad and they regarded the government's conduct as a violation of every decent impulse of a "true Norwegian." Their bitterness reverberated in the Special Committee meetings of September 27, 28, and 29, where the ministry, dissenters, and defenders spent hours in reviewing the agreements. At the second session on September 28, Michelsen presented variant aspects of the negotiations and marked the failure of hopes for foreign intervention. "When we went to Karlstad the first time we sought to mobilize Europe as well as we could," he said, but "no great power would take the initiative." During the recess the cabinet tried again, with Denmark's assistance, but direct pressure on Sweden failed and the Kaiser advised that "we must be reasonable and agree to the Swedish conditions."[2]

The Special Committee gave the anti-Karlstad forces ample opportunity for expression of their grievances, but they were unable to present any reasonable alternatives. Their lack of program was so obvious that these opponents of Karlstad were asked to present at least a report incorporating some concrete suggestions for the Storting. The committee's vote on September 29, in which four sided with Castberg and Konow, alarmed some members who looked at the one-third negative vote and forgot the original composition of the committee.

Outside the Storting the anti-Karlstad clique swung into immediate action with protest meetings. Their combination with antimonarchist agitation served to their advantage, but eventually republicanism was saddled with labels of "chauvinism," "war mongers," and other ill-deserved epithets which obscured pacifist and constitutional principles. A *Studentersamfund* meeting on October 1 opened the "great debate" on Karlstad, and speakers at points and places throughout Norway fought to influence the Storting. Such pressure, however, had only a marginal effect and it even appeared that some wavering Storting members swung to the government side. Fears of the consequences if the Karlstad Convention was vetoed brought greater solidarity of opinion

[2] Castberg, *Dagbøker*, I, 499-500.

to it than such intangibles as even national honor or patriotism could have achieved.

The Storting on October 6 began its consideration of government and minority reports on Karlstad.[3] Michelsen's main tactic was to stress the lack of alternatives and the unrealistic maintenance of forts which, according to staff reports, were ineffective. Following his prime minister's strategy, Olssøn laid his emphasis on mobile defenses as a substitute for the forts. The minority, approving only portions of the Karlstad Convention, planned an over-all attack with every one of the six carrying a share of the burden of debate. They urged first the rejection of the entire convention and especially the agreement on the forts. As an alternative they proposed settlement with Sweden on terms of equality and the full recognition of Norway. Even if this program was totally unrealistic, it merited some defense in view of the Liberal support it might gain in Sweden.

Progovernment adherents dominated the first two days of the debate, while anti-Karlstad representatives ineffectually sniped at the ministry. Eventually they had their chance and in well-planned and emotional appeals the six speakers presented full scale arguments against Karlstad. Michelsen's counteroffensive was cogent and reasonable, robbing many subsequent speakers of their most effective arguments. On Monday (September 29) Berner borrowed from Konow-Castberg strategy and heckled them with questions. In the evening Michelsen presented the final government defense of Karlstad so brilliantly that even Castberg admitted his forensic superiority.[4] Debate continued until nearly twelve o'clock that night, and between twelve and two the Storting members voted on Karlstad. The minority could muster but two votes to add to their six from the Special Committee, and the minority's proposition failed by 109 to 8. In final balloting the minority secured only eight more votes, and the government's proposal to accept the Karlstad Convention was approved 101 to 16. The sixteen voting against the government consisted of three moderates, two socialists, and eleven

---

[3] For full report of the debate see *Hemmelige møter*, 296-349.
[4] Castberg, *Dagbøker*, I, 507.

Venstre. Although the minority received applause as they left the Storting, few would agree with Castberg that October 9 was a "black day for Norway." As many have said, posterity proved Karlstad right and historic judgment fully confirmed its accomplishments.

The closing moments of the union's life rested in Swedish hands. Their treatment of the Karlstad Convention differed greatly from that of the Norwegians. The First Chamber spent brief time on it, with the "ultras" split on rejection; their leading member, Åkerhielm, defended both Karlstad and the ministry in its negotiations. The debate was tinged more with a sense of regret than with bitterness. The final vote unanimously favored acceptance of the Karlstad Convention. The Second Chamber did not debate and voted unanimous affirmation by voice. In quiet and calm the Riksdag cut union ties, and, as *Nya Dagligt Allehanda* wrote, October 13 would remain in Swedish history as that day when no voice was raised in the union's defense. Branting wrote in *Social-Demokraten* (October 14) that "the country draws a sigh of relief. Finally after this stormy summer is *peace* in port." On October 16 the Riksdag approved abrogation of the *Riksakt* and empowered the king to recognize Norway as an independent nation. The king's proclamation of abdication on October 27 went almost unnoticed. *Verdens Gang* and *Aftenposten* printed it, with comments on the bitterness shown in Oscar's last words as union king. The conclusion of the ninety-one year old union was not even an anticlimax, for the corpse was buried without mourners.

As for the Norwegians, they paid scant attention to Swedish actions, for debate on a form of government engrossed their interest. The lull during Karlstad in the diplomatic activity in behalf of the candidature of Prince Carl was broken by a government note to the Storting proposing an invitation to him and a constitutional monarchy for Norway. This debate on a form of government proceeded, as had the wrangling over Karlstad, into an open, public dispute in press and on platform. *Verdens Gang*, *Aftenposten*, and Conservative newspapers led the attack on republicans and defended monarchy. Only the Social Democratic papers, and some local *Venstre* organs, favored republicanism. The cabinet's choice was narrowed to the question of how soon and by what method monarchy could be inconspicuously installed. Both ministers and Storting members exaggerated reports of the spread of republicanism throughout the country. In the cabinet Gunnar Knudsen let his republican sentiments be known and refused to be convinced by Bothner's persuasive talk about a plebiscite. Bothner, after Knudsen's approval, went to Løvland to support a plebiscite, arguing that "otherwise the crown will be a crown of thorns."[5] But Michelsen answered Bothner in a noncommittal fashion and the cabinet did not discuss it. The only positive result was a statement that neither government nor country was committed to accept Prince Carl.[6]

The Scandinavian press, which hitherto phrased news items cautiously, began to remove its guards. Swedish Conservative papers accused the Danes of "playing fast and loose with Sweden" during the summer by promising a Danish prince for the Norwegian throne. *Politiken*, a Danish liberal paper, cautioned on a need for popular support for Prince Carl within Norway lest he should be a party king. The Danish historian and journalist, Aage Friis, asked Konow to sound the Norwegian government and Storting on a plebiscite. Konow, a bad choice for Friis since he was committed to republicanism, consulted no one before answering, "Cleared."[7] Schøning in articles in *Samtiden* and *Aftenposten* also requested a plebiscite, while republicans in the Storting began maneuvers to force before parliament constitutional amendments which meant an appeal to the people. The moderate and Conservative press opposed these republican efforts, and *Verdens Gang* began a personal attack on the Castberg-Konow parliamentary contingent. Nansen also attacked them in a speech defending monarchy before the *Studentersamfund*, which he hoped would launch a popular promonarchy movement similar to his March appeal for separation from Sweden. The Norwegian playwright, Gunnar Heiberg, in speaking to an overflow crowd

---

[5] Bothner, *op.cit.*, October 2.

[6] *Hagerup Bull*, 187.

[7] Konow Mss., University Library, Oslo.

of curious spectators and republicans at Trondheim, said that he would follow Nansen on a polar expedition, but not fishing after a king.

Conservative and moderate papers pleaded for their readers to maintain old Norwegian traditions and *Aftenposten* (October 13) even appealed to the "good, honorable Norwegian workers" who "will never stand for new developments which are in opposition to the Norwegian constitution." An Oslo republican meeting drew nearly 3,000 and one of its speakers, Halvdan Koht, broke with an old mentor, J. E. Sars, to protest his monarchist article in *Verdens Gang*. *Aftenposten* spiced its defense of monarchy with pictures of Prince Carl, Maud, and their young son, but unwisely reported Sweden to be making strenuous efforts for the election of Carl because of fear of a republic. *Verdens Gang* attacked a plebiscite because it would end all chances of internal peace or amity with neighbor countries. "What kind of republic do the Norwegian advocates want," asked its editor, "a type like that of the Swiss Confederation, or the American union?" If they wished the American variety, "the cost of presidential elections would be prohibitive and corruption on a grand scale would accompany it."[8] Socialist papers carried daily headlines, advertisements, and columns of articles beseeching workers and their friends to support a republic and reminding old republicans like Bjørnson, Sars, Løvland, Berner, and others of their betrayal of principle in supporting monarchism. At the height of the campaign *Social-Demokraten* threatened a crown of thorns for a king if he were forced upon the Norwegian people. Republicans mainly sought to force a plebiscite which, if a large enough minority favored republicanism, might eventuate in blocking election of a king.[9]

This noisy agitation extended even to the *Venstre* party. Castberg forced Berner to call a party caucus to discuss the constitutional question and there the party split on the question of republic or monarchy but voted for a plebiscite. At the same time, a conference of Storting presidents and cabinet officers posed

8 *Verdens Gang*, October 19, 20, 23.
9 *Social-Demokraten*, October 18, 19, 20, 21, 23, 26, 27.

two alternatives: immediate election by the Storting, or a plebiscite. Løvland, an old republican and *Venstre*, altered his principles and argued against a plebiscite, claiming that it would dis-
turb Norway's foreign relations and would make any occupant
of the throne uneasy. Those present preferred an immediate election by the Storting. Michelsen wished a plebiscite, but only on
the election of Prince Carl, and not on the choice of republic
or monarchy. Thus the majority opinion of the cabinet, as of
October 13, favored an immediate Storting election of Prince
Carl, but varied on procedures.[10] Three days later Michelsen
promised a *Venstre* meeting that a plebiscite would be held if
there were a sizable division among the people.[11] Cabinet ministers, alarmed by the agitation, insisted on a large Storting majority if they were to proceed and its *Venstre* members requested
action only if a hundred or more in parliament favored an immediate election.

With the cabinet in a quandary, Michelsen called for a secret
session of the Storting to report on the throne question.[12] His
opening speech told with a certain frankness of the summer's
negotiations which, he insisted, bound neither government nor
Storting. Naturally the radicals condemned Michelsen and the
cabinet for their policy during the summer and for the prime
minister's interpretation that they were not obligated in any
fashion. Konow pointed out that Norway, although under no
obligation to Sweden on the Bernadotte invitation, had made
promises to England and Denmark during negotiations and both
the foreign and home press showed Norway to be pledged and
unable to make a free choice between republic or monarchy. At
the end, tired of the incisive questions of Konow, Egede-Nissen,
Eriksen, and Castberg, Michelsen closed with a sharp refusal: "I
will not continue this debate." Michelsen's main objective had
been gained by that time: to show republican weakness in numbers and to persuade government supporters to follow the ministry once again.

[10] *Hagerup Bull*, 196, and Bothner *op. cit.*, October 13.
[11] Castberg, *Dagbøker*, I, 509.
[12] *Hemmelige møter*, 350-378.

Members of the cabinet moved slowly toward an immediate election of Prince Carl. Bothner partially abandoned his request for a plebiscite and, after a conference with Michelsen, Gunnar Knudsen promised not to cause a ministerial crisis over his republican sentiments. On October 19 and 20, by an exchange of telegrams and letters with Danish leaders, the cabinet learned that the plebiscite problem must go directly to Prince Carl. They also learned that the Danish government feared republican agitation, not for its effects on the selection of Prince Carl, but because of postelection difficulties which agitation would make for him. As a result the cabinet decided to request Storting for full powers for negotiations with Prince Carl. In that decision Michelsen's authority was used to its utmost.[13]

In Copenhagen Prince Carl, pushed firmly along by the Norwegian debate and press comments, moved toward requesting a plebiscite. Nansen's arrival helped to resolve the prince's doubts.[14] In a conference with Nansen, Wedel, and others, Carl argued for a plebiscite because this could be a means of procuring an idea of the wishes of the Norwegian people. But he did agree, after persuasion by Raben and Nansen, to land in Norway if a plebiscite gave him only a slim majority, even one vote. In Oslo the "one vote" was changed to "weak majority," which pleased the more cautious members of the cabinet. Nansen urged Carl to change his mind but failed completely. On October 23 Carl made his acceptance of the throne conditional on a plebiscite. Confirmation of his decision with its reservation eventually allowed the Norwegians to proceed.

These details reached the cabinet on October 23 through Michelsen. By the prime minister's plan, the Storting would grant the cabinet full powers for negotiations with Prince Carl and, upon his acceptance of the throne, it would elect him as king. The plebiscite would be concerned only with approval or dissent on the Storting action. The three Storting presidents and the

13 Cf. *Hagerup Bull*, 200-203.
14 Cf. Bothner, *op. cit.*, October 22 and Nansen, 126-134; Wedel, *1905*, 251-254, especially the last page where Wedel notes his advice to Prince Carl to request the plebiscite.

cabinet, with Gunnar Knudsen absent, gave unanimous consent to Michelsen's plan.[15] On October 25 a secret session of the Storting after debating this proposal granted its consent for negotiations and a plebiscite. A ten-man committee then drafted the plebiscite terms as both a government and Storting resolution.[16] Konow's parliamentary maneuver to postpone constitutional changes until the next year failed by an overwhelming majority. Desirous of an immediate election of Prince Carl, the Conservatives frowned on both the ministerial and Konow's courses of action. A *Venstre* meeting also consented, but showed no great pleasure in the government proposition, although the radicals kept quiet. Their silence was partially explained by their "victory over undemocratic measures" in forcing a popular vote and by the news that the Danish Rigsdag, royal family, and people wished a plebiscite.[17] They wished also to preserve their ammunition for the battle against the "real culprits"—Michelsen and the cabinet.

These radicals found their chance in the three-day debate on the future type of government for Norway which opened on October 28. This oratorical display ranks with the debate on the Karlstad Convention as the most hard-fought session of the year. Still smarting from defeat on Karlstad, Konow questioned the whole fabric of the ministry's policies. The constitutional grounds for action, he declaimed, were questionable and should be carefully examined only after delay and minute study. The so-called "good connections," of which cabinet members boasted, were in reality merely "secret treaties" and "secret relations" in violation of the Storting's powers. In his answer Løvland empha-

[15] It is this meeting which allows Hagerup Bull and Worm-Müller to state that the cabinet unanimously favored a plebiscite. However, before this meeting, the majority of the cabinet, excluding Bothner and Gunnar Knudsen, wanted an immediate Storting election and only these two wished a plebiscite. Cf. E. Hagerup Bull, "Fra 1905," *Samtiden*, XXXVII (1926), 539-542; Jakob S. Worm-Müller, "1905," *Samtiden*, XLII (1931), 159. Note also the latter's chapter, "Prins Carl blir konge i Norge" in *Haakon 7*, 120. Cf. *Hagerup Bull*, 205-206.

[16] *Hemmelige møter*, 379-406.

[17] Castberg, *Dagbøker*, I, 517; Aage Friis to Konow, October 26, Konow Mss., University Library, Oslo.

sized the unchanged nature of the constitution, which the election of a king could not alter in the least. He also tried to intimidate the Storting by pointing out the dangers of Norwegian isolation by the powers if her government chose a republican form of government.

Steadily the debate grew warmer, with personal remarks frequently marring formal address. Carl Berner, himself a *Venstre*, annoyed the radicals by repeating a question asked by *Verdens Gang*: "What kind of republic?" Castberg closed the session with a rough attack on Berner, Arctander, Hagerup, and other monarchists. The main gist of his argument was republicanism's greater democracy and, if monarchy were chosen, the domestic political strife that would follow the thwarting of popular wishes.

Hagerup Bull answered Castberg and the republicans by pointing out flaws in their arguments. Further speeches repeated familiar phrases and reasons for choosing one or another governmental form and, as time for adjournment drew near that evening, members began to drowse and to find pretexts for leaving the floor of the Storting. On the last day, Castberg, the opening speaker, resumed the bitter tone of the first session. Once, after stating that Karl Johan "bore arms against his own country and was banned by his own people," he was asked by the presiding officer to refrain from comments on the Bernadottes. His long speech extended over many diverse points and persons. Resentment against his sarcastic remarks, addressed to "the honorable Excellency the Foreign Minister" and to Arctander and his "polemics," naturally predominated among cabinet members who suffered most from Castberg's sharp tongue. Hagerup Bull, as he later wrote in his diary, thought during the morning that all was lost, for the majority of the Storting appeared unwilling and uncooperative. The cabinet's pessimism extended even to thoughts of resignation and a new government. But votes that night converted these pessimists, for Konow's propositions were defeated by three to one. The ministerial proposal, empowering the cabinet to negotiate with Prince Carl and to arrange a plebiscite, was accepted by a vote of 87 to 29.

The date for the popular vote was set for November 12 and 13.

The first two weeks of the month became a nightmare of meetings and demonstrations for and against monarchy, the election of Prince Carl, and republicanism. Prior to the Storting vote, the moderate and Conservative press disapproved of a plebiscite and now they turned their spite against republicanism which, it was assumed, had won a victory. Gunnar Knudsen's resignation from the cabinet on October 30 increased the effect of the emotional appeal even more. Rumors long preceded the event, but Gunnar Knudsen stuck to his post until acceptance of the government's proposition left him no alternative but resignation if he wished to be honest. After parting with his colleagues, he joined the fight in behalf of republicanism.[18]

Newspapers took a full share in the battle. The republicans had almost no press, except for *Social-Demokraten* and the local papers which carried advertisements of various gatherings. Admission, small though it was, was paid at some republican meetings. On one day seventeen speeches were announced. Castberg spoke ten times in the nine days from November 4 to 12 and his colleagues among the republicans carried even heavier schedules. At Fredrikshald promonarchists turned a Castberg meeting into a riot, and the speakers left by a rear exit under police escort. The Conservative and *Venstre* press accused republicans of a *revanchard* plot against Sweden since their prominent leaders had urged the rejection of the Karlstad Convention. The republicans, for their part, claimed that a large vote against the election of Prince Carl would mean *"We get a republic!"*[19] Out of Michelsen's final speech, delivered at Calmeyergade Bedehus in Oslo, the Swedish press plucked two statements which immediately shocked leaders in Denmark and Sweden. Prince Carl, so Michelsen said, was willing to come to Oslo in August if the Norwegian government had need for him, and, to compound his indiscretion, the prime minister continued with sneers at "the hesitant and backward Swedes." As his first official act, Ernst Günther, the newly-appointed Swedish minister to Norway ar-

---

[18] Cf. *Hagerup Bull*, 212-214, and Arne Björnberg, *Parlamentarismens utveckling i Norge efter 1905* (Uppsala, 1939), 19-20, and footnote.

[19] *Social-Demokraten*, November 11.

riving in Oslo on the same day as Michelsen's speech, protested his tactless remark.

At the plebiscite polls voters contradicted the pessimism of some cabinet members.[20] On Sunday and Monday, November 12 and 13, people flocked to vote as they had in August, without benefit of free rides on the Norwegian Railways. Like August 13 it was a national holiday, with flags flying, meetings, and everyone, in spite of bad weather, visiting and going from one place to another. On November 14 papers and people greeted the results with some feeling of relief. Michelsen's famous remark, "The new work day begins," now became a slogan for the new nation and new monarchy. The final count, not complete for two days, gave virtually the same percentage as the Storting vote on the election of Prince Carl; out of a total of 439,742 eligible voters, 259,563 favored the government proposition and 69,264 cast negative ballots.

Most parties either accepted the verdict calmly or expressed their approval without affronting the vanquished. Castberg wrote in his diary of his pleasure at the number of republicans.[21] *Social-Demokraten* had no complaints, but urged the government to accept liberal and progressive reforms. The party's battle was against capitalism, so the paper said, and if the new monarch stood with capitalism then both must be fought; the worker's defense and weapons lay in their economic power and not in a form of government. Newspapers supporting the monarchy began immediately to report from Copenhagen on all types of social activity of the new monarch and his family.

Swedish opinion on the plebiscite and the election of Prince Carl passed quickly from approval to a sense of indignation. The chief cause of this change was Michelsen's indiscretion in his Calmeyergade speech and other anti-Swedish remarks. Most Swedish editorials and criticism selected Denmark as a new target and spent lengthy columns on descriptions of Danish duplicity

[20] In a pool on the outcome of the election, the cautious Løvland guessed the vote would be 160,000 to 150,000; General Olssøn won with his estimate of 250,000 to 85,000, not far distant from the true vote. *Hagerup Bull*, 220.

[21] Cf. Schøning, *Dagbøker*, 429, and Castberg, *Dagbøker*, I, 519-520.

during the summer. They even sharply criticized Gustaf for his visit to Prince Carl and Princess Maud when he was in Copenhagen. Michelsen, according to *Nya Dagligt Allehanda*, was a *condottiere*, achieving his will by subterfuge, hypocrisy, deception, and ill-advised strategy. *Vårt Land* (November 15) claimed that a sinister Danish-Norwegian conspiracy behind Sweden's back plotted procurement of a Norwegian king even before rejection of the Bernadotte invitation, and credited Swedish alertness with having foiled the scheme. This press debate forced an inquiry by the Swedish foreign office into the circumstances and the truth of Michelsen's statements. To the Swedish minister at Copenhagen, Raben denied the veracity of Michelsen's purported comments, and he said that "Prince Carl . . . has expressed his sharpest disapproval and deep complaint over Michelsen's deceitful utterance. The foreign minister has asked the larger newspapers and Ritzau bureau officially to deny simultaneously."[22] Both Oslo and Copenhagen statements, which somehow seemed to miss confirmation of each other, furnished the Swedish press with an opportunity for acid comments on quotes from Danish and Norwegian papers. *Dagens Nyheter* (November 15) asked if the future of Norway would be like that of Portugal—a tail to the British kite. Even *Social-Demokraten* (November 16) caustically criticized the "king at any price" policy followed by the Norwegian government. The Danish liberal paper, *Politiken* (November 16), blamed Michelsen and hinted at a Danish investigation. The Danish cabinet and Rigsdag did mull over the topic, but decided to let the whole matter die by ignoring it.

The Norwegian government, Storting, and people, already recovered from the political combat on the plebiscite, paid little heed to the press war of Swedish and Danish papers. From November 15 to 25, when Prince Carl arrived in Oslo, the Norwegian press was filled with nationalistic articles on the new monarch, his family, and the traditions of royalty. On November 18 the Storting confirmed the popular mandate by the unanimous election of Prince Carl, who adopted the name Haakon VII

---

[22] Ramel to foreign office (telegram), November 15, 4M1a, *UDS*.

because of its historic traditions. Republicans voted for the new
king and were assisted by Berner who, as Storting president, ruled
that the plebiscite was binding on all parliamentary members.[23]
On November 25 King Haakon arrived in Oslo amidst a great
festivity and jubilation undampened by snow and grey skies. The
first king in over five hundred years now occupied the Norwegian
throne. The royal state reception and formal dinners during the
week formed part of the final drama of 1905—a drama which
officially closed with the coronation of Haakon VII in the cathe-
dral in Trondheim in June, 1906.

The attitudes of the Swedish king and press toward the new
regime showed an acceptance of the situation with good wishes
expressed for Scandinavian cooperation. Oscar's reaction was that
" 'Any upright attempt at good relations between the two countries will always be met with sympathy from my side.' "[24] *Dagens
Nyheter* (November 25) expressed concern over anti-Scandinavian feeling, both in Sweden and in other countries. A commercial treaty with Germany, reducing possibilities for Swedish
trade with either Denmark or Norway, the paper thought non-
sensical. *Verdens Gang's* plea for cooperation was answered by
Svenska Dagbladet with the comment that Sweden awaited the
"outstretched hand [which] we have not yet seen, but if it comes
and without reservation, then we here have learned not to be
late in grasping it."[25] At the same time *Verdens Gang* (December
14) could not help stating that "the Swedish bad humor for the
time is understandable. But they ought to seek to find expression
in forms that are otherwise in agreement with common usage
between two peoples." In Sweden the shift of tone found its
best expression in *Svenska Dagbladet's* columns on December 31:
"For us isolation is now best. In this hard air we should gain will
and strength to be ourselves." But any retreat from Scandinavian
cooperation proved impossible. What did change for a time was
the tempo of Scandinavian collaboration.

The two governments expressed their wish to cooperate, and,

---

[23] Cf. Castberg, *Dagbøker*, I, 520; *Hemmelige møter*, 425-438.
[24] Schøning, *Dagbøker*, 433.
[25] *Verdens Gang*, November 29; *Svenska Dagbladet*, December 1.

officially, Sweden recognized Norway by the appointment of
Ernst Günther as the Swedish minister. Yet when Michelsen telegraphed Staaff, now prime minister, to offer his New Year's
wishes, Swedish Conservatives acidly pointed to this "betrayal
of Swedish honor."[26] During the spring of 1906 Günther anticipated unpleasant reactions to the celebration of June 7, but he
was surprised at its quietness and its conversion into "The Voluntary Child Aid Day." In 1955 on its fiftieth anniversary Norwegian and Swedish prime ministers and kings joined in celebrating their future cooperation and ignoring past troubles. The coronation of Haakon VII in June 1906, also raised a delicate diplomatic puzzle. If any member of the Swedish royal family or official delegate attended, howls of distress would come from
Swedish die-hards. By agreement with Løvland, Günther took a
vacation and let it be publicly known that his absence from
Trondheim was not an insult but a stratagem to avoid embarrassment.

These small indications of pique and discomfort could not
obscure the almost unnoticed arrival of the two countries at
the threshold of integration. More than any other event, the
razing of the frontier forts, completed in August 1906, and certi-
fied by German, Austrian, and Dutch colonels, marked the transi-
tion from hostility to integration of a pluralistic type. Now the
long frontier between the two countries lay open and undefended except for the mountain barrier with its rugged terrain.
This final event of 1905, the first large step in the direction of
deepening and broadening the path to a fuller integration than
had ever existed under the union, symbolized a pledge by the two
peoples of a "no-war" community. It was much easier for them
to proceed with the process of "healing the wounds of 1905" with
these fortifications destroyed, for now peoples in both countries
could feel the absence of threats to peace and security.

Indicative of the new feeling and of the will to implement this
integration was the friendly spirit with which both countries
entered into negotiations for settlement of the disputed boun-

[26] Michelsen to Staaff, Staaff Mss., Uppsala University Library.

dary in the south. The area's numerous islands and inlets made establishment of claims to sovereignty difficult, and, since there was no main channel (*thalweg*) to follow, ordinary rules of international law could not be applied. The region, called Grisbådarne, served as fishing grounds for both countries. Løvland queried Günther about its settlement in October 1906, and asked Benjamin Vogt, the Norwegian minister in Stockholm, to initiate discussions with the Swedish foreign office. No headway was made until September 1907, when Lindman, the Swedish foreign minister, accepted in principle the Norwegian position and arranged a temporary agreement. A convention for arbitration of Grisbådarne was signed in 1908 and a Norwegian, a Swede, and a neutral (J. A. Loef, the Dutch minister of justice) were appointed. Later in the year a decision gave Sweden rights to Grisbådarne. Newspapers in both countries commended the decision and the methods by which it was achieved; apparently no irritation developed from the settlement in favor of Sweden.

Another unsettled problem from Karlstad showed in its solution the trend toward a sense of community. The Lapp question, which even today continues to trouble Norwegian and Swedish foreign offices, became again a topic of negotiations when the Swedes wished to permit Lapp migration earlier than June 15 as prescribed in the Karlstad Convention. A commission studied the question for some months and, on the basis of their report in 1907, the Riksdag passed a resolution granting rights to the Lapps. But a Storting committee, headed by Carl Berner, reported unfavorably. During the secret debate Norwegians used harsh words about Swedish wishes to revise 1905's arrangements, but eventually Løvland's influence overcame hostility and the Storting passed a proposition granting the alteration.[27]

Yet it would be a mistake to say that echoes of 1905's bitterness ceased abruptly in 1906. In the Norwegian elections of that year *Venstre* expelled Løvland, Arctander, and Bothner for their policies in 1905 and gave the radicals under Castberg and Konow complete control. *Venstre* had in its campaign emphasized anti-

[27] Christian Günther, *Minnen från ministertiden i Kristiania åren 1905-1908* (Stockholm, 1923), 46-55; Vogt, *Indtil 1910*, 128-131.

Swedish sentiments and urged the Norwegian people "to rally to protect the monarchy and Karlstad." Some voters swung to join *Venstre*, and that party's gains in the election stemmed in part from these old animosities. When Günther failed to fly a flag on Norwegian Constitution Day (May 17), as other foreign envoys did, the Norwegian press again hoisted the old memory of 1905. Yet, not a month later, flags flew in Oslo celebrating the golden wedding anniversary of Oscar II and Sophia. Both private and state telegrams went to the royal couple from Norwegians and their government. At the end of 1907 Norwegians rose nobly in memory of their former king in ceremonies commemorating his death. The government ordered all flags to be flown at half-mast, and private citizens of all political beliefs joined Løvland in a procession to the Swedish legation to leave their cards. Without reference to political beliefs, individuals and press expressed their regrets at the death of the Swedish king who had reigned over Norway for thirty-five years. At the formal presentation of the Nobel Peace Prize, which came simultaneously, Løvland offered a moving, impromptu memorial speech as the spectators stood. At a commemorative service at Trinity Church (Trefoldighet-kirken) in Oslo, a Swedish bishop from Karlstad gave the sermon and stirred his audience of cabinet, Storting, and citizens by reference to the benevolences and openheartedness of the late king. For the first time, Günther said, he realized how much Norwegians loved and respected the old monarch.[28]

In direct political relations the two states maintained a discreet distance. A Norwegian integrity treaty[29] of 1907 displayed an exceptional degree of Norwegian and Swedish bitterness toward each other. Sweden blamed both Norway and Denmark for what Swedes supposed to be a Norwegian-Danish entente against them. *Nya Dagligt Allehanda* reviewed past discords, drawing the moral that Sweden needed a new foreign minister and better envoys abroad.

At the same time official cooperation slowly took shape. During 1907 Swedes attended an official government-sponsored Scan-

---

[28] Günther, *Minnen*, 60-61.
[29] Cf. Chapter XIII.

dinavian Agricultural Congress in Oslo despite grumblings from the Swedish ultraconservative press. The first meeting of the Scandinavian Inter-Parliamentary Union the same year indicated the possibility of former antagonists joining together in a common effort; official groups, such as the Scandinavian marine and medical congresses, held their sessions without a note of protest. Defense plans of a new *Venstre* ministry in 1908 aroused scant attention in Sweden even when Norwegian debates referred to "the neighboring enemy." In 1909 Castberg employed latent bitterness from 1905 in forcing the passage of a concession law whose primary target was Swedish investments in Norwegian power installations.

But as time progressed, the traces of 1905 became fainter and fainter. Bjørnson's death in 1910 was sincerely mourned in Sweden, and Verner von Heidenstam's poem on the great Norwegian author was reprinted in several Norwegian and Swedish papers, representing truly popular Swedish sentiments.[30] In 1910 the Scandinavian Education meeting in Stockholm found Swedes standing and listening to *Ja, vi elsker* for the first time since 1905. Interestingly, *Nya Dagligt Allehanda*, always alert for sources of friction, called the meeting practical Scandinavianism in operation.[31] In 1914 the meeting of the three Scandinavian kings at Malmö symbolized the closing of the book on 1905, despite future references to that famous year. Within ten years of the union's end a majority of Norwegians and Swedes could refer to 1905 without undue recrimination. The celerity with which this animosity disappeared as a factor of friction and antagonism is a phenomenon almost unique in international politics. The next forty years were to see the achievement of an even more exceptional broadening of integration and to focus attention upon a Scandinavian sense of community exceeded nowhere else in the world.

[30] Cf. Helge Gullberg, "Unionkrisen 1905," *Samlaren*, xxv (1944), 110-111.
[31] August 9, 15, 1910.

CHAPTER XIII

◇◇◇

THE NORWEGIAN INTEGRITY
AND STATUS QUO AGREEMENTS

◇◇◇

ALTHOUGH cooperation could occur in many aspects of Norwegian-Swedish relations, it was clear that the two countries must fix their foreign policies on separate courses. The manner of the union's dissolution and the nature of its causes dictated for Norway some form of foreign support. Immediate efforts to secure recognition and a guarantee of her defenseless condition arose from unfounded fears of Swedish aggression. While the treaty of integrity for which Norway schemed was a restraint on the major powers, in the last analysis it was more a check on Sweden.

For Sweden the dissolution constituted a great blow from which only the worst might be expected. Norway was now among Sweden's potential enemies, because, in combination with Denmark, she would attempt a balance of power in the Baltic. Swedish leaders in foreign policy, whether Conservative or Liberal, sought therefore protection in absolute neutrality, nonparticipation in Scandinavian affairs, and abstinence from European international politics. Although Sweden's withdrawal from an active foreign policy was often called "licking the wounds of 1905," it stemmed primarily from domestic and defense problems and could hardly be attributed to the union's end.

For nearly a decade this isolation formed the obstacle in Norwegian-Swedish relations. What was created was a pluralistic political community wherein many interests and joint or common[1] associations developed but no plans could be made for

[1] The terms "joint" and "common" have been used systematically. "Joint" is defined as laws, actions, or conventions of a Scandinavian character which have been negotiated or arranged by the several governments. "Common" is defined to mean domestic laws or procedures which have been altered to conform to those of another Nordic country, but without a convention to solemnize their Scandinavian character.

political or defense cooperation with each other. Swedish unwillingness to seek cooperation fed Norwegian fears, and radical
Venstre made political fodder of these factors. The government
could seek an international guarantee of the neutral zone, and
moved slowly toward that objective. But its attainment showed
traces of 1905 again and again, and the worst possible connota-
tion was placed on either country's policies by the other. But
once the guarantee of integrity agreement was signed, Norway
and Sweden found few obstacles hindering the creation of good
relations with each other.

A guarantee of neutrality and integrity could be easily asked
of the powers by either state. The November Treaty of 1855, with
its guarantee of integrity of Norway-Sweden, which England and
France had signed as a part of their Crimean War diplomacy,
lapsed with the end of the union.[2] During 1905 the question of
the November Treaty's abrogation arose several times. Crown
Prince Gustaf spoke of its renegotiation with several leaders in
England and Germany,[3] receiving confirmation of British and
German interest in a new treaty. Upon his return to Sweden
Gustaf turned to matters more closely related to the union, and
the Swedish foreign minister showed more interest in arriving
at a satisfactory settlement with Norway than with the foreign
powers.[4] Except for passing references during the summer the
Swedes paid slight attention to it.

[2] Cf. *Sveriges historia* . . . , XII, 115-135, on the treaty and its historic context; cf. British official opinion as expressed in the memorandum in *B.D.*,
VIII, 83-84.

[3] Memorandum of conference with Rodd, May 17, 1O1O, *UDS,* and *B.D.*,
95; June 6, *Aus. Amt,* 2958, *UDN; G.P.,* XXIII, pt. 2, 403-404, and footnotes.
Aide-mémoire of conference of crown prince and Bülow, June 3, 1O1O, *UDS.*
Note also the draft proposal for an integrity treaty which Gustaf handed to
Rodd, *Bernadotte Arkiv,* Stockholm, and Trolle to Gyldenstolpe, June 4,
4M1b, *UDS;* Richtofen memorandum, June 10, *Aus. Amt,* 2956, *UDN.* While
this book was in press Professor Folke Lindberg published his very important
study, *Scandinavia in Great Power Politics 1905-1908* (Stockholm, 1958), which
gives a detailed account of the negotiation of the Norwegian integrity and
the North Sea and Baltic status quo agreements. For a full and complete
rendition of these negotiations see his book; this chapter attempts to deal
mainly with relations between Norway and Sweden.

[4] Cf. Lansdowne to Gustaf, 1O1O, *UDN;* Bildt to Gyldenstolpe, June 17,
4A15, *UDS;* Lundeberg *Anteckningar,* June 18, Uppsala University Library.

As Swedish interest declined, the Norwegians began hopefully to entertain the idea of an integrity treaty. Løvland stated that his foreign policy would be to arrange a recognition of Norwegian neutrality which would serve as a basis for a similar guarantee for Denmark and Sweden.[5] During August and September a guarantee played a minor role in Norwegian negotiations to procure British support of the choice of Prince Carl for the Norwegian throne. Of far greater importance was its use in the Karlstad negotiations where it became a great power pledge for the neutral zone. There the delegates agreed unofficially that either government could seek a guarantee, not only of the neutral zone, but of the integrity of the country as a whole. The subject caused some difficulty with the Swedes, for it was complicated by its combination with foreign pressure on the conference in September.[6] The Swedish delegation opposed any great power intervention and Sweden was already started on her road to isolation.[7] At the end of September, the guarantee was still unsettled. Several times during October, the British foreign secretary made it clear that England's policy would suit Norwegian wishes, but that personally he favored only a convention on integrity and not on neutrality.[8] In a letter from Nansen to Lansdowne, the guarantee of the neutral zone was mentioned with approval as being "very welcome" in connection with the renewal of the November Treaty.[9]

Rumors about the guarantee of Norwegian integrity appeared in Swedish papers.[10] *Nya Dagligt Allehanda* (November 20) offended sensitive Norwegians by its contemptuous reference to Norway as a Scandinavian Portugal and its warning to both Norway and Denmark that beside England there was no room. Be-

---

[5] Cf. Løvland, *Menn og minner*, 154, 155-156; and Count Frijs to Løvland, July 4, 1905, P8A, *UDN*.

[6] Cf. Chapter XI.

[7] Michelsen to Arctander, September 5, P8A, *UDN*; Lindman, *Anteckningar*, September 17, Lindman *Samling*, RAS.

[8] Cf. *Nansen*, 68, 78, 116-117.

[9] *Ibid.*, 107; cf. Bothner, *op.cit.*, October 14; *Hagerup Bull*, 194.

[10] Cf. *Svenska Dagbladet*, October 17; *B.D.*, 95; Rodd's statement, November 14, 1O10, *UDS*.

cause of this publicity, the Russian envoy told Løvland of his government's objections to a straight renewal of the November Treaty with its anti-Russian terms. If Norway wished a treaty guaranteeing her boundaries, the envoy said, it would be only correct to include Russia among the signatories. Løvland agreed with the proposal, but pointed out the obvious fact that even the first steps were yet to be taken.

These same rumors caused the Swedish foreign office to order Günther to pry information from Løvland. The Norwegian foreign minister frankly stated his policy to be the procurement of a guarantee of Norwegian neutrality and integrity. No hidden anti-Swedish motives were involved in Norwegian policies and, in apparent confirmation, Løvland promised to conduct no negotiations behind Sweden's back or without informing Günther.[11] However, to the British minister, Løvland expressed his expectation of some Swedish opposition, for Sweden considered a guarantee of neutrality as implying a "certain abdication of national position which she does not consider compatible with her traditions and history."[12] Later in March 1906, Løvland carelessly spoke of progress on the renewal of the November Treaty when in reality nothing had yet been done.[13]

Germany was also informed of the guarantee by Løvland. And from Stockholm the German government learned of Sweden's approval of the new treaty. It might even be directed against Russia, which would favor Norwegian interests in Finmark. If the treaty specifically exempted Russia, so Swedish opinion ran, it would nevertheless be pointed towards that country.[14] Through Haakon the Norwegian foreign office also let the Kaiser know of their eagerness for an early date for the signature of the guar-

[11] Günther, *Minnen*, 73.

[12] *B.D.*, 95.

[13] The British denied his statement and suggested to the Swedes that some preliminary agreement be arranged between Norway and Sweden before a guarantee by the powers. *B.D.*, 95-96. Note also *Norge og stormaktene 1906-14*, ed. Reidar Omang (Oslo, 1957), 60. Hereafter cited: *Norge og stormaktene*.

[14] *G.P.*, XXIII, pt. 2, 404-405. Hereafter simply cited as *G.P.*; Müller to Bülow, June 28, 1906, *Aus. Amt*, 2958, *UDN*.

antee. German policy, as seen through the dispatches from this conference and its memorandum, sought to avoid entanglement in any policy offensive to England, Russia, or France.[15]

During the summer of 1906 the powers became involved in the first Morocco incident and paid almost no attention to northern Europe. Revival of the integrity treaty was largely due to Løvland's determined pursuit of the subject. Upon orders to talk with the British foreign secretary, Nansen found England insisting upon giving Sweden a share. If two treaties were signed, it would mean a great power guarantee of Norway and Sweden against each other which would be an obvious interference in Scandinavian affairs.[16] As he described the treaty to Günther, Løvland outlined the new agreement as a "recognition of neutrality and a guarantee of integrity," the former comparable to the status of Switzerland and Belgium, and the latter in the manner of the November Treaty. The main Norwegian objective was to avoid involvement in a great war between Britain and Germany.[17] Sweden was willing to join in a guarantee of integrity, but not neutrality, and the differences between the two types of treaties were emphasized in the diplomacy at the time.[18]

Matters began to move more rapidly in December 1906, when the powers indicated a readiness for negotiations. At the same time, Sweden expressed an unwillingness to approve signature immediately, although her government would "accept with understanding any honorable Norwegian attempt in this direction."[19] On this basis, Løvland submitted a draft of a guarantee of neutrality, independence, and territorial integrity, with a clause reserving to Norway her right to aid Sweden and/or Denmark in case of war. Its pledge to maintain Norwegian neutrality was

[15] *G.P.*, 406-407, Tschirschky to Metternich, 407-408; for a full discussion see memorandum of Arnold Raestad, *Norge og stormaktene*, 72-78.

[16] *B.D.*, 96; cf. Metternich's comments on Sweden, *G.P.*, 408.

[17] Schoen (St. Petersburg) to *Aus. Amt*, November 22, and Tschirschky memorandum, November 25, *G.P.*, 408-409. On the several drafts and memorandum, see *Norge og stormaktene*, 82-112.

[18] Cf. *B.D.*, 96; Günther, *Minnen*, 76; foreign office circular, November 11, 1010, *UDS*.

[19] Günther, *Minnen*, 77-78.

immediately rejected. As both Germany and Britain stated, their troops would be sacrificed for Scandinavia.[20]

Even though their opinion was not asked, the Swedes protested. On several counts, Sweden opposed the Norwegian project. A conference between Løvland and Günther failed to clarify either Swedish objections or Norwegian counterproposals. Later, Denmark refused to be drawn into any negotiations on a Scandinavian defense pact, and Løvland dropped this part of the treaty.[21]

Because of these several objections, the powers agreed that Russia would present a counterproject, since she was involved in the November Treaty and most central to negotiations. A conference in St. Petersburg between the German ambassador and Isvolsky resulted in a joint draft treaty.[22] It eliminated offending parts of the Norwegian proposals and phrased quite generally most of what Løvland had made specific. Article 1 abrogated the November Treaty and Article 2 established perpetual neutrality for Norway, both for the powers and for Norway herself, and dropped the reservation for a Scandinavian defense pact. Article 3 guaranteed that the signatory powers would "respect" the neutrality, independence, and territorial integrity of Norway; Article 4 left the treaty open for signature by other powers, obviously intended for Sweden. The treaty was reduced to harmlessness by "respect" for Norwegian neutrality and integrity. The Russians assumed the unpleasant job of offering the Norwegians the bitter pill.[23]

Norway rejected the Russian draft, for it gave her nothing of Løvland's plan. "Maintain" was changed to "respect," releas-

[20] For details concerning the draft and objections of Britain and Germany see *B.D.*, 98-99, 99-101 (E. A. Crowe's minute, dated December 28); *G.P.*, 413, 411-412. For the Norwegian side with Løvland's explanations, see *Norge og stormaktene*, 126-131.

[21] Cf. Hammarskjöld to foreign office, January 10, 1010, *UDS*: Henckel (Copenhagen) to Bülow, January 18, *Aus. Amt*, 2958, *UDN*; Günther's conference with Løvland is in his *Minnen*, 78-80, 80-81; Swedish foreign office to Günther, December 17, 1010, *UDS*.

[22] *B.D.*, 101-102; *G.P.*, 416-418.

[23] Schoen to *Aus. Amt*, *G.P.*, 419. Tschirschky, for the German foreign office, agreed to the Russian views, approved Isvolsky's draft, consented to the sig-

ing the powers from any pledge and placing Norwegian foreign policy in a strait jacket. Norway wanted no guarantee of neutrality, but only "acknowledgement of neutrality, and a guarantee of integrity."[24] Løvland defended the proposed Scandinavian defense alliance, for he wished to avoid any appearance of anti-Swedish bias and to promote Scandinavian cooperation. As Bülow was told, "the Norwegians have suddenly discovered their Scandinavian heart."[25] Løvland refused completely the inclusion of the other two Scandinavian countries as signatories, for that would imply an inferior status for Norway.[26] The sum of these and other objections[27] lay behind Løvland's request for omission of neutrality provisions and the treaty's limitation to a guarantee of integrity.

Within two weeks the Norwegian foreign office issued its draft after a conference with Günther.[28] In the draft appeared several new features: an open-ended Scandinavian clause, a guarantee of the neutral zone, a twenty-year duration proviso, and a blank check on the steps to be taken by the powers to make effective their "respect" of Norwegian integrity. On the Scandinavian clause a British Foreign Office under-secretary wrote: "This seems a heroic solution, the significance of which we must assume Norway has fully weighed."[29] An escape clause for the powers stipulated that if Norway herself engaged in military operations the treaty ceased to be effective. The curious apathy of the powers to Norwegian-Swedish differences regarding the neutral zone seems

---

nature of a final treaty at Oslo, and expressed a desire to have Russia maintain the initiative in negotiations. For Isvolsky's note and counterproject see *Norge og stormaktene*, 156-163.

[24] *B.D.*, 97.

[25] Scheller-Steinwartz (Oslo) to Bülow, *G.P.*, 427; cf. full dispatch of February 5, *ibid.*, 426-428, and Scheller-Steinwartz's previous dispatch of January 30, *ibid.*, 425-426.

[26] Schoen to Bülow, February 5, *Aus. Amt*, 2958, *UDN; G.P.*, 428-430.

[27] Nansen wrote to Løvland suggesting the idea of limitation of the treaty to integrity, and when he spoke to Sir Edward Grey about it received his suggestion to sound out the powers with the altered text. The British ambassador at Paris either had a similar French proposal or he thought of it himself. *Norge og stormaktene*, 181-182; *B.D.*, 97.

[28] Günther to Trolle, March 12, 1010, *UDS*; Günther, 82-83; *Norge og stormaktene*, 204-206, 198-206.

[29] *B.D.*, 111.

to warrant an assumption that none knew of Sweden's hostility toward it. The powers appeared also to have disregarded the natural interpretation that a pledge on the zone would be directed against Sweden.

During the spring and summer of 1907 negotiations on the Norwegian treaty lagged. The Swedish foreign office understood the delay to be due to objections of the powers. The Norwegians blamed the Swedes for the delay and offered the powers an unappealing treaty of alliance if the agreement failed to materialize. At the same time, Løvland's charges of British obstructionist tactics succeeded in starting an acrimonious diplomatic exchange in which England and Germany sought to throw blame on each other. The impasse ended with the presentation of a new Russian draft.[30] Even it would have been allowed to simmer if the French minister at Copenhagen had not let slip the rumor that Germany was attempting to secure Danish consent to an alliance and to the closing of the Belts and Sound during war. Life suddenly returned to the integrity treaty and by the middle of July the British were suggesting limitation of the Norwegian treaty to integrity which would be "respected" and not "maintained." After securing the approval of the Russian government, a German-British joint memorandum was sent around to the principals.[31]

The Swedes viewed the new proposal with considerable misgivings. Their foreign office informed the British minister that it had embarked on a study of an alteration in policy in which the integrity treaty, while not objectionable, "could only appear directed against Sweden, and would make it impossible for her to some day follow [the] precedent of Norway."[32] The shift which Sweden contemplated, so Rodd wrote, was "how she could best safeguard her position by a change in policy, which I gathered meant drawing nearer to Germany." Russia's pressure for denunciation of the neutralization of the Åland Islands alarmed Sweden, as did the apparent anti-Swedish policies of both the

[30] *B.D.*, 112-115; *G.P.* (Schoen to *Aus. Amt*, June 8), 438; *Norge og stormaktene*, 249-254.

[31] Cf. *G.P.*, 443-444, 444-445, 443, 445-446; *B.D.*, 116-117.   [32] *B.D.*, 117.

great powers and Norway. In order to reassure her, Grey told the Swedish minister that an integrity treaty would contain no threat against Sweden, but *"that Norway itself would not attempt anything against any country which could endanger this integrity."*[33]

When it came time to seek a power willing to propose a counterdraft meeting the Norwegian and Swedish objections, Russia proved lukewarm. Eventually, however, a Russian draft was circulated among the powers, but Sweden again objected that the form of the treaty seemed to be motivated by fears of Swedish *revanche* against Norway for 1905. Any guarantee of integrity which pointed at Sweden would harm good relations among the Scandinavian countries. Sweden had proved her peaceful intentions regarding Norway, so the Swedish foreign minister argued, by expressing her willingness to enter any reasonable integrity treaty, by the 1905 arbitration agreement, and by the settlement of the Grisbådarne dispute.[34] Both directly and indirectly the Swedish foreign office sought deletion of Article 2 of the integrity treaty which set up a great power warranty over the neutral zone.[35] At Oslo Günther asked to see Løvland to discuss the treaty in its entirety.

Günther's interview with Løvland was a long and stormy affair. After a summary of the Russian draft, the Norwegian foreign minister interposed some verbal reflections on the treaty, but failed to mention the inclusion of the neutral zone. Günther objected angrily to the anti-Swedish nature of the treaty, stressing its harmful effects on the Scandinavian interests of both countries. At Karlstad, Løvland pointed out, Sweden had refused to con-

---

[33] Wrangel to Trolle, July 22, 1010, *UDS*. Cf. also Vogt to Løvland, July 26, 1907, *Norge og stormaktene*, 278-279. Britain's policy was the cause of a maneuver which involved Haakon, Edward VII, and the German government and brought Nansen several times to the British Foreign Office. Norway now wanted to avoid her earlier commitment on a simple treaty of integrity. Cf. Scheller-Steinwartz to Bülow, July 22 and July 29, *Aus. Amt*, 2958, *UDN*.

[34] Memoranda of September 14 and 16, 1010, *UDS*.

[35] The Swedish foreign minister telegraphed to Paris: "We earnestly desire that paragraph 2 be entirely and completely stricken." The German ministers at Paris and Stockholm were asked to inform their government and the British minister at Stockholm relayed the same message. Trolle to Gyldenstolpe, September 16, 1010, *UDS*; *G.P.*, 447; Hindenburg to Bülow, September 18, *Aus. Amt*, 2958, *UDN*.

sent to an international guarantee of the neutral zone, but left
Norway free to secure her own assurances later. Günther agreed
to these truths, but objected to the treaty's intentions which
would arouse Swedish bitterness against Norway and impair good
relations. Løvland contended that the treaty could not be given
such an interpretation. Rather Norway feared a war between
Germany and England in which Britain would request the opening of some Norwegian ports. Günther, unable to foresee events
in 1940, broke out: "That's unreal." Then, Løvland continued,
if Sweden wanted a guarantee, why not extend the neutral zone
the entire length of the frontier? He concluded the conference
by promising to furnish Günther with the full contents of the
treaty before completion of negotiations.[36]

While appearing to comply with Swedish wishes, Løvland pursued another course with the foreign powers. In a British minute
on the Russian draft the revealing comment was added: "It
seems . . . a pity the Swedish view could not be met, by omission
of 2nd part of Art[icle] 2, but the Norwegians w[oul]d not have
it."[37] Günther, for his part, attempted to procure Russian aid in
arguing the Swedish case and to ask the Russian minister at Oslo
for the text of Article 2.[38] At the same time the Swedes tried to
secure German and French support for a revision of the offending passage. The Swedes wished Article 2, guaranteeing the neutral zone, to apply solely to the four powers, or, as an alternative,
to have Sweden as a signatory.[39] This alternative, previously
refused by Løvland, was revived by the French government at
Oslo and St. Petersburg. The Russians tried mediation at Oslo,
but an irritated Løvland refused again and added a complaint
against Swedish agitation among the powers.[40] The Swedish foreign office immediately ordered Günther to reassure Løvland of

[36] Günther to Trolle, September 18, 1010, *UDS*; Günther, *Minnen*, 86-88.
Cf. Løvland's memorandum, *Norge og stormaktene*, 291-293, which promised
neither consultation nor provision of full contents.

[37] *B.D.*, 119; see also the Russian draft, pp. 118-119, and Grey to Rodd,
117-118.

[38] Trolle to Günther, September 23, 1010, *UDS*.

[39] Memoranda, September 25 and 26, 1010, *UDS*; Lindman *Samling*, RAS;
Günther, *Minnen*, 90. Cf. copy of letter of Lindman to Günther which was
shown to Løvland, *Norge og stormaktene*, 299-300.

[40] Günther to Lindman, September 26, 1010, *UDS*.

Sweden's noninterference with the treaty and of her nonagitation among the powers. The Swedish denial of opposition to the treaty is confirmed by conferences between the Swedish foreign minister and Isvolsky at Carlsbad. Isvolsky divulged parts of Russo-German negotiations on the Åland Islands and Baltic status quo agreements which would compensate Sweden for compromises in the Norwegian integrity treaty.[41] To gain a favorable reception on these treaties Sweden must not press too hard on the Norwegian integrity agreement. At the same time, the Swedes would not be displeased if it completely failed.

Through several courses the Swedish foreign office succeeded in establishing two choices: either deletion of the offensive clause or acceptance of Sweden as a signatory. When asked regarding the latter, Nansen misunderstood momentarily, thinking of Sweden as being guaranteed and not a guarantor. Upon his recovery from his surprise, Nansen absolutely refused for "that would indeed place Sweden as a great power." To Løvland he wrote of his wish to avoid an appearance of nervousness, but that on his visit to the royal palace at Balmoral he would ask Edward VII to use his influence with his government.[42]

The Swedish *démarche* on their participation in the treaty as a signatory, arranged at St. Petersburg with the French chargé d'affaires on orders from Paris, received German passive support. Tschirschky wrote that Germany had no objections and added that it would solve the problem of abrogation of the November Treaty. The inclusion of Sweden as a signator soon became a compensation for Russian refortification of the Åland Islands.[43] A Swedish endeavor to secure British support for the *démarche* failed completely. As explained to the Swedish minister, Nansen had said that "this proposal never could be accepted by Norwegians since it would be viewed as a Swedish protection over Norway which Norwegian self-respect would under no condition accept."[44]

[41] Günther, *Minnen,* 89-90; Miquel to *Aus. Amt,* October 3, *G.P.,* 450.

[42] Løvland to Nansen, October 2, P8A, *UDN;* Nansen to Løvland, October 2 (two dispatches); Nansen to Løvland, October 3, *ibid.*

[43] Cf. *G.P.,* 451-452, 452-453; Memorandum of Lindman, October 5, 1O10, *UDS.* Hindenburg to Bülow, October 9, *Aus. Amt,* 2958, *UDN.*

[44] Wrangel to Lindman, October 5, 1O10, *UDS.*

When asked directly whether Sweden could not be a signatory Løvland compromised a bit by suggesting a Norwegian-Swedish treaty after the signature of a guarantee by the five powers. In addition, he employed complaints about Swedish press agitation and the use of "violent language against Norway" to advise an early signature of the integrity treaty.[45] Nansen added that a *fait accompli* "would be the right means of improving the relations between Norway and Sweden, whilst if the present uncertain state of things lasts much longer, the heat in Swedish minds will soon rise to a boiling point."[46] Caught in a dilemma the Norwegian foreign office sought to preserve the treaty, and, at the same time, to prevent the entry of Sweden. On the other side, Sweden strove to secure either the deletion of the offensive clause, which she did not want at all, or her own inclusion among the signatory powers. But her ultimate objective aimed to make the treaty impossible.

Britain, for her part, faced the task of refusing the Swedish *démarche*, and looked for a compromise. Nansen was asked to request his government to accept Sweden as a signatory. But nothing happened. Nansen either failed to inform his government or he decided to ignore the question. Only England, on Sweden's behalf, opposed the treaty and sought Sweden's inclusion. The trump card was in Swedish hands, for they could refuse to "find the moment ripe for the abrogation of the November Treaty."[47] Although only a technical matter, this abrogation might hold up signature of the Norwegian treaty for months and, perhaps, weary the powers until they dropped the subject. Løvland, when informed by the British of the *démarche*, immediately sent a circular to various Norwegian legations to explain that the November Treaty's abrogation could not be blocked by Sweden, for its denunciation was entirely separate from the integrity treaty. Løvland's understanding of the legalities of the case failed him somewhat, for Sweden possessed sound

[45] Günther to Lindman, October 5, 1O10, *UDS*; Løvland to Norwegian Legation at London, October 10, P8A, *UDN*.

[46] Nansen to Grey, October 11, P8A, *UDN*.

[47] Lindman to Rodd, October 19, 1O10, *UDS*; Günther, *Minnen*, 91.

legal grounds for her views, and the British insisted upon abrogation of the November Treaty before signature of the integrity convention.[48] Various compromises failed. One, suggested by Grey, included the words "et après avoir communiqué avec Sa Majesté le Roi de Suède" after "les bénéfices de la paix" to convince Sweden of the treaty's application to the powers.[49] But such efforts failed to budge the stubborn Norwegians. Løvland rejected any new negotiations even while agreeing to accept specific suggestions from Sweden for small editorial alterations in the treaty's text. Günther offered the idea of signature of a Norwegian-Swedish pact simultaneously with the integrity agreement, but Løvland declined even after further protests.[50]

Eventually the Swedish foreign minister telegraphed Günther that Sweden desired no alterations and, in a following letter, wrote of the futility of prolonging the argument. When neither the powers nor Norway would propose changes, the Swedish government could not, in good conscience, offer any.[51] Günther conveyed Trolle's wishes to Løvland and asked only slight changes in wording which sought to make the treaty less obnoxious. The full report, the Swedish minister said, would be available in three days.[52] At this last minute, Løvland resisted a British move to forestall the signature of the treaty, refused their request for omission of "et avec sa zone neutral," and demanded the treaty's signature. On November 2, before Günther presented his editorial changes, the representatives of the four powers and Løvland signed the treaty guaranteeing the territorial integrity of Norway. To experts in the various foreign offices, the treaty and the furor it caused "was much ado about nothing," but for Nor-

[48] Løvland circular, October 23, P8A, *UDN*; Nansen to Løvland, October 24, *ibid.*

[49] Wrangel to Lindman, October 24, 1O10, *UDS.*

[50] Günther to Løvland, October 27, P8A, *UDN*; Günther, *Minnen*, 82-83; Løvland memorandum, October 27, P8A, *UDN*; Günther to Lindman, October 28, 1O10, *UDS*; Løvland to Günther, October 30, *ibid.*

[51] Trolle to Günther, October 31; see also protocol of the cabinet meeting of October 31, 1O10, *UDS.*

[52] An accompanying apology for delay in presentation of Swedish points of view was a jibe at Løvland for failing to fulfill his September promise to furnish Günther with the contents of the treaty. Günther to Løvland, November 1, P8A, *UDN.*

wegian-Swedish relations the negotiations, the terms of the treaty, and the methods used in handling the Swedes were regretted and long remembered.

The Swedes reacted immediately by charging Løvland with dishonesty, and criticizing both the treaty for its anti-Swedish nature and the Norwegian government for its policy. Günther's first letter to Løvland so greatly offended the Norwegian foreign minister that he sent it back to the Swedish envoy, after a copy had been made, for corrections and emendations.[53] In the letter, and the subsequent conversation of the two,[54] Günther poured out his bitterness. He accused Løvland of negligence, of broken promises, and of prevarications. As he said, he must report to his government of his betrayal, since he had written confidently in earlier reports of Løvland's honest and sincere promises to keep him apprized of negotiations. Lacking the confidence of, and in, the Norwegian foreign minister, he could only resign. According to Günther, Løvland turned white and asked him not to take such a drastic step over such a small affair. Günther indignantly replied that a "broken promise was no small affair." Løvland promised to give the Swedish minister a note with an accompanying explanation. In a letter the next day, Løvland further tried to cover the "broken promise" by stating that there had been a misunderstanding, "whether my method of explanation [is] to blame, or your understanding of it, I shall not attempt to judge. It is in any case a misunderstanding, which I, as well as yourself, Herr Minister, regret."[55]

By telephone Günther received instructions to tell Løvland that he intended to leave Oslo, and that perhaps he would not return. Simultaneously the Swedish foreign office released details of the treaty through the *Svensk telegrambyrå* with a deliberate twist intended to arouse antagonism. The Günther-Løvland conflict, which remained secret from the public, almost caused a cabinet crisis in Norway and forced Michelsen to act as a mediator. Representatives of the foreign states, through their *doyen*, presented Løvland with a statement approving Günther's ac-

[53] Günther to Løvland, November 3, P8A, *UDN.*
[54] Günther to Foreign Office, November 3, 1010, *UDS.*
[55] Løvland to Günther, November 4 (copy), P8A, *UDN.*

tion. In Stockholm, Vogt, the Norwegian minister, asked for an explanation and requested the foreign minister to order Günther to remain at his post. Trolle would do nothing, and, to irritate the Norwegians further, held a press conference in which he revealed enough of the negotiations to make Norway appear as a malefactor.[56]

The Swedish press commented on the completed treaty in mixed fashion. The Liberals upheld the Scandinavian aspects of the agreement and the Conservatives damned it as a Swedish diplomatic defeat. In view of its subsequent history, since it was abrogated after Norwegian entry into the League of Nations, *Nya Dagligt Allehanda* accurately forecast future Norwegian reversals of opinion. But the same paper revived echoes of 1905 in its diatribes on the treaty and Norwegian methods of achieving it. Günther, in commenting later on its ratification, claimed that only "chauvinist" Swedish papers attacked it.[57]

Swedish ill will soon disappeared, however, with the almost simultaneous announcement of the signatures of the Baltic and North Sea status quo agreements which ensured Sweden's security in the Baltic. The two agreements, from which Norway was omitted because of her guaranteed position, compensated partially for Norway's exclusion of Sweden from negotiations on the integrity treaty. But beyond that, the continuation of the neutralization of the Åland Islands and the certainty of German support mollified most Swedes. Security in the Baltic and protection from Russian aggression, which Germany's participation in the Baltic agreement connoted, made Swedish leaders more willing to forgive Norway.

[56] See dispatches from November 5 to 7 in 1010, *UDS*, and comments and interview of Trolle in *Nya Dagligt Allehanda* of November 6 and 7; the paper editorially condemned Trolle, but supported his retention in the foreign office, as his resignation would be a victory for the Norwegians.

[57] Norwegians in part agreed with the Swedish view. *Venstre* disapproved of the treaty and always regarded it as one of Løvland's mistakes. In debate on its ratification members of the same party argued that its anti-Scandinavian nature and its obstruction of Nordic cooperation made it necessary to reject its ratification. Brunchorst to Thommessen, January 18, 1913, Thommessen Mss., Oslo University Library; Sigurd Ibsen, *Udsyn og Indblik* (Oslo, 1912), 14-22.

The two agreements on the Baltic and North Seas originated in the nullification of the November and Åland Islands Treaties of 1855-1856. In 1905 the powers wished to avoid upsetting the power balance in the Baltic, but they altered Sweden's position by signing the integrity convention. During the last months of negotiations on it, the threat of Sweden's nonabrogation of the November Treaty forced Russia to placate the Swedes. Other powers joined in the move, and early in 1907 the British Foreign Office prepared a report on the Baltic's importance which caused them to inquire of France concerning negotiations on the 1855-1856 treaties. Both the British and French governments recognized Russia's wishes to abrogate the neutralization of the islands and to open the Baltic.

In August 1907, Isvolsky made his move without informing either of Russia's allies. The Russian foreign minister sought the maintenance of status quo in the Baltic and avoided the more dangerous open sea and fortified Åland Islands which Sweden, France, and England feared. Russia's proposal for exclusion of the non-Baltic powers was absolutely rejected by Germany on the grounds that such exclusions would make Germany appear to be attempting to detach Russia from France. "Our policy requires us not to create any special movement directed against England," Bülow told Isvolsky, and, in a marginal note on a letter of Tschirschky, added "richtig" to the latter's suggestion that England be included in the agreement. At a meeting between the Kaiser and the Czar at Swinemünde, a protocol established the principle that restrictions on Russia's freedom of control over the Åland Islands might be lifted, but this venturesome step was later rescinded. A Baltic status quo agreement must include the British, and thus make a German-Russian Åland Islands treaty both inconsistent and dangerous.[58]

The German foreign office, acutely sensitive to English policies, planned the arrangement of a North Sea status quo treaty as a possible compensation for Britain if she failed to sign a Baltic agreement. A draft of such a treaty was even sent to the

[58] For the British views see *B.D.*, 122 ff.; for German documents see *G.P.*, 463-474, which includes the Swinemünde protocol.

German ambassador in London so that German initiative might forestall English questions and intervention in the Baltic negotiations.[59] A new Åland Islands convention formed the basis for discussions at Carlsbad between Isvolsky and Trolle, the Swedish foreign minister, and cleared the path for Swedish consent to an alteration in the status of the islands. In this, England's omission would not concern Sweden, who would be most likely to call upon the Germans for assistance in resisting Russian demands. Evidently the Trolle-Isvolsky conversations found the Swedes eager, not to say impatient, to sign some form of agreement.[60] These discussions pursued the objective of a public treaty guaranteeing the status quo in the Baltic and a Swedish-Russian convention on the Åland Islands backed by a separate secret agreement between Germany and Russia.[61]

Britain held the balance, and the German foreign office refused any commitment to Russia on the Åland Islands. The German ambassador at London, Count Paul von Wolff-Metternich, suggested a frank approach to the British, for secrecy would create mistrust.[62] In making this suggestion he assumed correctly that England interested herself in the fate of Sweden and feared closing the Baltic. France, suspicious of Germany and wary of the activities of her ally, Russia, grew increasingly worried over secret negotiations. Sweden might close the Baltic out of pique and might sign an alliance with Germany.[63]

British policy on the Baltic, quite simply, consisted of an admonition to the Swedes to ask Russia for assurances on the Åland Islands and on the 1855 and 1856 treaties. The latter protected Sweden, for it remained in force, even though the dissolution of the union nullified the November Treaty of 1855.[64]

[59] Cf. esp. Tschirschky to Metternich, October 4, *G.P.*, 478-479.

[60] Count Carl von Wedel to Bülow, October 5, *G.P.*, 479-481.

[61] Cf. Memorandum and Schoen to Bülow, October 29, *G.P.*, 481-482, 483-485.

[62] Metternich to Bülow, October 29, *G.P.*, 485-490.

[63] Cf. Bertie to Grey, October 31, and November 1, *B.D.*, 133-134, 134-135.

[64] Grey to Bertie, November 7, *B.D.*, 135-136. An interesting point is that Gustaf wished England to remain out of the Baltic question. Schoen to Pourtalès, November 8, *G.P.*, 493-494.

The British hardly expected to prevent closure of the Baltic and only hoped "that Russia and Germany should not enter into a mutual engagement to help each other to close the Straits [Sound and Belts]."[65] Grey's easy consent to the principles involved in a North Sea treaty without raising the Baltic question mystified the German foreign office. But Grey assured Metternich, who later told the British foreign secretary of pending negotiations on a proposed Baltic treaty, of British sympathy for German views regarding a status quo convention. England wished only the maintenance of free navigation in that sea. Grey did ask, however, about the possibility of a new arrangement on the Åland Islands. If one were contemplated, it would be best to discuss the matter with France, both as an ally of Russia and a signator of the 1856 treaty.[66]

At the same time, Sir Arthur Nicolson talked with Isvolsky at St. Petersburg about these negotiations and received a reasonably frank explanation of them. Isvolsky answered Nicolson's questions regarding the Åland Islands by pointing out the possibility for some separate agreement with Sweden. Nicolson's request for instructions was answered by both Grey and Sir Charles Hardinge by an assurance that none were necessary. "If Russia can come to terms with Sweden about the Åland Isl[and]s it can only be a matter of satisfaction to all concerned."[67] On the North Sea agreement Grey expressed the opinion that it meant little, but that he would oblige Germany.[68] Germany and England agreed except for a British insistence upon the inclusion of France. The Germans tried to prevent it since France possessed no North Sea littoral. The main pressure on both agreements came from France, who had been, as Hardinge put it, stupidly handled by Isvolsky.[69]

[65] Grey to Lord Tweedmouth, November 19, *B.D.*, 136-137.

[66] On German views and suspicions see *G.P.*, 496-505; on Grey's conversation with Metternich see Grey to Count de Salis, December 4, *B.D.*, 137-138.

[67] Nicolson to Grey, December 4, and notes, *B.D.*, 138-139; Metternich to foreign office, December 12, *G.P.*, 506-507.

[68] Grey to Count de Saolis, December 9, *B.D.*, 142-143.

[69] Cf. Lister to Grey, December 11, and Hardinge to Nicolson, same date, *B.D.*, 145-146.

The French eagerly wished to discover the secrets of Russo-German diplomacy and to punish Isvolsky for his precipitate action. They especially wanted Isvolsky to clarify his purposes in undertaking negotiations which, as an ally, France considered unfriendly. Grey sided with France by conveying his complete disapproval of the fashion in which negotiations had been conducted.[70] On the other hand, British Foreign Office officials showed no suspicion of Isvolsky's motives and thought the agreements quite clear. They confidently expected Sweden, in view of the necessity of abrogation of the 1856 treaty, to prevent any anti-French or British action on either Isvolsky's or Germany's part. In a German draft of a North Sea agreement, submitted in January, 1908, a few British changes were made: "respect" replaced "maintain" and "entrances to the Baltic" was substituted for the specific names of the Kattegat, Skagerrak, Belts, and Sound.[71] Although further discussion revolved around this last alteration, the two governments, and, therefore, the majority, agreed on the North Sea status quo agreement.

France, England, and Germany wanted to maintain security for Sweden in the Baltic at the expense of Russia's release from servitudes on the Åland Islands.[72] When provided with a draft agreement, the Swedish government promptly sought reaffirmation of British support. Grey wrote to Rodd that Britain would have Russia "make an arrangement which would be satisfactory to Sweden" before abrogation of the 1856 treaty. Rodd replied from Stockholm that the Swedes considered the form of both North Sea and Baltic agreements quite satisfactory, and they could now be signed simultaneously. Sweden recognized, of course, that Russia must be compensated for the failure to de-neutralize the Åland Islands and sought to provide it by her willingness to withhold opposition to the two conventions. Russian consent to separation of the Baltic and Åland Islands questions seemingly resulted from the personal intercession of Prince Wil-

[70] Radolin to foreign office, December 14, *G.P.*, 511-512; Nicolson to Grey, December 15, *B.D.*, 150-151.

[71] Cf. *B.D.*, 161-168; *G.P.*, 521-541.

[72] Cf. Schoen's two memoranda of February 20 and 21, *G.P.*, 534-541.

helm of Sweden when he was in Russia for his marriage to a Russian grand duchess.[73] Sweden's position on the fortification of the Åland Islands was evidently made clear by a *démarche*, delivered by Sweden's minister to Russia, in which Sweden refused her consent to an alteration of the status of the islands.[74] By April the North Sea and Baltic agreements could be signed simultaneously. Swedish-Russian diplomacy on the Åland Islands left their status unchanged, and, as the Swedes hoped, left little prospect of any future revision. Since the treaty of 1856 was not abrogated, Sweden could indefinitely continue to use two of its signatories, France and England, against Russia. On April 23, 1908, the North Sea and Baltic treaties were signed, the former in Berlin and the latter in St. Petersburg. The great powers refrained from further interference in Scandinavian affairs and the Nordic states quite willingly approved their indifference.[75]

The settlement of these vital treaties and problems meant much to Sweden and Scandinavia. Sweden rested easily now with assurances of German, French, and British support against a possible future Russian expansion. The union's weak alliance was replaced by a more secure defense of Sweden's Baltic frontiers through continued neutralization of the Åland Islands, the Baltic status quo treaty, and the friendly support of three great powers. Sweden depended upon German support in her future foreign policy, but isolationism and self-imposed neutrality in great power rivalries lessened the need for foreign aid. In some measure the Swedes received compensation for 1905 and the Norwegian treaty of integrity, and their resentment partially subsided. The three treaties forced both Norway and Sweden to display less diplomatic animosity, at least to foreign eyes, and made them both distrustful of foreign assistance. Since they could lean neither to East nor West, the three Nordic governments turned more to each other in foreign policy to create a firm rapport as a substitute for outside support in their isolation and neutrality. With

[73] Pourtalès to foreign office, *G.P.*, 545.
[74] Cf. *G.P.*, footnote, 550.
[75] See *B.D.*, 175-177, 184, for texts of the two treaties.

threats of war becoming more serious after Austria's occupation of Bosnia-Herzegovina in 1908, Scandinavian leaders reconsidered their national isolation and conceived of a united Nordic neutrality which offered hopes of protection in war and against power politics.

CHAPTER XIV

◇◇◇

THE ACHIEVEMENT OF INTEGRATION

◇◇◇

THE signature of the guarantee of integrity for Norway, and the North Sea and Baltic treaties, allowed both states to attain a better perspective on their future foreign relations. Norway emphasized neutrality and depended on Britain and her economic power for protection. Sweden coupled neutrality with a pro-German orientation to resist the fancied aggressive designs of Russia. After adjusting themselves to the new circumstances, the two governments slowly sought ways for a rapprochement with each other. Scandinavian cultural and economic cooperation had been halted briefly in consequence of the storms of 1905, but within two or three years most of the Nordic associations operated once again. The threats of militarization, increasing armaments, and international tensions arising from power politics even speeded the two governments toward integration.

Formation of several peace societies prior to 1905 hastened the progress of northern integration. The Scandinavian Peace Congresses, which met nearly every year during the decade preceding the dissolution of the union, offered popular proof of peaceful intentions. Through their resolutions they reminded Scandinavian peoples of their sworn intent to maintain peace with their Nordic brothers and with the world. Scandinavian dependence on neutrality, arbitration agreements, submission of the Grisbådarne dispute to an arbitration board, and collaboration in cultural, economic, and social measures received the support of these Scandinavian organizations.

Two years after the dissolution of the union, Danish members of the Inter-Parliamentary Union succeeded in creating a section for northern Europe. Their motives for such a program stemmed from an ardent spirit of Scandinavianism and a strong international peace program which received the backing of Liberal and Social Democratic parties. In 1906 Niels Neergaard, member of the Danish lower house of parliament and of the Inter-Parliamentary Union, invited representatives of the three states to a meeting at Copenhagen. Two objectives dominated the minds of its nine members: to increase Scandinavian cooperation and to prepare for Nordic unity in the Union. Opinion in Norway and Sweden opposed formation of the new group, but Neergaard persuaded Norwegian and Swedish delegates to approve an official second meeting. In September 1907, the Scandinavian Inter-Parliamentary Union came into being with a council acting in an administrative capacity.

Although a full congress did not meet until 1910, Scandinavian leaders began moving toward complete cooperation. At a meeting in 1911 at Oslo proposals for arbitration of the chief Scandinavian disputes and formulation of principles for increased activity of peace agencies were fully studied. Committees prepared specific proposals for consideration by congresses. These efforts, backed by Scandinavian cabinet officers, parliamentary spokesmen, and long-time leaders in the movement, stimulated collaboration during World War I. In each advance the Inter-Parliamentary Union pressed forward, and the establishment of a secretariat in 1918 enabled the Union to publish its proceedings and to extend its information services. Finland joined in 1924, and Iceland the year after, so eventually five countries participated in the Union. Two decades after 1905 a semiofficial body represented one aspect of regional integration.[1]

A second predominant and increasing influence was the growing power of both Social Democratic and labor groups. Their programs of internationalism, disarmament, peace, and Scandinavian cooperation served as blocks for building a Nordic unity. Although the domestic program in each country fitted its own

[1] For the early period of the Scandinavian Inter-Parliamentary Union see O. J. Falnes, *Norway and the Nobel Peace Prize*, (New York, 1938), 115-116; Edvard Wavrinsky, "Några personliga minnen," *Årsbok för interparlamentariska grupperna*, 1919, 22-35; Eric C. Bellquist, "Inter-Scandinavian Coöperation," *Annals* of the American Academy of Political and Social Science, 168 (July, 1933), 183-184, 186-187; Louis de Geer, "Nordiskt samförstånd," *Nordisk tidskrift*, I (1925), 323-324.

national milieu, their natural similarity caused a growth of identification with each other. As these political and labor movements came to dominate the domestic scene they partly aided the development of a sense of community. After 1889 the three national Social Democratic parties met periodically in Scandinavian congresses, and national labor organizations likewise initiated their Nordic meetings at an early date. A Scandinavian labor congress of the 1890's conceived the idea of national federations. Started in 1898-1899, these national unions in due course united in a Scandinavian federation which served as an administrative clearing organ during industrial conflicts and collected funds to assist colleagues in other countries. Acting as carriers for integration, they tended to submerge nationalism and to increase international Scandinavianism and its symbols.

The expanding peace movement stressed the necessity of stating clearly Scandinavia's attitude toward war and armed belligerents. During the Russo-Japanese War in 1904 the northern states issued identical declarations of neutrality, but the Hague Convention of 1907, and its changes in rules, forced them to revise their statements. Austria's occupation of Bosnia-Herzegovina, with its threat of war, stimulated further action, and in 1909 Günther, now Swedish minister to Denmark, received instructions to negotiate a revision of these neutrality rules preparatory to another identical Scandinavian declaration. The Danish foreign minister, Count Carl William Ahlefeldt-Laurvig, gave his approval and a Danish delegate from the Hague Conference drafted a revision of the 1904 declaration. Denmark wished to bring Norway into these negotiations, but the integrity treaty prevented her inclusion. Obviously, also, Sweden remembered too much of 1905, and Denmark, sensitive to Swedish criticism, was unwilling to push the issue. Hjalmar Hammarskjöld, as the Swedish expert on international law, prepared a counterdraft which both countries approved.

Quiet on the international scene caused negotiations to lag until the second Morocco crisis in 1912 spurred both Danes and Swedes into action. Hammarskjöld went to Copenhagen to settle the remaining areas of disagreement, especially differences in

Danish and Swedish interpretations on territorial waters, pilot and navigational rules, and wartime services expected of neutrals. An exchange of notes, and some negotiations, easily removed these conflicts. At the same time serious consideration was given to a request of the powers for a permanent Scandinavian neutrality during hostilities, which Denmark approved, provided Norway and Sweden would also approve. Out of these negotiations came the elements of the neutrality declaration of 1912 when the Balkan wars required statements of policy from the Nordic states. Norway became a participant, preferring Scandinavian unity to isolation; she also agreed to the 1912 principle that changes in neutrality rules must have the consent of the other Scandinavian states.[2]

At the time of Archduke Ferdinand's assassination the concept of a neutral Scandinavia was firmly fixed with a joint up-to-date declaration ready for use upon the inception of hostilities. Immediately upon the outbreak of war the Swedish envoy at Oslo approached Norwegian Foreign Minister Nils Claus Ihlen with a proposal for an agreement that neither country would go to war against the other. In July Knut Wallenberg, the Swedish foreign minister, had broached the subject of a Norwegian-Swedish alliance with the Norwegian minister in Stockholm, and in August it was combined with the new proposal. The Norwegian government, while endorsing further negotiations, refused to sign an immediate agreement. Wallenberg, in making these proposals, sought to prevent a Norwegian alliance with the Entente which might result in Sweden, pressed by her pro-German Conservative faction, joining the Triple Alliance. Wallenberg hoped that an alliance with Norway would silence both pro-German and anti-Russian elements. He, therefore, sent instructions to the Swedish minister at Oslo to begin his negotiations.

Brief talks at Oslo and Stockholm sufficed for the drafting of a statement, even though an alliance scheme never materialized. The following public declaration came out of these discussions:[3]

2 Günther, Minnen, 115-122; Torsten Gihl, Den svenska utrikespolitikens historia, Volume IV (Stockholm, 1951), 14.

3 Eric C. Bellquist, Some Aspects of Recent Swedish Foreign Policy (University of California Publications, I, Number 3 [Berkeley, Calif., 1929]), 256.

"Inasmuch as war has broken out among several foreign powers, the Swedish and Norwegian Governments have mutually declared their determination, in the state of war that has arisen, each to maintain to the utmost of its ability, its neutrality in relation to all the belligerent powers. At the same time the two Governments have exchanged binding assurances, with a view to precluding the possibility that the condition of war in Europe might lead to hostile measures being taken by either country against the other." A Swedish proposal, which was not accepted, would have added: "Should either government find itself unable to defend its neutrality it shall, before agreeing to ally itself with any of the belligerents, inform the other government in order that it may in this eventuality prepare to join simultaneously on the same side."

On the same day this agreement was signed, August 8, 1914, it was announced in the Riksdag and Storting amidst approval from all sides. Within eight days another symbol, voluntary and spontaneous, was raised in the form of a memorial stone on the Norwegian-Swedish border whose inscription stated the fundamentals of integration: "Hereafter is war between the Scandinavian brothers impossible." These words of Oscar I, whose ideal neither Norwegians, Danes, nor Swedes had been able to achieve, now became a reality with a world at war. The process of integration long kept from realization by union discord, matured within nine years after dissolution of the union. Future generations and numerous Scandinavian leaders may be expected to deepen and broaden that integration, and establish amalgamated institutions to strengthen economic, social, cultural, and political ties.

With war on the continent actually begun, parliaments and peoples of both countries greeted with pleasure the no-war pledge and its symbols as a manifestation of the increasing collaboration of the Nordic countries. They could see in them evidence of a sense of community which had long been fostered by those who wished Scandinavian peoples to live together in amity and good will.

The Norwegian-Swedish agreement, however, was not extended to Denmark, and her government expressed some concern over

Scandinavia's future. Rumors indicated that Swedish anti-Danish
sentiments were responsible for the treaty. But a declaration of
common Scandinavian neutrality evidenced mutual good relations without expressing the unanimity of Nordic goals. When,
in November, Britain closed the North Sea to neutral shipping
in violation of the status quo agreement of 1908, the three countries joined in their dissent from the British action. Although of
no effect in altering Britain's action, or her attitude toward neutrals, her maintenance of an open channel for neutral shipping
north of Scotland evidently was the result of the Scandinavian
protest.[4] In drafting the identical notes, leaders also expressed a
wish for a more formal show of Scandinavian unity.

This desire materialized in the Three Kings' Meeting at
Malmö on December 14, 1914. It embodied a spectacular symbol
of integration. Although the three kings had met at the funeral
of Frederik in Copenhagen in 1912, neither Gustaf nor Haakon
had yet visited the other's country. The words of the declaration
and the invitation clearly indicated that integration was now to
be given greater substance. The three monarchs standing on the
balcony of their hotel in Malmö represented the disappearance
of animosities of 1905 and the achievement of a sense of community.

The firm accord begun by the Malmö meeting continued to
develop new strengths. Before Denmark notified the powers of
her decision to mine territorial waters, she carefully planned it
with Sweden to avoid violation of Swedish rights in the narrow
Sound. It was necessary, and actually easy after this, to venture
further and to establish naval cooperation in mine clearance. The
defense ministers, meeting in Oslo in February 1915, planned for
naval units of the three countries to cooperate in the common
task of keeping their territorial waters clear of floating mines and
of protecting merchant shipping. It deepened integration, although no joint command was created.[5]

In fiscal affairs Scandinavian integration received a setback

[4] Eli Heckscher, Kurt Bergendal, *et al., Sweden, Norway, Denmark, and
Iceland in the World War*, 58.
[5] *Sveriges historia* . . . , xiv, 182.

which could not be overcome. The finance ministers, fighting against inflation and discrepancies in their common currencies, found themselves overwhelmed by war's financial effects. Rapid inflation in Norway and Denmark in 1914-1915 made Sweden uneasy and caused her to prohibit the free sale of gold to the *Riksbank*. Although understandable, Sweden's action damaged beyond repair the forty-year currency convention. On the other hand, Danish and Norwegian trade representatives found that comparison of notes and frequent conferences prevented repetition of mistakes and an unfriendly and competitive atmosphere such as the British Trade Ministry tried to create when trade pacts were negotiated in 1915.[6] When Norway refused to join Denmark and Sweden in presenting a joint note on contraband, and the three countries attempted unilateral action, the poor bargain each made and the subsequent stiffening of Britain's policy on war materials revealed how beneficial a Scandinavian entente could be.[7] The joint protest in 1916 against British nullification of the Declaration of London had an immediate practical result.[8]

Even in serious incidents the three countries stood together. When Norway in 1916 protested the sinking of the Norwegian ship *Ravn* off North Cape, the Danish and Swedish ministers at Berlin intervened to secure a peaceful settlement and a more favorable Norwegian-German trade agreement. Germany expected Scandinavia to split at this point, but both Denmark and Sweden refused to yield. Gustaf V personally asked Wallenberg "to do what you can to solve the conflict for Norway," and urged the German minister at Stockholm to counsel his government to satisfy Norway.

Not all was pleasant in Scandinavian cooperation, and in this joint effort Norwegians and Danes found Hammarskjöld's "dictatorial manner" displeasing. At the same time, while resenting too hasty judgment or action by any Scandinavian leader, foreign and prime ministers willingly followed the dictates of necessity

---

[6] Alex. Foss, *I krigsaarene, 1914-1919* (Copenhagen, 1920), 259.
[7] Gihl, 91-92.
[8] Nils Ørvik, *The Decline of Neutrality, 1914-41* (Oslo, 1953), 92-103.

when they met in Copenhagen and Oslo in 1916. These sessions reaffirmed Nordic neutrality and the Oslo conference set forth a joint policy on handling belligerent violations of neutral rights. The Oslo principle of improvement of inter-Nordic commercial exchanges advanced further in the direction of full-scale economic cooperation. For example, severe crises in domestic production and consumption had resulted from restricted access to overseas markets. Although powerless to initiate concrete proposals, the foreign ministers plunged into the ramifications of a trade agreement to solve these crises.

This economic cooperation, which the three ministers discussed, was begun first by private individuals and companies. Assured of government approval of import-export agreements, they set out to provide their market needs. The necessity for alleviating rationing, either initiated or about to be, caused the utilization of inter-Scandinavian resources of food and industrial production. In May 1917, governmental exploration of the terms on which an inter-Scandinavian trade could be conducted broadened the scope of activities.

But the Three Kings' Meeting at Oslo in 1917 specifically organized the program of inter-Scandinavian trade. Christian X had proposed the meeting, but the Swedish government and King Gustaf V hesitated because of the unpleasant aspects of a Swedish return to the Norwegian capital after twelve years. Gustaf must be credited with persuading the Swedish cabinet to agree to the royal visit and to his statement of the "new union" which was the high tide of wartime cooperation. At Oslo a special committee worked out details of the program and adopted the principle of "reasonable bounds" for prices and amounts of commodities to be exchanged. Each country pledged itself to abstain from any trade agreement with another state if such agreement were harmful to Scandinavian interests. Each country's needs were roughly outlined: Denmark wanted finished products, steel, some raw materials for textile and steel industries, parts for railroads and streetcars, and raw materials for paper industries; Norway needed iron ore from Sweden, foodstuffs from Denmark, hides and wool; Sweden desired foodstuffs, grain, and wool.[9] The value of Danish exports to Sweden showed a seventy percent increase and to Norway almost twenty percent. Norway's lower demands on Denmark resulted from differences in population, and from strenuous efforts by the Norwegian government to maintain self-sufficiency. Although the agreement ceased to function early in 1919[10] it pointed out obvious lessons in Scandinavian cooperation which proved useful in the later "Oslo Bloc."[11] Economic collaboration proved clearly in monetary and material terms the value to be gained from integration, especially in crisis periods.

Political cooperation of the Nordic countries during the war period showed strong neutralism and a special interest in a postwar juridical organization. The colorful note in the Three Kings' Meeting at Malmö and later at Oslo obscured the real nature and practical results of these conferences. Gustaf's visit to Oslo symbolized the movement toward deepening Scandinavian integration, but, while kings displayed their unity outwardly, their ministers embarked on planning for future economic and political cooperation. All Scandinavia heartily applauded him when he spoke of a ". . . new union, not of the old sort, but an understanding and a hearty union whose life force I hope shall be of a more enduring nature than the previous."[12] The clasped hands of Haakon VII, Christian X, and Gustaf V denoted the living faith in the unbroken unity of Scandinavia. This scene and that of the balcony at Malmö were reprinted often during the

[9] *Sveriges historia* . . . , xiv, 427; Gihl, 312-313. For the last eight months of the war this barter pact put pressure on the Allied Powers in their economic relations with the North and was vitally important to the Scandinavian peoples. In specific terms, comparing the first two months of 1917 and 1918, figures show the following gains: Butter to Norway from Denmark, 27,000 kg. and 290,000 kg. respectively; meat, 490,000 kg. and 1,990,000 kg.; butter from Denmark to Sweden, 17,000 and 1,266,00 kg.; pork to Sweden, none and 376,000 kg.; meat to Sweden, none and 1,680,000 kg. Foss, *I krigsaarene*, 88-89.

[10] Cf. Gihl, 394-395, for ministerial conference of May 26-28, 1919, which officially concluded the economic agreement.

[11] On economic agreements of 1917-1918, see two speeches of Foss, *I krigsaarene*; Wilhelm Keilhau, *Norge og verdenskrigen* (Oslo, 1927), 249.

[12] Rütger Essén, *Sverige upplever världen* (Stockholm, 1935), 325.

ensuing years to show the vigor and vitality of the mutual trust and interest of Nordic peoples.

On the more practical side two committees were appointed at Oslo to plan economic cooperation and to study problems of neutrality and international law. The first committee's labors produced beneficial results in the trade pact which has been discussed. The second committee's report to the respective governments in May 1918 rested partly on similar labors of the Scandinavian Inter-Parliamentary Union. The Committee presented an interesting political conformation with its Conservative and Social Democratic Swedes, its two *Venstre* Norwegians, and its *Venstre* Danes. Ten years previously the Norwegians and the Conservative Swede would not have been associated together in any enterprise. Their report, published at the end of January 1919, planned for a juridical international organization with a secretariat, council, and other adjuncts of the League-to-be. The report had little effect on the eventual League of Nations Covenant, but it showed Nordic interest in avoiding the "political League" which received much support in France, England, and the United States. The Scandinavian states on request sent representatives to Paris to advise on the Covenant, but these arrived too late to participate in the Hotel Crillon conference of the neutral states. Their objections to what was accomplished there rested, however, on wartime planning in Scandinavia.[13]

In other planning sessions the Scandinavian states mainly attempted to establish common policies for an era of peace. Ministerial conferences of 1918, 1919, and 1920 dealt to a great extent with these topics and in the last year the Stockholm meeting concentrated on discussion of the League of Nations, ending with an agreement to confer together before asking admission. At another conference in Paris financial experts laid out Nordic schemes on national credits to foreign countries and postwar pay-

[13] On these meetings and the plan for an international organization see S. Shepard Jones, *The Scandinavian States and the League of Nations* (Princeton, N.J., 1939), 26-46; Bellquist, *Some Aspects of Recent Swedish Foreign Policy*, 265-272; Gihl, 394-397.

ments. But these conferences proved, unfortunately, the last for a decade.

By 1920, however, institutions had developed which could serve as carriers for Scandinavian integration if governments neglected their opportunities. The Scandinavian Inter-Parliamentary Union continued to act as an advisory body for political ends, while the Scandinavian Administrative Union, organized in 1918, also bore some of the load of integration through representatives of the national civil services and government staffs. The inauguration of *Foreningen Norden* (Nordic Society) in 1919 served partly to achieve this purpose. It owed its conception to the Three Kings' Meeting in 1917 and to ministerial conferences during the following two years. Its central figure during its formative stage was a Dane, C. J. Heerfordt, who worked through friends and political leaders of Scandinavia. His ideal envisioned an organization to assist governments in the creation of common or joint Nordic programs. The strong opposition to his scheme for political-economic unity under Swedish leadership, however, caused the creation of private organizations within each of the countries to avoid any diminution of national sovereignty. A small Swedish group started the idea of a Scandinavian information agency and Danes, Swedes, and Norwegians joined in exerting their influence in its behalf.[14] In 1922 Iceland joined, and Finland followed in 1924, with small local societies, in addition to the national parent body, being created in each country. *Foreningen Norden* started to publish a series of brochures on Scandinavian subjects and with the assistance of the Letterstedt Foundation assumed responsibility for *Nordisk tidskrift*, which has now served for over thirty years as a journal of information and propaganda on Scandinavian affairs.[15] The society promotes

14 Members of this group were the Danish historian, Aage Friis; Eli Heckscher, the Swedish economic historian; J. L. Mowinckel, president of the Norwegian Storting and later prime minister; Niels Neergaard; Alex. Foss, Danish leader of Scandinavian causes; E. Hagerup Bull, Norwegian politician and lawyer. The heads of the three national societies were Harald Grieg (Norway), Thorsten Nothin (Sweden), and C. V. Bramsnaes (Denmark). The latter for over a generation was a leading spirit in the work of *Foreningen Norden*.

15 It might be, as Julius Lange said, "that menfolk do not read *Nordisk tidskrift*, but God's angels do it," but its information circulates among an

study trips, lectures, meetings, publication of books, and reading circles. Its purposes, as set forth in the first paragraph of its charter, supplement a deepening integration.[16]

> The organizations will set as their task to deepen the feeling of sympathy between the Scandinavian peoples, extend the cultural and economic connections between them, and forward their internal cooperation. They will, in so far as their ability extends, give support to the cooperation which has started, and give impulse to new cooperation, in so far as natural conditions exist. . . . In this work the organizations will have as their goal to strengthen the Scandinavian peoples' cooperation inwards and outwards.

Since the trend of Scandinavianism continues, and is increasing its importance, it cannot be judged lightly. The rapid advances in such activities sprang naturally from wartime cooperation and from the labors of devoted men like Alex. Foss, who spent their lives in seeking the expansion of Scandinavian integration. In part, too, this growth served as an example and a stimulant, for a wide variety of groups joined in the trend toward formation of Scandinavian organizations. Bishops of the Lutheran churches of the Nordic states formed a congress; a Scandinavian Journalist Committee was established. The Scandinavian Peace Society and the Joint Committee of the Scandinavian Royal Sports' Societies both concerned themselves with peace, since the latter organization handled Scandinavian participation in the Olympic Games. Scandinavian housewives banded together in 1919, as did tourist agencies, orthopedists, nurses, and football players; and throughout the 1920's this tendency to form Scandinavian regional associations continually expanded.

The cooperative societies, stimulated partly by integration,

---

elite of active Nordic leaders and active Scandinavianists. For information on *Foreningen Norden* see Aage Houken, *Det nye Norden* (Copenhagen, 1940), 31-37; Louis de Geer, "Nordiskt samförstånd," *Nordisk tidskrift*, I (1925), 325-326.

[16] Quoted in Otto Leroy Karlström, "The 'Scandinavian' Approach to Political Integration" (Ph.D. Thesis, University of Chicago, 1952), 35. Used by permission of the author.

formed a central regional organization in the *Nordisk andels-forbund* in 1918. Its factories today produce light bulbs, rubber boots, automobile tires, and a variety of products; it mills flour; its sales cooperatives market farm products abroad; its purchase cooperatives buy materials from foreign producers to supply their wants. Likewise, Nordic labor and employer associations, which formed Scandinavian central bodies prior to 1914, emphasized conciliation and collective bargaining agreements, thereby aiding attainment of industrial peace. Business firms formed central Scandinavian offices, thus facilitating the rise of pooling and cartel arrangements. Scandinavian shippers' associations agreed upon passenger and freight rates and upon rules of navigation, and assisted in information services. Scandinavian tourist agencies banded together to encourage travel in northern Europe and to assist in easing difficulties in communication. The northern pulp industries cartel of 1920 merged with the European forest products cartel in 1936, with controls over prices, quantity, quality, and type of production. Pooling arrangements in shipping, electrical supply industries, fish products and their processing, manufacture of cellulose products, and in a multiplicity of industrial commodities established relative economic peace and taught lessons of regional economic cooperation. Reduction of competition in agricultural products has been achieved; for example, dairies agreed to make complementary types of cheeses to avoid both duplication and price competition. This functional approach meets hardly any obstacles in its trend toward regional integration.

The admission of Finland to these Nordic associations created no particular problem. Some objected to the term "Scandinavian" being applied to Finns, but in spite of language and racial backgrounds, they have been accepted as equals in any Scandinavian association. The terms "Norden" and "Nordisk" were devised in part to encompass the Finns, and the prevalence of the terms in Scandinavia shows their general acceptance.[17] Finland first joined the *Nordisk andelsforbund* and, thereafter, became a member of

---

17 See Karlström, *op cit.*, 5-6, esp. 6, for definition and analysis of the terms Scandinavian and Norden, *ibid.*, 8-13, and appendix.

Foreningen Norden and the Scandinavian Inter-Parliamentary Union. Finland's defense problems, her racial and linguistic dissimilarities, and her competition with Norway and Sweden in forest products proved no source of conflict. Of course, Swedish cultural and religious traditions aided Finland's participation in schemes of Nordic cooperation.

During the decade of the 1920's, in the absence of ministerial conferences, the main point of contact was the League of Nations. The brunt of political cooperation was borne by the Scandinavian Inter-Parliamentary Union and *Foreningen Norden*, but to foreign eyes the sharing of ideas and policies in the League of Nations justified the use of the term Scandinavian Bloc. The Nordic states' entry into the League came partly from an Inter-Parliamentary Union meeting in 1919 and from the Scandinavian Peace Congress session at Stockholm the same year. Each country decided for itself whether or not to join the League, but it seems no accident that the Storting, Riksdag, and Landsting simultaneously approved applications to the League in 1920.

In the League the three countries and Finland pursued similar policies, with exceptions mainly on details of procedure. On numerous occasions their decisions resulted from conferences of their delegates at Geneva and their common approach to League problems encouraged the growth of cooperation. The principle of universality in membership in the League received Nordic support. They heartily favored Germany's admission, and Sweden, backed by Denmark and Norway, arranged preliminaries for her entry. They conferred and agreed on a policy on the nonpermanent members of the Council and urged, naturally, the election of a Baltic state. They fought jointly for rotation of membership of the nonpermanent seats on the Council and approved together their increase in 1923. After conferences with the Swedish delegate, the Danish and Norwegian representatives favored Sweden's plan for no increase in the number of permanent members of the Council in 1924; their united effort was chiefly responsible for a defeat for Poland and Spain on this issue.[18]

[18] Jones, *The Scandinavian States and the League of Nations*, 116.

A main policy, however, of the Nordic states in the League was to bolster its legalistic and juridical functions. Codification of international law held chief interest for the three states and this led them to support Hammarskjöld for the chairmanship of the Committee of Experts for the Progressive Codification of International Law. The committee received both common and joint Scandinavian support, and in 1930 the resolution calling for a Council inquiry commission on codification came from a joint Scandinavian proposal. Their enthusiasm for juridical aspects of international organization diverted them to an interest in the Permanent Court and conciliation and arbitration treaties.

Denmark consistently advocated compulsory arbitration conventions, while Norway and Sweden clung to reservations on security, sovereignty, and "vital interests." Between 1922 and 1925, however, their attitudes changed, and in 1924 the Swedish Social Democratic cabinet accepted the principle of compulsory arbitration. A series of treaties were signed by the Scandinavian countries, which were "substantially alike." In Sweden the treaties received full support and passed without a recorded vote in both houses of parliament; in Denmark the lower house approved unanimously. In Norway the Conservative and Agrarian parties and their newspapers stirred up a furore, with *Tidens Tegn, Nationen,* and *Drammens Tidende* leading the journalistic fight against their acceptance. The reluctance of some Storting members to accept them arose out of the Danish-Norwegian dispute over Greenland, but, after protracted debate, parliament approved the treaties in 1927 by a vote of 90 to 53. Of the minority, however, only thirty were Conservatives and Agrarians, indicating splits in other parties. For Scandinavian integration the most important aspect of these arbitration treaties was their deliberate discarding of principles of sovereignty. This partial elimination of nationalism effected a popular willingness to yield on inter-Scandinavian controls over some sections of national life.[19]

[19] See Jones, *The Scandinavian States and the League of Nations,* 201-206, on these treaties; cf. Bellquist, *Some Aspects of Recent Swedish Foreign Policy,* 322-335.

Two of the Scandinavian countries have the dubious honor of submitting the first international conflict to the League. Sweden and Finland agreed to arbitration of the Åland Islands case and approved the council's decision, although groups in both countries grumbled briefly over the peculiar status of the islanders, who, incidentally, were mainly Swedish-speaking. The dispute, stemming from Swedish fears of their possession by a great power and of their subjugation to a Finnish majority on the mainland, arose in 1921 when it appeared that Swedish and Finnish troops were ready to battle over their possession. With cultural autonomy of the islanders assured and with guarantees of status quo on neutralization, the Swedes accepted gracefully the decision of the Council.

A later dispute between Denmark and Norway further illustrated the Scandinavian intent to use peaceful means for the settlement of conflicts. Norway claimed the eastern part of Greenland as *terra nullius*. An oral agreement on Greenland accompanied Danish recognition of Norwegian claims to Svalbard in 1919, which was not withdrawn in 1921 when Denmark claimed sovereignty over all of Greenland. Denmark accepted an agreement in 1924 giving Norwegians rights of residence, trade, and admission to scientific work in Greenland, but failed to clarify sovereignty over the eastern part. Motivated by nationalism and beset by economic difficulties, Norwegian members of a whaling and scientific expedition, with the support of the Norwegian government, landed on Eastern Greenland to claim the portion lying between 71° and 75°. Under terms of the arbitration agreement of 1927, however, Norway could not refuse submission of the case to an arbitration board.

In 1933 a Hague decision gave Denmark full rights and sovereignty in Greenland. Norwegians wrote newspaper articles, brochures, and books denouncing Denmark. Even a former Norwegian foreign minister, Arnold Raestad, published anti-Danish articles and pamphlets, and W. C. Brøgger prophesied that a future date would see Norway's rights rectified. The Greenland case weakened rapport for a time between Denmark and Nor-

way but did not noticeably hinder continued Nordic cooperation.[20]

A partial reason for Dano-Norwegian difficulties in Greenland
was the depression and its stress on an autarchic system of economy. The Nordic countries resolved to counteract this tendency
and proposed that the smaller nations sign conventions for a reduction of restrictions on trade. The leading force behind the
effort to eliminate trade restrictions was Norway and her foreign
minister, Mowinckel. In 1930 he invited the Scandinavian states,
together with Belgium and the Netherlands, to a meeting at
Oslo to explore further the possibilities of either elimination or
reduction of trade restrictions and tariffs. The conference produced a limited convention which specified that no duties would
be increased without advance notice of fifteen days. It went into
effect in 1932 with Finland assenting to it the following year.
This Oslo convention, and the bloc it created, exemplified both
Scandinavian and small state solidarity. It gave impetus to a
limited effort to alleviate economic distress produced by economic
depression. Halvdan Koht said of the convention when he was
foreign minister in 1938:[21] "Practical obligations . . . did not go
very far, and the practical results of the agreement could not be
of great importance in the economic life of the world. But at a
moment when ruthless economic warfare was prevailing and
when even such modest agreements in favour of a partial truce
as attempted by the Geneva Convention of March 24th, 1930,
had proved impracticable, the Oslo Convention was of great
moral importance as an omen of peaceful tendencies."

As a consequence of the pact, Norway dropped plans for increased duties on a few industrial articles from Sweden. Likewise,
tariffs on rubber tires, which affected Belgium and the Netherlands, were not imposed, and Belgium abandoned her proposal
for higher duties on cardboard and paper products. In 1934
Mowinckel proposed extending information on prospective
changes into all fields of commercial restrictions. Finland, Swed-
en, and Norway later carried this proposal into effect. At the

[20] See Houken, *Det nye Norden*, 80-86, for discussion of the Greenland case.
[21] Koht, "The Oslo Convention and After," *Le Nord*, i (1938), 39-40.

Hague meeting in 1936 these states drafted a convention to limit the application of quotas within the Bloc, especially on such articles as glass, furs, and paper. This convention also made more effective the nondiscrimination principle of the original Oslo Convention.

Further economic crises in 1937 drove the Oslo Bloc countries in the opposite direction toward strengthened domestic subventions and restrictions. At Oslo in 1938 the members disagreed so completely that only the skeleton of the original Oslo Convention remained in an agreement on mutual information on commercial restrictions. In eight years of economic cooperation Scandinavia failed to achieve a goal of united action because of international economic forces and self-interest that left the small states impotent.

Efforts of the Nordic states to attain mutual assistance programs were mixtures of success and failure. In 1934 the Nordic countries established the "Nabolands Boards" to encourage "commercial and economic co-operation between the countries of the North, taking into consideration, on the one hand, the possibility of extending mutual trade between the Northern Countries, and on the other, the investigation of opportunities for achieving closer co-operation between the countries of the North with a view to safeguarding their general commercial interests."[22] Delegations to the "Nabolands Boards" examined areas of economic collaboration and recommended changes and reforms to their respective governments. Annual meetings took place at Stockholm in 1935 and, successively, at Copenhagen, Oslo, and Helsinki. In addition the "Boards" agitated for application of "Northern reservation clauses," exempting special agreements among the Scandinavian countries from trade pacts with other states.

A Nordic tariff union also found its strong advocates even in the midst of depression and economic rivalry. During the 1920's *Foreningen Norden* conducted essay contests on the subject and published the prize pamphlet. Its meeting in 1923 dealt solely

[22] H. J. Procopé, "Economic Co-Operation between the Northern Countries and the Joint Delegations for its Promotion," *Le Nord*, 1 (1938), 54-57.

with the subject, and here hearty advocates of the tariff union appeared. During the period of the Oslo Bloc success, *Foreningen Norden* revived the project in 1934 and appointed the Scandinavian Committee to explore various alternatives on customs preferences, joint agreements on common business interests, further improvement of trade mark, copyright, business and corporation laws, and other matters. Its report served as a basis for a ministerial conference in 1934 when Rickard Sandler, *Foreningen Norden* member and Swedish foreign minister, urged positive consideration of either a customs union or first steps leading to that goal. But by 1937 Scandinavian governments placed a defense pact as first priority and defined as unattainable the adjustments in currency, production, and trade to make a customs union possible.[23]

In the two decades after World War I, political and diplomatic relations between the northern states were limited to cooperation in the League and profitable conventions for compulsory arbitration of disputes. Economic cooperation lagged until the depression forced Scandinavia to try the Oslo Bloc convention. The Bloc attempted an economic integration on a small scale, but competition and restrictions on free international trade, in their larger setting, thwarted this effort. The tendency to think as Scandinavians in both economic and political areas constituted a first step, however, toward creating a definite ideal of Scandinavian regional unity and solidarity. The experience gained in these first steps also became useful after World War II when the climate was more conducive to experiments in the direction of both political and economic collaboration on a deeper plane.[24]

[23] Houken, *Det nye Norden*, 62-65, 73-74.

[24] For good reviews of general Scandinavian problems and some aspects of Scandinavian collaboration see Herbert Tingsten, *Svensk utrikesdebatt mellan världskrigen* (Stockholm, 1944) and his English edition of the same work *The Debate on the Foreign Policy of Sweden, 1918-1939* (London, 1949), together with Rowland Kenney, *The Northern Tangle* (London, 1946).

CHAPTER XV

◇◇

WAR AND PEACE

◇◇

THE two past decades have seen the growth of integration to a point where Scandinavian countries are establishing important institutions with some political powers. The movement has not come smoothly or in a steady flow but with spurts in which success exceeds failure. During these years the major advances have been in social, cultural, and economic collaboration, and the most notable failure in the creation of a defense alliance. Twice in these decades the Scandinavian countries have tried to attain such a pact and twice they have had their efforts go for naught because of conflicts in policies or outside factors. During the 1930's optimism among various pro-Scandinavian groups, spurred by the creation of the Oslo Bloc, favored a Nordic defense union. Many articles and speeches drew attention to such an idea when Germany occupied the Ruhr and rearmed in 1936. Two Swedish military experts, writing in *Nya Dagligt Allehanda*, pointed to Nordic isolation as a result of excessive national emphasis on neutrality and disarmament.

This rising public interest in a defense union received a sharp check when Danish Prime Minister Thorvald Stauning said a defense union constituted the sheerest utopia. His realistic statement of Scandinavia's inability to defend itself, or to prevent aggression, seemed most unfeeling and blind when Denmark, as the most vulnerable, needed such guarantees. In Sweden the editor of *Göteborgs Handels-och Sjöfartstidning* wrote that "Stauning has taken the nerve out of Scandinavian cooperation." Both Norwegian and Swedish foreign ministers joined with Stauning in calling the defense union project chimerical. Rickard Sandler, always an earnest supporter of Scandinavian unity, feared that the Soviet Union and a rearmed Germany would assume Nordic aggressive designs in creation of a defense community. Halvdan Koht, with realistic sense, commented on the absence of a common enemy against which Scandinavia could direct a defensive military alliance. However, he differed from Sandler and Stauning by advocating a coordinated defense program to improve Scandinavia's chances of escaping war. These statements and public attention on a defense union at least made apparent the question of Nordic policy if war came.

The two meetings of foreign ministers in Stockholm and Oslo in 1937 and 1938 dealt indirectly with Koht's suggestion. At Stockholm in September 1937, the ministers, drawing on experiences of World War I, drafted a Nordic plan of action in case of hostilities. They agreed to revise the 1912 neutrality rules in view of alterations in Scandinavian attitudes, and in 1938 signed an amended agreement. An exchange-of-goods convention, similar to the one devised during World War I, was arranged, giving a rough outline of quotas and terms of trade. A year later at Helsinki the four foreign ministers studied other similar proposals, while Sweden and Finland drafted a defense plan for the Åland Islands. Their possible occupation by either Germany or the Soviet Union, and their use as bases for aggression, vitally affected Finno-Swedish defense policies. The two states easily arranged outlines of an agreement, but stopped negotiations because of the effects which any change in the status of the islands would have on Soviet and German Baltic policy. These negotiations, and the general unease of the Nordic states, caused Hitler to invite them to sign nonaggression treaties with Germany. The four ministers, speaking as a unit from their meeting at Stockholm, refused the offer. But, since each state could respond as it wished to Germany's invitation, Denmark signed such a pact with Hitler, thus shocking the other Nordic countries by this clear exposition of Danish defenselessness. At the final prewar meeting of the Scandinavian states in August 1939, the four governments drafted a joint declaration of neutrality.

After the outbreak of war in September 1939, the Scandinavian states held several ministerial conferences. The prime ministers and chiefs of the foreign offices and the Icelandic minister at

Copenhagen formally declared Scandinavia's neutrality and pledged their mutual assistance in attaining respect for their position. In October the chiefs of state and prime and foreign ministers met in Stockholm. Christian X, Haakon VII, and Gustaf V, once again as in World War I, symbolized unity and peace, and at their side stood Finnish President K. B. Kallio. The conference further revised neutrality rules and then drafted a joint declaration on Nordic nonintervention in the war. By this move they sought primarily to avert a Soviet attack on Finland, against whom a Russian propaganda campaign was in progress. But Nordic unity could not stop Stalin, and Finland's war status and Scandinavian policy took precedence at the December meeting of the three foreign ministers. Prior to the conference Rickard Sandler, for years an advocate of mutual assistance and now proposing military aid to Finland short of intervention, was forced to resign because neither Per Albin Hansson, the Swedish prime minister, nor Gustaf V would permit so bold a program.[1] Consequently no one advocated a united stand in Finland's behalf. The meeting did agree to permit civil and military volunteers for Finland, however, and as individual states they granted some financial assistance.

Despite strong pro-Finnish groups in Sweden, the government did not deviate from its stringent policy. When, early in 1940, France and Britain asked permission for transit of their troops over Swedish territory to aid Finland, Sweden refused on grounds of her neutrality. Norway also rejected the same request on the assumption that it would involve her in war. Nordic attempts to remain neutral and to respect all the rules proved fruitless, and in December Germany began a propaganda campaign against Scandinavia and completed military plans for an invasion. During these months until April 9, the Nordic states constantly exchanged information on their policies, considered together notes from the belligerents, and protested jointly both German and British violations of Nordic neutrality. Since Finland's treaty with the Soviet Union restricted her freedom in foreign policy,

[1] For background on Swedish attitudes on Finland see Tingsten, *Svensk utrikesdebatt* . . . , 312-387.

she was not a part of these diplomatic ventures. Although Sweden and Denmark could not join Norway in protesting against violations of her territorial waters, their foreign offices kept abreast of the latest news and assisted Norwegians in every possible way. Scandinavian military and naval attachés in Germany exchanged information and warned the Norwegian government of an impending German attack prior to its inception.

The invasion of Denmark and Norway on April 9, 1940, left Sweden to pursue her neutral course alone. When Norway resisted German aggression, Sweden extended no aid and even permitted transit of German troops across Swedish soil. The argument for Swedish submission to Hitler's demands still remains a debatable point. On one result of Sweden's staying out of war, there can be no valid disagreement. Had Germany occupied Sweden, the latter's subsequent role as a haven for Danish and Norwegian refugees would have been impossible.[2] Sweden intended no harm to Norway or Denmark, but sought only to avoid her own entanglement. Although her neutral position benefited the three other Nordic countries greatly, Sweden was roundly criticized, chiefly by Norway. The Danes, hoping for better treatment at Swedish hands, complained much less than Norwegians. The revival of old Norwegian-Swedish tensions ultimately made Norway hesitant about entering any defense union with Sweden as a member.

Before the conclusion of hostilities, Norway found greater reason for qualms about Sweden. In April 1945, the Norwegian government asked for Sweden's intervention in the war to prevent the devastation of northern Norway. Plans called for Swedish troops to join Norwegian "police forces" stationed in Sweden and to invade Norway, forcing German troops to surrender. After detailed study of the proposal the Swedes refused, since a Ger-

[2] Literature on the subject of Norwegian-Swedish and Danish-Swedish relations is extensive and mention need be made only of the documents published after the war: *Sveriges förhållande till Danmark och Norge under krigsåren* (Stockholm, 1945); *Transiteringsfrågan* (2 vols., Stockholm, 1947); *Norges forhold til Sverige under krigen 1940-1945* (3 vols., Oslo, 1947-1950). These publications clarified and quieted public and governmental opinion, especially the outraged feelings of those who suffered under occupation. A minority, however, remained dissatisfied.

man defeat on the continent seemed so imminent. Norwegian military leaders, fearing that their country would be the great and terrible *Götterdämmeruung* of the Nazis, expressed their bitterness over Swedish hesitancy. In an official Norwegian White Book in 1950 these same Norwegian leaders recognized Sweden's policy as wholly correct and reasonable.

Norwegian fears proved unfounded, and with the war's end in 1945 the Nordic states turned to new problems in their relations with one another. The revival of economic and cultural cooperation came easily, because of necessity, the number of carriers, and the existence of institutions able to cope with animosities bred in wartime. Political conflicts, however, proved more difficult to solve and such imperfections as do exist in Norwegian-Swedish relations find their origin in the aftereffects of the war. The entrenched majority position of Labor-Social Democratic postwar governments in both countries, and Danish socialist strength, has proved of major value in the re-establishment of an easy relationship productive of further integration. When Sweden offered financial loans and grants for immediate use, Denmark, Finland, and Norway accepted gratefully. Swedish grants or loans totaled over a billion dollars, the payment of which immediately after the war's end enlarged their value and helped to eradicate some latent hostilities. Sweden's willingness to provide these funds arose in part from a sense of guilt, but, even without that motive, her government still would have been eager to assist her neighbors to achieve stability.

In international organization as in the area of economy, the Nordic countries resumed their collaboration. Norway participated in plans for the United Nations from the first, while Denmark waited for liberation in May 1945 before sending representatives to the United Nations meeting in San Francisco. Sweden was seated in 1946 with strong support from both Danish and Norwegian governments.[3] The views of the three countries on the United Nations paralleled each other so closely that Norway

[3] For a review of Swedish discussion of the United Nations see Herbert Tingsten, *Debatten om nordisk enhet, Norden serie*, Number 3 (Stockholm, 1943).

represented all three, and Denmark and Sweden even issued a formal declaration approving Norway's actions. The declaration symbolized their reunion as a Nordic community.[4]

In the work of the United Nations, representatives of the three countries resumed their League custom of caucus prior to General Assembly sessions. While on the Security Council, the Norwegian representative kept the other two delegates informed daily of his activity and, therefore, his statements in the Council's chamber echoed the sentiments of the Nordic states. At frequent intervals and prior to United Nations' sessions, the three foreign ministers, often joined by an Icelandic official, issued joint communiqués revealing Nordic foreign policy in respect to both the United Nations and to problems outside that organization. The Scandinavian sense of community appeared, for example, prior to the Big Four meeting in Berlin in 1953, when the three foreign ministers issued a joint plea for peace and for settlement of the conflict between East and West. Similarly, before other conferences of the major powers, Nordic joint notes supported the purposes of the meetings. Scandinavian solidarity became so notable in this period that Trygve Lie, then Norwegian foreign minister and later Secretary-General of the United Nations, felt impelled to say:[5] "Within the framework of the Charter some small nations would naturally collaborate more closely between themselves, a collaboration that should not be interpreted as having any bearing on their relations to any other Powers."

On specific problems the Scandinavian states have shown a higher degree of unanimity than in League days. For example, when divergences over membership and the principle of universality appeared, the Swedes altered their views to achieve unity among the Nordic countries.[6] They arrived, through several conferences, at a decision on a *de facto* recognition of Red

[4] On questions relating to the Nordic countries and the United Nations for the first seven years, see Martha Trytten, "The Scandinavian Countries and the United Nations: Some Political Problems" (Mss. Master's Thesis, University of Wisconsin, 1953). Used by permission of the author.

[5] Trytten, *op. cit.*, 19.

[6] Trytten, *op. cit.*, 203.

China and they attempted to secure membership for her in the United Nations and her recognition by other states. For them the basic principle on which acknowledgement of a regime rested was not its political complexion, but whether or not it could maintain order within its borders. When the U.N. voted sanctions against Spain, Norway, because of her own wartime stand against fascism, favored these penalties. Denmark and Sweden voted for a Norwegian amendment which struck a middle course between the Polish demand for diplomatic and economic sanctions and the American proposal for withdrawal of diplomatic representation. Norway outdistanced her Nordic neighbors in applying sanctions, but ministerial conferences narrowed this difference.

Other issues arising in the United Nations showed further Nordic unity. The Arab-Israel conflict illustrated quite well the extent of Scandinavian cooperation. A Norwegian compromise on the division of Palestine and an international commission was, in reality, a joint proposal. Although other states rejected it, portions of the Norwegian suggestion formed part of the plan utilized by Swedish Count Folke Bernadotte whose appointment was backed by the northern countries. The Danish representative, to conform to the views held by Norway and Sweden,[7] reversed his vote on a resolution for an international control of disputed areas. Throughout the settlement of the Greek issue, and the attempted solution of Balkan problems, Scandinavian policy and votes constantly presented a united front. On Korea and Red China it appeared several times as if the Nordic countries would split. When a resolution for the condemnation of Red China as an aggressor came before the General Assembly, the Scandinavian states did go their separate ways. Denmark and Norway joined with the United States in voting for the resolution while Sweden abstained. Perhaps Norwegian and Danish membership in the North Atlantic Treaty Organization had something to do with their votes being cast for the affirmative side which the United States strongly supported. But these two countries favored a Swedish proposition for a United Nations embargo on trade with Red China.

[7] Trytten, *op. cit.*, 278-279.

When Korea became the locale of a new war, or police action, in June 1950, the Scandinavian countries approved of sending troops and supplies to resist aggression. Their peoples, likewise, favored strong measures, even if their countries were themselves still recovering from occupation or straining to assist in reconstruction. During the first months of hostilities in Korea the Nordic states joined in approving actions of the United Nations and its commander in Korea. An American proposal to bypass the Security Council, after the Soviet delegate blocked action there, was jointly favored by the Nordic countries. Sweden, however, proved less willing than Denmark and Norway to pledge military forces in the war, but she did accept a proposal for an international police force. Hospital equipment, medical personnel, ships, and supplies were sent by each of the three states separately to Korea and evidenced the readiness of the three countries to sacrifice for world peace.

Nordic cooperation in the United Nations constituted a normal act with traditions of some decades behind it. But a defense union, although its advocates appeared prior to World War II, could not muster either tradition or practical experience in its favor. During the war, defense union ideas, similar to those of the 1930's, began to arise. Swedish debate on the issue, paralleled by nebulous proposals from the Norwegian government in exile in London, revealed Sweden's abandonment of her traditional alliance-free policy. Swedes naturally assumed that their country would be the center for a Nordic defense system whose members would be pledged to military support of each other. The union would be aloof from blocs and great power rivalries.

Debate on a defense union did not become acute until the Czechoslovakian crisis in 1948. In the spring Norway and Sweden opened negotiations for a definite proposal on a defense union. Later Denmark joined in and her prime minister, Hans Hedtoft, became a leader for the pact. Each country maintained clear lines of policy during these negotiations. Sweden wished an alliance-free defense union, while Norway wanted strong ties with the West. Sweden agreed to a system by which the resources of all three countries would be pledged for the defense of the other.

For her part, during negotiations, Norway gave up temporarily her demand for formal ties with the West. Both Norway and Sweden agreed to avoid commitments to either of the power blocs.[8]

By September these tentative proposals became the basis of formal negotiations. In a meeting in Stockholm the foreign ministers agreed to study construction of a defense union and in October, impelled by what they learned at Paris from American Secretary of State George Marshall, they selected a military committee. Its members, equally representative of ministerial, administrative, and legislative bodies,[9] laid out numerous specific items and postulates for further negotiations. Scandinavian consultations with Marshall produced clarity, if not hope, on the Nordic defense union. He saw Halvard Lange and Gustav Rasmussen, the Norwegian and Danish foreign ministers, together, and Östen Undén, prophetically enough, met with Marshall later. All three sounded out the American Secretary of State on possible delivery of war materials to a Scandinavian defense union and on the projected Atlantic Pact. Marshall was quite reserved in his answers, but from him, and a later Department of State news release, the ministers learned that members of the Pact and allies of the United States would have priority on procurement of war materials. Marshall was undoubtedly influenced by French opposition to any European defense plan which would scatter expenditures and military supplies. But American pressure for entry of the Scandinavian countries into the Atlantic Pact was most telling in its discouragement of negotiations for a Nordic defense union.

[8] For data on the defense union, the best are: Leroy Karlström, "Beginning and End of Norwegian Neutrality," *The Norseman*, IX (1951), 217-231, 289-298; Karlström, "The 'Scandinavian' Approach to Political Integration." Cf. also Lennart Hirschfeldt, *Skandinavien och Atlantpakten. De skandinaviska alliansförhandlingarna 1948-1949, Världspolitikens dagsfrågor* (Stockholm: Utrikespolitiska institutet, 1949), 4-5.

[9] Denmark: Vice-Admiral A. H. Vedel, Minister Frantz Hvass and Folketing members Poul Hansen and Harald Petersen; Norway: Trygve Brateli, Dag Bryn, W. Munthe Kaas, and Lt. General Ole Berg; Sweden: Landshövding Carl Hamilton, Riksdag members Elon Anderson and Sven Andersson (later G. F. Thapper as his replacement), and Defense Chief Major General Nils Swedlund.

In November the American elections, with their surprising victory for President Harry S. Truman, changed the schedule for negotiations on the Atlantic Pact. The State Department worked hurriedly to create the North Atlantic Treaty Organization (NATO) which hastened Scandinavian negotiations. Due to Norwegian insistence, a report from the military committee was moved forward a month, which meant only partial exploration of the international and Scandinavian scene. Its report, submitted in part to the meeting of ministers in December 1948, stated certain fundamentals: 1) a common defense would improve the military resistance potential of each country; 2) a defense union would be preferable to military cooperation; 3) both Denmark and Norway must increase their military expenditures, and Sweden would maintain her current level; 4) war materials would have to be procured outside the North; 5) a defense union would not participate in a great power bloc system or a war, if the latter could be avoided; 6) in event of an attack on a member state, outside aid would be imperative. After study of these recommendations the foreign ministers agreed upon the desirability of a defense union and the continuation of negotiations.

This decision and the military report laid the foundations for defense union talks. Halvard Lange, in answer to questions in the Storting, avoided the topic, and Norwegian parliamentary members showed their preference for merger with NATO. Lange wished to see what results arose from Nordic negotiations and he kept in mind the fraction of his own Labor Party which favored a defense union over Norwegian adherence to NATO. The skeptical Lange, distrusting the lengths to which Swedes would depart from their traditional neutrality, hurried matters by an interview in *Arbeiderbladet*. He said that because of[10] "modern techniques and possibilities they open, [we] must look to increasing cooperation with the people whom we recognize as befriending us, even outside Scandinavia's frontiers. We hope that Sweden and Denmark, for their part, will come to the same conclusion so that we can hold together even in the proposed co-

[10] Hirschfeldt, *op. cit.*, 34-35.

operation that is proceeding as we now do in the work on Europe's economic reconstruction."

Lange's maneuver forced Sweden to greater concessions than she normally would have given. When the ministers met at Karlstad on January 9, 1949, the Swedish government abandoned much of its reserved position to prevent Norway from joining NATO. Behind this Swedish yielding were the persuasive powers of Hans Hedtoft. Neither he nor his party wanted any share in the great power bloc system under construction and wished to maintain a Scandinavian alliance-free defense union. But in pushing the Swedes forward, the Danes raised the vitally important question of the proportionate share of the three states in a defense of their neutrality. Sweden, for her part, did not make any specific quotas as conditions for a defense union. But the American statement on priorities for shipments of materials made any Nordic defense union dependent upon its own financial and material resources. If neither the United States nor Britain would give aid, then the Swedes wished an evaluation of Scandinavian resources in combination with purchases abroad.

In an amplification of the military committee report, the Swedes displayed their willingness to go the extra mile. They proposed a joint strategic planning board and program, the standardization of all types of war materials, the creation of unified forces for certain areas (Øresund, Skagerrak, Kattegat, and the Swedish-Norwegian border), and the unification of the three air forces. The surprising aspect of these concessions was the degree to which Sweden relinquished her earlier emphasis on national rights. A Scandinavian general staff meant an inextricable coordination from which Sweden could not hope to escape.

Norway refused to meet Sweden's moves and insisted on a Scandinavian defense union with membership in NATO. When the Swedes declined to abandon an alliance-free policy, the Norwegians gave up hope even if they reluctantly agreed to continue negotiations. First, however, parliamentary groups, party leaders, and cabinets had to thresh out their variant opinions on a defense union. The several ministers agreed to meet at Copenhagen later in the month and to postpone an answer to the

United States until the completion of the Scandinavian conferences. The debate in Norway and Sweden showed how far from
agreement these two states were. Riksdag members expressed their
hesitancy about accepting Undén's radical Karlstad program, and
he countered by pointing out the readiness of Norway to join the
West in preference to an alliance-free system. In the Storting
Lange criticized the Swedish concept of a neutral defense union
which neither suited Norwegian needs nor guaranteed outside
financial and military support.

As a consequence, at the Copenhagen meeting the two states
refused to budge. With a formidable array of government officials present, as well as delegates from the three parliamentary
foreign affairs committees, this conference accepted the Karlstad program and added proposals for immediate defense preparations. They drafted and sent a joint note to Washington and
London on delivery of war materials, but, because of an American statement, a favorable answer seemed hopeless. In addition
they agreed to a later meeting in Oslo to consider alterations or
concessions in either Norwegian or Swedish conditions and an
American reply, if one came in time.

At Oslo the same delegations met once again, with the respective ambassadors from Washington, London, and Moscow joining in the discussions. Nothing had changed. Norway presented
a draft of a *démarche* to the United States which the Swedes refused to accept. Sweden then offered a treaty project which apparently the Norwegians cursorily examined. In the Swedish
treaty, however, had been incorporated a pledge barring Norway or Denmark from joining NATO. The Norwegian delegation appeared quite restive and evidently wished to end the
conference in order to begin negotiations for an entry into
NATO. In spite of many Danish compromise suggestions Norway refused to give up her demand for a Nordic defense union
in NATO, and Sweden would not renounce her alliance-free
plan. At the conclusion of the Oslo conference each nation was
free to solve its defense problems by itself.

The communiqué from Oslo, while explaining the failure to
attain a defense union, noted the continuance of Scandinavian

cooperation:[11] "The discussions have been conducted with frankness and in a spirit of mutual confidence and understanding. The three nations will continue to develop their cooperation in important spheres. The mutual consultations on questions of foreign policy will be maintained and strengthened." At the same time all three prime ministers offered public explanations of the failure of Scandinavian integration to sustain a heavier load. Prime Minister Gerhardsen of Norway spoke in much the same way as the leaders of the other two states:[12] "If sincere good will had been sufficient in itself to create agreement, we would have had agreement today on a northern defense union. The negotiations have not produced a positive result because our security problems are different, perhaps in their nature, and at least in the way we interpret them. We feel that it would not be right, by means of circumlocutory phraseology, to give the impression of agreement when it does not exist."

The failure of the Nordic countries to achieve a defense union effected no vital change in their relations with one another. As a matter of fact, subsequent events showed the Swedish policy to be more calculated to ease tensions in Scandinavia, and it allowed Finland to regain her position among the Nordic states. If Sweden had been in NATO, Russia would not have permitted Finland to join the Nordic Council in 1956. Yet, debate in Sweden, especially criticisms by defense chiefs, indicated some interest in having Sweden more closely tied to Denmark and Norway and the West. Military leaders thought Swedish policy to be shortsighted. General Nils Swedlund stressed the absolute necessity of procurement of military supplies from the West; in event of war such aid must be forthcoming or Sweden could not survive. In some quarters the failure to agree on a Scandinavian defense union was assumed to be a "Swedish defeat," but since Norway and Sweden together initiated discussions, with their policies clear from the beginning, that interpretation seems hardly correct.[13]

---

[11] *The Norseman*, VII (1949), 119.   [12] *Idem.*
[13] Cf. Wilhelm Keilhau, "Norway and the Atlantic Pact," *The Norseman*, VII (1949), 80-85.

An interesting and important sequel to the Scandinavian defense talks developed from half-hearted inquiries in Washington on military aid. The startling answer was given that no priorities for NATO members had been established and that any countries, barring Communist states, could buy war materials on an open market. If this answer has been given in January, it would have altered negotiations on the defense union. Likewise, a joint Scandinavian *démarche* in February, as Denmark requested, might possibly have resulted in some *modus operandi* for a loose connection between NATO and a regional Nordic defense union. The change in American views had been due, in all probability, to heavy fire from the *New York Times, Herald Tribune,* and the *Washington Post* which deplored the State Department's pressure on Scandinavia and its hasty negotiation of NATO.

It might seem that the Nordic split on defense policy would hamper and confine possibilities for political changes through cooperative action. However, international pressures forced the three countries to continue their joint planning, both in foreign policy and in defense matters. Thus continuous conferences of foreign and defense ministers followed the Danish-Norwegian signature of the Atlantic Pact. Swedish purchases of war materials in the United States and Britain brought about some standardization and conformity with the West and with Norway and Denmark, while Western utilization of some Swedish patents on armament served, even if faintly, as reminders that Sweden lay not too far from the Western orbit. A war among the Scandinavian countries continues to be unthinkable and, as Gustaf V said in 1917, "no brother's hand will be lifted against another."

Out of Scandinavian frustration on a defense union came increased demands for actions showing Nordic cooperation. In 1951 the Danish and Swedish parliaments simultaneously passed resolutions calling for the creation of a central body which would recommend measures directed at greater integration. Its chief Danish advocate was Hans Hedtoft, who had so strongly favored the Nordic defense union. In Sweden the proposal gained the support of the four major parties and the Storting in Norway unanimously approved the creation of a committee on economic cooperation.

At a meeting of the Scandinavian Inter-Parliamentary Union, Hedtoft urged the formation of a Nordic Council, composed of elected representatives of the national parliaments. Hedtoft planned that the Council would develop regular and coordinated cooperation in matters of common concern. The union adopted Hedtoft's motion in principle and selected a committee[14] to plan for such an organization. Foreign ministers of the five countries favored this new body, although Undén wished to avoid the error in the Council of Europe in excluding governments from deliberations and decisions. In other words, Undén favored more, rather than less, integration. Oscar Torp of Norway agreed with Undén, but his Conservative colleague doubted "the necessity of a new organ," and proposed that "a practical measure to bring the Scandinavian countries together would be to give Members of Parliament free travel facilities all over Scandinavia."[15]

Public debate in parliamentary bodies and in newspapers aroused popular interest. The new organization received high acclaim and neither Danes nor Swedes dissented from the plan. Norwegian Conservatives and Agrarians (*Bondepartiet*) voiced some objections. In Sweden *Svenska Dagbladet* wrote that it was "wise not to reject the proposal without further ado," and *Stockholms-tidningen* "referred caustically to the failure to solve such practical matters as Scandinavian passports and customs and a Scandinavian labor market, and said: 'As long as one is unable to master these and similar practical questions, one should avoid creating new organizations in order to cooperate on paper.' "[16] The Norwegian *Aftenposten* expressed its support of the Nordic Council, noting that it would not be a supergovernment, but

[14] It consisted of Hedtoft, Sigurdur Bjarnason (Iceland), Karl August Fagerholm (Finland), Nils Herlitz (Sweden), and Oscar Torp (Norway).

[15] *The Norseman*, IX (1951), 306.

[16] *The Norseman*, IX (1951), 306-307. This journal picked mainly derogatory statements and comments about the Nordic Council. Since then both passport freedom and a Scandinavian labor market have been adopted and only the customs union is still under discussion.

clearly fill a gap in Nordic cooperation. The powerful *Arbeider-bladet*, voice of the Labor Party, advocated its creation, while *Dagbladet*, most often anti-Scandinavian and anti-Swedish, wrote of the difficulties it would create for Norway in regard to the Atlantic Pact and the encouragement it would give opponents of NATO.[17]

Obviously, Norwegian opinion was divided on the Nordic Council, although the majority party favored it. A small group, when the time came, voted against the charter. Oftedal[18] thought the main reason for Norwegian opposition to be an instinctive reaction against Scandinavianism. *Venstre* split on the vote; the *Kristelig folkeparti* and *Bondepartiet* both opposed the Council; the Labor party almost unanimously approved. More Storting members probably would have voted against the Nordic Council's charter if a compromise had not been arranged whereby ministerial representatives participated in the Council without a vote. Norwegian fear of transgressions against constitutional limitations on ministers and of a transfer of sovereignty to the new Council were both lessened by this revision. In contrast both Danish and Swedish parliaments voted almost unanimously for the Council's charter. Thus, with considerable debate, but little real numerical opposition, formal approval for the Nordic Council was granted by the legislatures of Denmark, Iceland, Norway, and Sweden.

By its charter the new body was given recommendatory and advisory functions. Delegates are elected by the parliaments, and both prime ministers and foreign ministers of the respective countries are members. (Sixteen representatives each from Denmark, Norway, and Sweden and five from Iceland met in the first session; in 1956 sixteen Finns joined them.) Other cabinet officers can attend and address the Council but cannot vote. Any matter pertinent to the Scandinavian countries and tending to increase opportunities for integration can be brought before the Council. Sessions are held each year, more frequently upon de-

---

[17] *Ibid.*, x (1952), 82.

[18] Chr. S. Oftedal, "Nordisk råd og nordiske samvirke," *Samtiden*, LXI (1952), 210-211.

mand of two governments or twenty representatives, and alternate between the several capitals, starting with Copenhagen. Debate is public, but closed sessions can be held by application of parliamentary rules. Special committees have been appointed to study all types of cooperation and a permanent secretariat to coordinate the work of the Council is in process of creation.

The Nordic Council differs in many respects from *Foreningen Norden* and the Scandinavian Inter-Parliamentary Union. In both these groups representation is unofficial. A proposal from either organization would receive the same treatment as a petition of a private citizen, while Nordic Council recommendations are from elected parliamentary delegates and from ministers. In its prestige and its semi-official character the new Nordic Council has an authority unmatched by any previously existent body. Delegates to the Nordic Council can dissent, when discussing a recommendation of the Council in their own legislature, but having once agreed to a measure in a Council meeting their opposition before their parliament would be unlikely. For example, C. J. Hambro, Norwegian Conservative leader, who voted against some propositions in the first Council meeting, spoke in their favor when they reached the Storting.

In opening the first meeting in the Rigsdag chambers in Copenhagen, Frederik IX commented on Danish pride in the new Council. He went on to state that "the Scandinavian Council is the latest and most important expression and instrument of Scandinavian cooperation. It is my hope, and the hope of the Danish people, that it shall succeed in accomplishing much in the service of all the Scandinavian peoples, strengthening the cooperation and solidarity among them, and reinforcing the century-old ties which bind them together."[19] Statements of delegation leaders also make interesting reading, for they all desired to avoid "holiday Scandinavianism," and to concentrate on practical measures. In view of Norwegian opposition, Gerhardsen warned his own colleagues and delegates from the other three countries:[20] "In the Norwegian Parliament . . . there was disagree-

19 *The Norseman*, XI (1953), 93.
20 *The Norseman*, XI (1953), 93-94.

ment about the Scandinavian Council. Many were opposed to it, but a great majority decided that Norway should take part in it. Those who were opposed to the Council are also represented in the Norwegian delegation. I am also pleased to be able to say that a unanimous Parliament and a unanimous people are behind the desire for the best possible cooperation among the Scandinavian countries. It is only about what form that cooperation should take that differences may exist."

Among the Nordic Council's opponents of whom Gerhardsen spoke was C. J. Hambro, who had criticized its formation. At Copenhagen, sitting as a delegate, he confined himself to less rigorous utterances, warning Council members of the dangers arising from derogation of national sovereignty and the creation of superstate machinery. The answers of his Norwegian colleagues, and of Conservative members of other delegations, disclosed Hambro as pretty much alone.

The Nordic Council concentrated on limited objectives and expressed hopes for greater activity in Scandinavian cooperation. It adopted a resolution urging relaxation of Scandinavian travel controls, and by the year's end both passport and customs inspection were dropped. The Council advocated the creation of a Scandinavian university and more public health coordination.[21]

Later in the year the several ministers of health agreed on a series of proposals, since adopted both in principle and in some parts, which tend to make Scandinavia into a unified health district. Citizens of one country, living or visiting in another, may now receive full health and medical benefits. A Nordic university has now become reality through agreement on its location, budget, and other items, even if it has yet to admit its first student. Study of a northern postal, telegraph, and telephone union is now under way and it appears likely that it will be created. The Economic Committee assumed responsibility for a study of a customs union or elimination of restrictions on trade. And finally, a proposal for a tunnel or bridge across the Øresund, joining

[21] Cf. George R. Nelson, ed., *Freedom and Welfare—Social Patterns in the Northern Countries of Europe* (Copenhagen, 1953). On passport controls and other early work of the Nordic Council see Rolf Edberg, "Osynliga gränser i Norden," *Nordisk tidskrift*, xxx (1954), 197-207.

Denmark and Sweden, was adopted, but in later study it was shelved because of the expense and difficulties in planning.

The second meeting of the Nordic Council, held in 1954, devoted the major part of its ten-day session to problems of economic cooperation. It adopted a recommendation for elimination of trade restrictions and development of a common market or a Nordic customs union. Ministers of the four countries later prepared propositions for their governments on the subject. A common Scandinavian labor market agreement went into effect in July 1954, and converted the three contiguous countries into an integrated labor unit wherein laborers, regardless of nationality, might seek employment.

The revival of Scandinavian customs union proposals originated in the various efforts of the Marshall Plan countries to reduce or to eliminate economic barriers to world trade. In the Organization for European Economic Cooperation, the Scandinavian states also considered the possibility of some form of customs union and established their own Scandinavian Committee for Economic Cooperation. European signature of the General Agreement on Trade and Tariffs (GATT) also stimulated thoughts of a common Nordic market. Earlier even than this, at the Paris meeting on the Marshall Plan, the Scandinavian countries announced a conference to study a plan for the elimination "wholly or partly, of the customs frontiers between the four countries." When it came time for such a study, however, several objections arose. Elimination of restrictions would mean abolition of many bases for Scandinavian postwar economic policy. Subventions, currency differences, limited markets, and the Scandinavian region's dependence upon trade with non-European areas, stabilization programs of all varieties, differences in standards of living, variations in degrees of quality and quantity of production, and dissimilarities in credit and savings reserves formed barriers to any moves to eliminate restrictions.

At Copenhagen in 1956, however, the Economic Cooperation Committee reported to the Nordic Council on the subject of a common Scandinavian market or customs union. Extensive debate showed only the Norwegian Conservative and *Venstre* rep-

resentatives opposed to the recommendation. They feared sub-
mergence of Norway in the higher production ratios, the competition from better-equipped Swedish and Danish industries,
the higher standard of living in these two countries, and the reduction of national freedom of action with reference to foreign
markets. Other delegations, regardless of party, favored it, and
urged the advantages of greater trade opportunities, expansion
of market facilities and means of production, and the higher
standard of living eventually accruing to those in the program.
Because of the desire for unanimity on such an important subject the report was sent back to the committee for further study
and arose again at the Helsinki Nordic Council meeting in 1957.
It is not unlikely that action may be still further postponed; any
progress must be gradual, piece-by-piece, and made in a manner
which will leave all delegations satisfied with the steps taken.[22]
But the new element added to plans for a Nordic customs union
has been the arrangement of conventions by OEEC and its six-
state adjunct for establishment of a European customs union
which became effective in January 1958. The Nordic countries,
through the Economic Committee, decided to postpone further
planning for a Scandinavian common market and to enter discussions on the larger European common market. In these debates, the various arguments showed clearly that the economic
advantages of the larger area had greater pull than Nordic ties.[23]

The Nordic Council in its four years of operations from 1952-
1956 has proved itself capable of carrying fairly heavy loads and
of accommodating various types of Scandinavian integrative
activity. Even in the few instances where recommendations have
failed, the reaction has been one of thoughtful examination of
the proposal and often a feeling that it might be tried later, with
added features, or when the mood seemed more propitious. What
has been accomplished in these four years marks the Nordic
Council as a permanent organization carrying a great share of

[22] See Halvard Lange, "The Northern Countries and Europe," *The Norseman*, VIII (1950), 3-7, for a good discussion of the problems of creating a
customs union in Scandinavia.

[23] See the report of the Economic Committee, *Nordisk økonomisk samarbeid* (4 vols., Oslo, 1957).

further integration and even possessing some features tending toward an amalgamation. In spite of fears among Conservative groups, and especially Norwegian Conservatives, Agrarian, and *Venstre* parties, the Scandinavian peoples want more areas of integration that will lead toward a fuller sense of community. Even Norway and Sweden have found it practical and sensible to arrange for transit of goods through Trondheim to Sweden, for mutual sharing of hydroelectric resources, and for the arrangement of patterns of economic activity which benefit both peoples. In this sense the Nordic Council serves both as an example and an agency in bringing about a more complete union.

In another direction the Scandinavian countries worked toward a regional scheme of cooperation. In 1951 Denmark, Norway, and Sweden completed arrangements for the formation of the Scandinavian Airlines System (SAS) in order to provide for competition against American, British, and other international airline companies,[24] and to eliminate some of the economic and operational disadvantages of the small, individually owned airline. In establishing SAS the three countries shared in a ratio of 2:2:3, with Sweden carrying the largest capital outlay. Fifty percent of the stock in SAS is owned by the states, with the remainder in private hands.

In the operations of SAS the usual national rivalries have been reduced to a minimum and they have worked together very well. The main problem of serious dimensions is the share of maintenance for each country. A compromise provided Norway with a greater proportion of the European services for two-motored transports, while the larger ships, used in Polar flights, have been serviced in Denmark and Sweden. Some friction resulted also from the pooling arrangement wherein competition for participation in the best schedules and longest hauls showed some divergencies of opinion. After the normal adjustment period, however, these differences and frictions have been reduced to a minimum, and the SAS continues an efficient and quiet operation with staffs

[24] See Robert A. Nelson, "Scandinavian Airlines System Cooperation in the Air," *The Journal of Air Law and Commerce*, xx (1953), 178-196; also his doctoral thesis on SAS at Boston University, 1953.

drawn from the three countries. In certification of maintenance and pilot personnel national boundaries have been largely disregarded. As arranged, the licensing of pilots by one country, for example, must be validated in the other two. The SAS carriers also pay only one customs duty on the import of company property. Much economic integration has been necessary for the elimination of national rivalries and frictions. As the American expert on SAS, Robert Nelson, says,[25] "it is perhaps to the everlasting credit of the Scandinavian countries that they have had the vision to recognize their common lot and to overcome the nationalistic inclinations which so often sabotage a proposal of this nature." It has not been an easy or trouble-free road to cooperation, but it has been economically profitable and convincing proof of the advantages which collaboration brings to its participants.

Steps taken in the economic sphere have been matched, and in some instances even exceeded, by those taken to achieve cultural integration. Efforts to eliminate nationalism and prejudice from history textbooks have been initiated on the model of the *Foreningen Norden's* program of the 1930's. The ministers of education, meeting at Copenhagen in February 1954, considered stimulation of more intellectual activity through reorganization of the Scandinavian Cultural Commission. Subventions for Scandinavian cultural congresses and the establishment of a cooperative organ for educational and research activities received much support, and later a Nordic atomic research center proposal was adopted. Plans have been made for Scandinavian student examinations whereby a student of any Nordic country might take his examinations at another university than his own. Basically the establishment of nearly similar curricula and identical requirements were presupposed. Teachers from another Scandinavian country were to be paid their normal salary, plus expenses of travel, and programs of exchanges were to be further developed.[26] These recommendations grew out of earlier projects begun in 1947 which had met with general approval throughout Scandinavia.

[25] *Op. cit.*, 196.
[26] See *Politiken*, February 5 and 11, 1954, for reports of the meeting.

Cultural integration has frequently been concerned with problems of linguistic variations among the five Scandinavian states. Finnish and Icelandic are too dissimilar to be amalgamated with the other three languages, but nationals of these countries use either Swedish or Dano-Norwegian in communication with other Scandinavians. Attention has especially centered on the gradual reduction or elimination of dissimilarities in the three languages commonly used.[27] Several quantitative tests have been made on the relationship of language to Scandinavian unity, and show some trends. A Swedish Gallup Poll in 1946 found that there was some understanding of the language of another Scandinavian country, but that it ought to be greater than indicated because of the slight actual differences.[28] A study undertaken by Einar Haugen in 1951-1952 indicates other aspects of the language problem.[29] He has concluded that, due to increases in travel and communication, the language barrier has become less noticeable and less bothersome. The problem in Norway of two languages, *riksmål* or *bokmål* and *nynorsk*, does not alter the relationship with either Swedish or Danish and constitutes a national or local

[27] Note especially the work of such scholars as Professors O. V. Friesen of Uppsala, Sven Clausen of Denmark, and Elias Wessén of Sweden. Clausen established the *Årbog for nordisk målstraev* in 1938 and in 1941 the Danish Society for the Promotion of Scandinavian Language Unity. Requests for governmental study of orthographic changes on a Scandinavivan basis prior to any adoption has resulted in keeping the languages from spreading further apart. A weak movement for Scandinavian spellings has produced some modification of the Danish capitalization of nouns and shows some progress is being made. Cf. Elias Wessén, "The Scandinavian Community of Language," *Le Nord*, IV (1941), 233-236.

[28] For full figures and their interpretation see Karlström, *Scandinavian Approach*, footnote, 135.

	Yes	Some	No
Do you understand			
Norwegian	44	41	15
Danish	17	41	42
Can you read			
Norwegian	32	28	22
Danish	13	22	43
Haven't tried			
Norwegian	18		
Danish	22		

[29] "Nordiske språkproblemer—en opinionsundersökelse," *Nordisk tidskrift*, XXIX (1953), 225-249.

issue.[30] The development of either *nynorsk*, with its slightly closer proximity to Swedish, or *samnorsk* (a blending of *nynorsk* and *bokmål*) does not harm communication, but, as some scholars insist, might even increase fluency in linguistic communication.

Relatively easy understanding of the language of another country has been achieved, but Norwegian occupies a favored position. An amusing note was added on the preference for one's own language in comparison with another. Both Norwegians and Swedes chose their own language, but the Danes preferred the beauty of Norwegian and Swedish. In his conclusion, Haugen states that the four forms of Scandinavian are not receding from one another, but neither are they approaching one another with any speed. A high percentage of persons, however, would agree to language reforms to procure greater Scandinavian similarity.[31] The various "Language Commissions" in the three countries indicate also the serious consideration given to linguistic reforms and the necessity of preserving some common Scandinavian character to the language of the future.[32] Yet, language remains one of several indices of the extent to which peoples are willing or unwilling to resolve their differences within a scheme of integration.

In Scandinavian cultural, social, and economic integration the extent to which carriers of a sense of community have developed is greater than casual observation might suggest. The trend toward formation of regional economic associations of many

[30] An analysis of the statistics on alterations or changes in preference for *nynorsk* or *riksmål* shows that, from 1930 to 1954-1955, the former has increased eight percent, and the latter decreased by the same amount. However, over the same period, those who state that they are neutral has increased seven percent, indicating their unwillingness to be involved in the language controversy and their desire for a blending of the two languages. Cf. Alf Sommerfelt, "Norwegian Languages," *The Norseman*, xv (1957), 165-172.

[31] Haugen, data not included in his article, but available to the author.

Do you favor language reforms	Yes	No
Danes	43	38
Norwegians	33	27
Swedes	57	20

[32] K. G. Ljunggren, "Den nordiska språkvården och de nya orden," *Nordiska tidskrift*, xxxii (1956), 217-227. Note also the tables in Knut Dahl Jacobsen, Stein Rokkan, and Normann Vetti, "Kontakt og samarbeid mellom de nordiske folk" (mimeographed report, Oslo, 1956), 51-54.

kinds has increased steadily. Cultural associations beyond the possibility of listing foster movements toward eradication of cultural differences. The degree to which common or joint social legislation laws have been adopted inclines one to say that these five countries, in this regard, are nearly a unit. Likewise in other fields the Nordic countries have continued to add to the list of institutions, agencies, laws, and organizations which now defy description.

During the decade and a half since the first attempt at a Nordic defense union, the Nordic countries have experienced war, threats of war, economic crisis, and reconstruction. During that time, in spite of differences of opinion, these countries have clung to their resolve to maintain their regional unity within the United Nations and in their own geographic area. The Scandinavian approach to integration has revealed that political amalgamation would be strongly resisted, even when great changes have taken place in other fields. Practical reforms have tended to further integration, and leaders have given it a progressively heavier burden to bear. Their caution in the creation of the Nordic Council came from a reasoned judgment that simple and easily-performed tasks and objectives serve as stepping stones for future strengthening of their organization.

Over the century and a half since the formation of the Norwegian-Swedish union, the Nordic states have seen attempts at Scandinavian integration finally succeed. The frictions within the union to 1905 permitted no sense of community to develop. But, as Norwegian and Swedish leaders said, the union's end brought about a lessening of Scandinavian tensions. In place of that troubled union, Norway and Sweden achieved an integration in 1906, when they destroyed the frontier forts, and symbolically continued it in 1914 with their public resolve not to war upon each other. Since that time, this integration has been deepened and broadened so that today the people of Scandinavia look with pride to what they have accomplished. They view the future with satisfaction, knowing that they will never war against a member of their community nor lose that sense of identity which marks the integrative process.

CHAPTER XVI

◆◇

POSTSCRIPT AND CONCLUSIONS

◆◇

THE willingness of the Scandinavian countries to cooperate with each other in a pluralistic security-community is founded on solid factors of mutual responsiveness. Their cultural similarities, as the past has proved, did not always foster integration or even amalgamation. Their close affinities in language, religion, ethnography, and common traditions of law, government, and philosophical values at times failed to prevent conflict. Yet, these several common characteristics assisted rapid integration once political barriers were removed in 1905-1906. Without these similarities, there could not have developed that sense of community which, in combination with other conditions, made impulses toward integration effective.[1]

Of deeper significance for Scandinavian integration are the set of social conditions allowing for the inception of integration and stimulating the growth of a sense of community. It seems apparent that common systems of social thought and similar reactions to social change are basic to integration. Thus Scandinavian political reforms and social progress displayed domestic trends and effected a growth of identification with each other, since, basically, these impulses sprang from identical or similar patterns of social thought. When other courses of action were valued more highly, the Scandinavian countries did not find sure grounds for association. Some common social values seem to be necessary also, even though these might not always be in complete agreement. A degree of latitude of difference must be permitted in social attitudes or else the sense of community encounters obstacles. Social equality must be recognized fully by the two countries committed to an integration process; without mutual re-

---

[1] For further information on results from the more general study see *Political Community and The North Atlantic Area*, Chaps. II and III.

spect for the opinions of another country's representatives, any framework of amalgamation could not but fail. While the responsiveness of the Scandinavian peoples to social changes is now fully established, Norwegians and Swedes during the union found it difficult to respond adequately and quickly to each other's concepts. In partial explanation of this slow response, Scandinavian integration required considerable communication and mobility between classes and among the peoples of this area. The members of the elite groups in the several Scandinavian states responded to the opinions of others, and these channels of communication increased the tendency to regard one another as part of a common group. At the same time, this identification of themselves as an "in-group" emphasized the "out-group" character of non-Scandinavians. Another social factor of considerable importance in the trend toward Scandinavian integration seems to have been the involvement of farmer and worker groups in the movement. As they grew in political importance, their approval of measures tending toward integration became dominant and assured its achievement. From the beginning, farmer groups opposed integration, and their leadership of intellectual elite, perhaps out of a feeling of inferiority, advocated disamalgamation. As agrarian groups diminished in importance, socially and politically, the prestige and weight of worker groups, aligned together in labor unions and socialist parties, took over the burdens of the integration process.

In this study the main economic factors causing integration were economic growth and satisfaction of expected economic rewards. In the first instance, the rate of this growth exerted a vital influence upon reactions of large groups of people. When Norway and Sweden industrialized in the last half of the nineteenth century, their national economies did not keep pace with each other; when Sweden forged ahead, tendencies toward disintegration and disamalgamation began to appear. During the twentieth century, these differences in economic growth have been reversed so that Norway exceeded Sweden's rate. As a consequence, resistance in Norway to establishment of common economic institutions has decreased, and the dependence of both countries upon each other has increased proportionately. Yet, this problem remains to be solved in discussions of the common market scheme of these past four years. As the community expanded, these differences also tended to merge and to diminish in importance with the appearance of other factors and the complementation of national economies by the industrial, financial, and agricultural production of other systems.

The economic rewards of integration must appear in some form.[2] It appears that expectations develop group positive responses favorable to the contemplated event; these responses, however, are converted into hostile, or opposition, attitudes if some tangible form of reward is not forthcoming. The Scandinavian Airlines System is an instance in point where the rewards in traffic volume and income have exceeded expectations to such a degree that no group within either of the three countries in SAS would now advocate discontinuation of this economic cooperation. Other examples would be private ventures in the fields of industry and agriculture, such as the Northern Cooperative Union, which have proved their value economically in improving the standard of living of all three peoples. The limited version of a tariff union which connected Norway and Sweden during a major part of the union's existence failed to appeal to broad sections of the population and its abandonment met no large scale opposition. In other respects, the development of mutual economic organs with national representation promoted a sense of community.

It is, however, in political factors and conditions that most items of influence upon integration are found. From this study, a set of essential conditions appears. First of these would be recognition of political equality and national independence in making decisions, even to the elimination of some aspects of national sovereignty. The subordinate position of Norway within the union proved an obstacle, especially when accompanied by governmental technicalities, such as foreign consular representation. It was on this point that most of the heated controversy centered during the last decade of the union's existence.

2 See *Political Community and the North Atlantic Area*, 49-50.

When the union was dissolved, however, the Swedes recognized the equality of Norway in international relations and within a brief period the two states were integrated.

As an accompaniment, there must also be a perception of peaceful change and some provision for it. The growth of arbitration and conciliation machinery with public support increased the depth of integration, just as the arbitration agreement in the Karlstad treaties provided Norwegians with a sense of security making possible the destruction of the frontier forts. At the same time, Norwegian latent fears of Swedish aggression ceased to be effectual in arousing antagonism between the two peoples. Another factor was the entry of new social groups into the political relations between the two nations which often resulted in harm to integration, especially when these new groups fought against domestic entrenched groups with fixed political orientations. Thus the *Venstre* party in Norway, opposed to Conservative political viewpoints, adopted an antiunionist position because Conservatives were prounionist. The newer socialist parties, with their stress on unity and coordination of programs, steadily won out over the *Venstre* nationalist policies and furnished the avenues for mutual understanding and cooperation.

More important in the political conditions, however, was the possession of similar sets of political values and a willingness to act together on political problems in ways commensurate with these values. The Norwegians found these values minimized while in the union, as compared with the national rewards which independence would bring. Once the union ceased to be, however, these values were flexible enough to accommodate a wide range of new standards conducive to integration. In agreement with this point, it seems apparent that some political symbols representing these value systems must arise and these must be comparable. Such a small symbol as the word "Norden" seems to have arisen from this need. With a common set of values it is easier to judge the predictability of another national group. If peaceful change, social welfare, democracy, and political participation are values common to several groups inside each country, the political responses of leaders and peoples will be more certain to coincide and to be much less erratic. The value system of socialist parties, for example, would be nearly identical, regardless of political boundaries or nationalism.

Neither the danger of war within Scandinavia nor the threats of war from a non-Scandinavian aggressor had an appreciable effect on integration. Twice during the union's existence war between Norway and Sweden seemed imminent, but its dangers apparently caused no diminution of Norwegian or Swedish popular hostility toward one another. When the union was dissolved, the major event which preceded integration was the destruction of the frontier forts. For Norway this meant a great power guarantee and the adoption of a foreign policy based on neutrality. During World War I, cooperation between the Scandinavian countries came from a desire to preserve trade, commerce, a high standard of living, and other economic and social demands, rather than the prevention of outside intervention in Scandinavian affairs. Likewise, during World War II, Sweden avoided involvement for national reasons. But a better example of the effect of external war threats would be the twice-attempted Scandinavian defense pact. It failed mainly because of resistance to an amalgamation which would lessen national sovereignty. Even the grave danger of involvement in conflict between East and West has failed to push the Scandinavian states into amalgamation. On the other hand, this tendency has been matched, contradictorily, by an increase in integration; for example the creation of the Nordic Council stemmed from a desire to preserve a high degree of cooperation in pushing integration forward. On the economic front, as another example, the Scandinavian states have had an extended and serious consideration of a common market proposal.

These conclusions deal, for the most part, with political factors. Yet, the stress in Scandinavian cooperation of the last decade has been on social, cultural, and economic amalgamation, and the political has been deliberately avoided. Inevitably, the question will arise of whether to amalgamate or not, and Scandinavia, already an integrated pluralistic security-community, must recognize that the choice lies before it.

◇◇◇

BIBLIOGRAPHY

◇◇◇

MATERIALS on the union of Norway and Sweden extend from documents in the two foreign offices to articles and brochures written in the heat of controversy. Newspapers in Norway and Sweden resound with the language of battle, with its stereotypes, its invective, and its edged innuendoes. In this bibliography are compiled only some of the more important materials that might be conveniently used for an understanding of the union and Scandinavia since 1905. In the footnotes are other citations which have proved useful.

The basic documents for this study came from the two foreign offices where even some cabinet dispatches can be found. The Norwegian *Utenrikesdepartment* has both these materials and those relating to the negotiation of the integrity treaty under the listing of P8A. Part of the treaty's documents, up to October, 1907, are published by Dr. Reidar Omang under the title *Norge og stormaktene 1906–14*, Oslo, 1957. Dr. Omang, the foreign office archivist, was of great assistance in preparation of this study and allowed the use of photostats of captured German documents. The British Foreign Office gave final permission for their incorporation in this study. They go under the long title of *Auswärtiges Amt. Abteilung A. Norwegen No. 7 Verhandlungen über die Unabhängigkeit und Integrität Norwegens*, Band 1-4. *June 1905-October 1907*. To supplement these documents, *Die grosse Politik des europäischen Kabinette, 1871-1914*, eds. Johannes Lepsius, Albrecht Mendelssohn Bartholdy, Friedrich Thimme, 40 vols. in 54, Berlin, 1922-1927, has been used. From these documents has come information regarding German policy in the Baltic.

On the Swedish side the *Utrikesdepartment* archives, formerly headed by Dr. Uno Villers (now librarian of the Royal Library) and presently by Mr. Åke Kromnow, contain a variety of both diplomatic and domestic materials relating to the union. The several bodies of documents are listed according to groups, sections, and subject; thus Group 4, Section A, Subject 14, contains documents relating to the union and post-June 7 period, as does Group 4, Section M, Subject 1b. On the integrity treaty the documents are in Group 1, Section O, Subject 10. Also in Stockholm I was given access to the Bernadotte archives through the help of Professor Torvald Höjer. Here are dispatches and personal correspondence of Oscar II, Gustaf V, and Princes Eugén, Carl, and Wilhelm, and some of their letters to and from foreign dignitaries.

In England at the Foreign Office Library I was granted the privilege of checking the documents cited in Vol. VIII, *British Documents on the Origins of the War, 1898-1914*, eds., George P. Gooch and Harold W. V. Temperley, 11 vols., London, 1926-1938, and I found that publication so complete and the memoranda so accurate that it was unnecessary to have attempted my check.

The personal memoirs and correspondence span such a wide range of subjects and bulk so large that they appear impossible to cover entirely. In Norway the *Riksarkiv* (Royal Archives) and *Universitetsbiblioteket* (University Library) have extensive manuscript sources. It might also be mentioned that the University Library is a depository for all books published in Norway; in the same way the Royal Library in Stockholm functions for Sweden. The main sources for the story of 1905 are the diaries (*Dagbøker*) of Hagerup Bull (*Statsråd Edvard Hagerup Bulls dagbøker fra 1905*, Oslo, 1955) and Bothner, the latter in the Royal Archives (RAN). In the University Library are also the diaries and letters of Nansen, now published under the title of *Dagbok fra 1905*, Oslo, 1955. Sophus Arctander's correspondence and some notes are there also, together with the manuscripts of Konow which are most valuable. Two most interesting diaries are published—those of Jakob Schøning and Johan Castberg. I owe thanks to Professor Frede Castberg, former Rector of Oslo University, for his permission to use his father's diary. Since my use of it, however, it has been published in two volumes and I have preferred to cite from them. The same is true of Hagerup's notes and letters at the RAN, which have been published. Also at the Royal Archives are some materials of Vinje, which were useful because of his moderate position. Through selection, then, there are represented here two Conservatives (Hagerup Bull and Hagerup), two moderates (Vinje and Bothner, the latter *Venstre*), and four *Venstre*, three of whom were radicals (Konow, Castberg, and Schøning; Arctander the exception).

The Swedish archives are likewise filled with personal and public correspondence and diaries from the time of the dissolution. But the Swedes have not attempted to publish them, with the exception of Arne Wåhlstrand's magnificent collection on Karlstad (*Karlstadkonferensen 1905*, Stockholm, 1953), which is a model of completeness to delight the historian. The main sources are the Karl Staaff and Christian Lundeberg papers at the University Library at Uppsala. These cover more than the 1905 period and are full of miscellaneous items. Included in the Staaff manuscripts is a typewritten copy of Gustaf Axel Berg's notes (*Anteckningar*) from 1905. Also in the University Library are the papers of Harald Hjärne to which his son, Professor Erland Hjärne, gave me access. In Stockholm the Royal Archives (RAS) have the Boström and Lindman collections, both extremely valuable because of the prominence of these men in union affairs. Lars Tingsten's papers, some of which are in the *Krigsarkiv* in Stockholm, were used in Göteborg under the friendly eye of Professor Wåhlstrand. Use also was made of Fridtjuv Berg's copy letter book, and my thanks are owed to Mr. Tor Berg for the chance to use it. On the Swedish side, I did not seek quite the same completeness as in Norway because of the availability of good accounts in Wåhlstrand's two works (*1905 års ministärkriser*, Stockholm, 1941, and the previously mentioned *Karlstadkonferensen*). I would be ungracious, however, if I did not express my thanks to Professor Wåhlstrand for the hours of his time spent in talk about 1905—*nittonfemshistoria*.

Norwegian memoirs are appearing regularly and so far several have been published. Castberg's diaries (Johan Castberg, *Dagbøker, 1900-1917*, 2 vols., Oslo, 1953) are full of the radical case and probably will rate highest in their human value. Likewise

Schøning (Jakob Schøning, *Dagbøker*, Oslo, 1950) reveals the angry radical side of the story of 1905, but from outside the Storting and cabinet. Francis Hagerup was so far distant from the political scene in 1905 that his diary, including its letters and notes (*Dagbok ført i 1905*, ed. H. Falck Myckland, Oslo, 1951) depicts a man standing still in the midst of a flowing stream of ideas and events. Benjamin Vogt has also published his ramblings (*Indtil 1910*, Oslo, 1941, and *Efter 1910*, Oslo, 1945), but they are almost useless in giving insights into his large part in 1905's history. Jørgen Løvland's memoirs (*Menn og minner fra 1905*, Oslo, 1929) have been edited by his son and are valuable on Karlstad. Vogt has also written a brief note on the Karlstad Conference which is one of the most interesting pieces of polemics yet published on 1905, "Les négociations de Carlstad 1905," *Le Nord*, III, 1940, 52-63). Edvard Hagerup Bull published some sections of his diary (*Fra 1905. Erindringer og betragtninger*, Oslo, 1927; "Fra 1905. Erindringer og betragtninger," *Samtiden*, XXXVII, 1926, 197-207, 269-280, 333-345, 449-463, 521-542; "Om kongevalget i 1905," *Samtiden*, XXXIX, 1928, 1-15), but these are trivial when compared to his diary. Halvdan Koht has also written about his share in 1905 ("Da den norsk-svenske unionen vart sprengt," *Historisk tidsskrift* [Norwegian], XXXIV, 1947, 285-320, and "Kongs-vale i 1905. Fordhandlingane utanlands," *Syn og Segn*, LIII, 1947, 14-29, 64-76), as has Frederik Wedel Jarlsberg (*1905 Kongevalget*, Oslo, 1946). If a view of the military front and its tensions in 1905 is desired, they will be found in Angell (H. Angell, *Fortaellinger fra Grænsevagten 1905*, Oslo, 1905). Of the older memoirs the best is that of Blehr (*Møt frigjørelsen*, ed. Sigurd Blehr, 2 vols., Oslo, 1946-1948), although many more personal accounts of the union in the nineteenth century can be found.

Two Norwegian documentary collections are indispensable, that of Heiberg (*Unionens opløsning 1905*, ed. J. V. Heiberg, Oslo, 1906) and the Storting secret session reports (*De stenografiske referater fra de hemmelige møter i Stortinget i 1905*, Oslo, 1951). Other than Sam. Clason's unreadable notes in the RAS, on which a scholar is presently working, no attempt has been made to bring together the Swedish parliamentary materials in this same fashion.

The Swedish side is otherwise also sparse in materials. Wåhlstrand has published the documents on Karlstad, and Lars Tingsten (*Hågkomster*, Stockholm, 1938) his memoirs, but nothing of importance remains to be mentioned. Bishop Gottfrid Billing, (*Anteckningar från riksdager och kyrkomöten 1893-1906*, Stockholm, 1928) has more on the earlier period. Christian Günther (*Minnen från ministertiden i Kristiania åren 1905-1908* and *Minnen från ministertiden i Köpenhamn åren 1908-1914*, Stockholm, 1923), minister to Norway and then to Denmark, has given some insights into the aftermath of Karlstad. Mention also ought to be made of the article by the Swedish secretary at Karlstad, Johannes Hellner ("La conférence de Carlstad d'aôut-septembre 1905," *Le Nord*, III, 1940, 30-51), which contrasts so strangely with the similar article of Benjamin Vogt mentioned before.

Norwegian and Swedish newspapers all shared in making the break and thus give an insight into the suspense of 1905. Representative papers have been selected, which for Norway were *Verdens Gang, Social-Demokraten, Dagbladet, Vort Land* (some numbers), and *Aftenposten*. These five papers give *Venstre*, socialist, Conservative, and moderate opinion on the crisis. In Sweden a similar choice was made, *Social-Demokraten* for the socialists, *Dagens Nyheter* for the Liberals, *Vårt Land* and *Nya Dagligt Allehanda* for the Conservative, with *Stockholms Dagblad, Svenska Dagbladet*, and *Aftonbladet* thrown in for good measure. Likewise added for the sake of completeness were the Danish *Politiken* and *Social-Demokraten* for the year 1905. Newspapers are difficult to use and even more confusing when they take one into the intricacies of nearly a century's quarrels.

The secondary materials are extensive on the Norwegian side, but virtually nonexistent on the Swedish. The only mark of Swedish interest are Wåhlstrand's works and those of Folke Lindberg (*Kunglig utrikespolitik*, Stockholm, 1950 and in English, *Scandinavia in Great Power Politics 1905-1908*, Stockholm, 1958), to whom thanks should also be given for opening materials he collected and for listening patiently while an American explained his reasons for studying 1905. More general items on the Swedish side used in the later part of this study are Torsten Gihl's *Den svenska utrikespolitikens historia*, Vol. IV, 1914-1919, Stockholm, 1951, and Eric C. Bellquist's *Some Aspects of Recent Swedish Foreign Policy* (University of California *Publications*, I, No. 3, Berkeley, Calif., 1929). On 1905 the Norwegians have published three works of some interest: Bernt A. Nissen (*1905*, Oslo, 1930); S. C. Hammer (*Det merkelige aar*, Oslo, 1930); and Yngvar Nielsen (*Norge i 1905*, Horton, 1906). Of more general interest and serving a broader expanse of Norwegian history are the works of Nils Orvik (*The Decline and Fall of Neutrality 1914-41*, Oslo, 1953), O. J. Falnes (*Norway and the Nobel Peace Prize*, New York, 1938, and *National Romanticism in Norway*, New York, 1933), Theodore Jorgenson (*Norway's Relations to Scandinavian Unionism 1815-1871*, Northfield, Minn., 1935), Wilhelm Keilhau (*Norge og verdenskrigen*, Oslo, 1927), Arne Bergsgård (*Året 1814*, 2 vols., Oslo, 1943-1945), and Sverre Steen (*1814* in *Det frie Norge*, Oslo, 1951).

Of the more general materials used for the last two chapters of this book probably the best are still themselves manuscripts: Otto Leroy Karlström's doctoral thesis at the University of Chicago ("The 'Scandinavian' Approach to Political Integration," 1952) and Martha Trytten's master's thesis at the University of Wisconsin ("The Scandinavian Countries and the United Nations: Some Political Problems," 1953). S. Shepard Jones (*The Scandinavian States and The League of Nations*, Princeton, 1939) is the only account of Scandinavian cooperation in the League. Eric C. Bellquist has a provocative and informative article ("Inter-Scandinavian Coöperation," *Annals* of the American Academy of Political and Social Science, 168, July, 1933, 183-196), giving a part of the details of integration and its functional aspects. The wartime cooperation of the Scandinavian countries is covered in two works, that of Foss (Alex. Foss, *I krigsaarene, 1914-1919*, Copenhagen, 1920) and the Carnegie Endowment economic studies (Eli Heckscher, Kurt Bergendahl, *et al.*, *Sweden, Norway, Denmark, and Iceland in the World War*, New Haven, Conn., 1930). Another survey of Nordic cooperation is that of Aage Houken (*Det nye Norden*, Copenhagen, 1940) which fits well with Finn T. B. Friis' account ("Dansk deltagelse i det nordiske samarbejde" in *Danmarks Kultur ved Aar 1940*, Vol. VIII, Copenhagen, 1943). On the Scandinavian defense union two works are essential, that of Karlström, mentioned above, and Lennart Hirschfeldt (*Skandinavien och Atlantpakten. De skandinaviska alliansförhandlingarna 1948-1949. Världspolitikens dagsfrågor*, 4-5, Stockholm, 1949). The Scandinavian economic experiment in the Scandinavian Airlines System is well told in Robert Nelson's article "Scandinavian Airlines System Cooperation in the Air," *The Journal of Air Law and Commerce*, XX, 1953, 178-196, which is an abstract of his longer doctoral thesis at Boston University.

In the end, the historian returns to the two magnificent national histories of Norway (Edvard Bull, Wilhelm Keilhau, Haakon Shetelig, and Sverre Steen, *Det norske folks liv og historie gjennem tidene*, 10 vols., Oslo, 1929-1935) and Sweden (*Sveriges historia till våra dagar*, ed. Emil Hildebrand, 15 vols., Stockholm, 1919-1935), and their appropriate volumes and historians, for a general version of the union. In places the story must be supplemented with other materials, especially in the twentieth century, but what historians of both countries have done is to bring alive these times of trouble.

As this bibliographical essay began with a comment on the lack of completeness so it must close with an apology to all those historians whose works have not been mentioned. But the American reader can turn to Ingvar Andersson's *History of Sweden*, New York, 1956 and Karen Larsen's *History of Norway*, Princeton, N.J., 1948 and find a convenient summary of both the troubles of union and each country's history. Actually, however, the historian must dig into archives and manuscripts to bring out the real story of the Norwegian-Swedish union and Nordic integration. Even then there are some who will not believe what is written because they remember too well and hold a caricature of their neighbor across the border.

INDEX

PUBLICATIONS OF THE CENTER
FOR RESEARCH ON WORLD POLITICAL INSTITUTIONS

These printed publications, and others not in printed form, are obtainable from the Center for Research on World Political Institutions, Princeton University, except where noted.

Research in the International Organization Field: Some Notes on a Possible Focus, by Richard W. Van Wagenen (1952), 70 pp. Center Publication No. 1.

The Individual and World Society, by P. E. Corbett (1953), 59 pp. Center Publication No. 2.

An International Police Force and Public Opinion: Polled Opinion in the United States, 1939-1953, by William Buchanan, Herbert E. Krugman and R. W. Van Wagenen (1954), 59 pp. Center Publication No. 3.

Multiple Loyalties: Theoretical Approach to a Problem in International Organization, by Harold Guetzkow (1955), 62 pp. Center Publication No. 4.

Political Community at the International Level: Problems of Definition and Measurement, by Karl W. Deutsch (September, 1954), Short Studies in Political Science No. 3, 70 pp. Available from Random House, New York.

Political Community and the North Atlantic Area: International Organization in the Light of Historical Experience, by Karl W. Deutsch, Sidney A. Burrell, Robert A. Kann, Maurice Lee, Jr., Martin Lichterman, Raymond E. Lindgren, Francis L. Loewenheim, and Richard W. Van Wagenen (1957). Available from Princeton University Press.

The Habsburg Empire: A Study in Integration and Disintegration, by Robert A. Kann (Praeger, 1957). Available from Frederick A. Praeger, New York.

Norway-Sweden: Union, Disunion, and Scandinavian Integration, by Raymond E. Lindgren (1959). Available from Princeton University Press.